The Idea of a Liberal Theory

The Idea of a Liberal Theory

A CRITIQUE AND RECONSTRUCTION

David Johnston

PRINCETON UNIVERSITY PRESS

PRINCETON, NEW JERSEY

Library of Congress Cataloging-in-Publication Data

Johnston, David, 1951–
The idea of a liberal theory / David Johnston.
p.   cm.
Includes bibliographical references and index.
ISBN 0-691-03381-1
ISBN 0-691-02913-x (pbk.)
1. Liberalism. I. Title
JC571.J57 1994   94-4089
320.5'1—dc20

This book has been composed in Bitstream Caledonia

Third printing, and first paperback printing, 1996

Printed in the United States of America
by Princeton Academic Press

10 9 8 7 6 5 4 3

For Margaret Chambliss Johnston
and in memory of Stuart Marcus Davis

Contents

Preface and Acknowledgments   ix

INTRODUCTION   3

CHAPTER ONE
Political Theory and Liberal Values   11

CHAPTER TWO
Rights-Based Liberalism   40

CHAPTER THREE
Perfectionist Liberalism   68

CHAPTER FOUR
Political Liberalism   100

CHAPTER FIVE
Humanist Liberalism   137

CONCLUSION   186

References   193

Index   201

Preface and Acknowledgments

I HAVE WRITTEN this book to defend liberal values. To some readers it may appear that those values need no defense. Is not liberalism already triumphant throughout the developed world? Perhaps it is, for now. Yet the fall of despotisms that plagued the world for decades with momentous results has given rise to a new danger, the danger of complacency. As feminists, neo-Marxists, and others have demonstrated amply, liberal complacency is unwarranted. If liberalism appears triumphant today, responsibility for that triumph rests as much with the weakness of the illiberal regimes of the past as it does on the vitality of liberal political-economic systems. Those systems are in need of reform. The task for liberal political theories today is to help guide these reforms. But our liberal theories will be able to undertake that task only if those theories themselves are revitalized. It is my hope that by tracing my way back to the theoretical roots of liberalism in this study, I can help to achieve the needed refashioning of liberal political theory.

.   .   .

In preparing this study, I have incurred many debts. I first began to think about the subject of this book in a sustained way in the spring of 1988, at which time I was on leave with the generous financial assistance of the American Council of Learned Societies and the National Endowment for the Humanities, whose support I acknowledge with gratitude. During that year Bruce Jennings, with the financial assistance of the Exxon Educational Foundation, hosted a series of meetings of distinguished moral and political thinkers at the Hastings Center, which helped me to focus my thoughts. I first attempted to put some of those thoughts into written form later that year, producing a paper on which I received valuable comments from Joshua Cohen, Bill Galston, Amy Gutmann, and Joseph Raz.

I then began to work on a draft of the book as a whole. Several students provided helpful criticisms during the process, including Nathalie Sylvestre, Brian Walker, Steve Wall, and the members of my seminars on Rawls's theory of justice in the spring semesters of 1992 and 1993. I also benefited from comments on a draft of chapter 3 from Robert Amdur, Glen Stassen, and the members of the Columbia Seminar on Studies in Political and Social Thought and the Princeton Colloquium on Political Philosophy. John Christman, Philip Green, Amy Gutmann, George Kateb, J. Donald Moon, Nancy L. Rosenblum, Alan Ryan, and Rogers Smith all read a draft of the book and provided comments that helped me to identify many problems, as did a shrewd and well-informed anonymous reader. I also benefited from readings by several colleagues at Columbia, including Julian Franklin, Raymond Geuss, Mark Kesselman, and Ira Katznelson. Charles E. Lindblom and Henry Shue read the penultimate draft and helped me to correct some final mistakes. All these people helped me to shape my thoughts, and for that I am extremely grateful.

I wish to express special thanks to four people. Dennis F. Thompson has been supportive to me over many years, through good times and bad. Without his help, I would not have been able to write this book. I have also benefited from numerous conversations with, and the support of, Charles E. Lindblom over the years. Many of my thoughts about liberalism and political philosophy were shaped in part through our discussions and are stronger than before as a result. Quentin Skinner has also been unfailingly supportive of my efforts to make sense of political philosophy, as has Julian Franklin.

I would like also to take this occasion to express my gratitude to two people who have no direct connection with this book but who helped me at crucial times in my career. Sir Isaiah Berlin, as a reader of my dissertation at Oxford, gave me advice that was both critical and supportive. His words had a formative influence on my thinking and have helped to guide me through the maze I have been exploring ever since. The late Judith N. Shklar gave me invaluable and unstinting support at a more recent, dark and difficult period of my career. I hope this and my future work will be worthy of her.

Ann Wald of Princeton University Press helped guide me through the rewriting of large parts of this book and has been a generous and supportive editor throughout the process. Finally, Wendy Johnston, Katie Johnston, and Victoria Johnston made the sacrifices that enabled me to write this book, for which I am deeply grateful.

New York City
November 1993

The Idea of a Liberal Theory

AT ITS INCEPTION and for much of its early history, the liberal tradition of political theory was radical both in its intentions and in its principal effects. Locke was a revolutionary and, in his best-known political writings, a shrewd opponent of the absolutist tendencies that had been manifest in England throughout much of the seventeenth century. Adam Smith brilliantly exposed the crude assumptions and calamitous consequences of the mercantile system that dominated the economic and trade policies of most European states in his day. In France liberal principles justified a wide-ranging program of legal and social reforms, including abolition of aristocratic privileges, termination of the widely abused institution of benefit of clergy, and abrogation of deeply resented sumptuary laws regulating dress, among other measures. One source of liberal radicalism was the insistence of Hobbes—who was antiliberal in most of his key political conclusions, but liberal in many of his theoretical premises—that human associations must be founded on an acknowledgment that all individuals are equal by nature.[1] Regardless of their source, however, to their early proponents liberal ideas represented a radical, liberating vision of the future.

As parts of the liberal program gained acceptance, the radicalism of its earlier years began to fade. Two grand alliances contributed to the attenuation of these radical tendencies. The first was between the liberal movement and those with a stake in the capitalist organization of economic life. The second alliance was between the liberal movement and the growing administrative state. As these alliances gained strength, the political theory associated with the liberal movement began to exhibit a tendency toward ossification. Liberalism was beginning to acquire the identity of an ideology of the status quo.

Even after these developments, the liberal tradition of political theory retained some of its radical impulses and tools of criticism. Two of these tools remain important today. The first is the concept of individual rights. The concept of rights gained its critical edge by being turned against the state. The second tool of liberal criticism is the idea of distributive justice, which acquired much of its importance by being turned into a means of

---

[1] According to Hobbes, the ninth law of nature is "that every man acknowledge other for his Equall by Nature." "The breach of this Precept," he adds, "is *Pride*," and for Hobbes pride is the passion most antithetical to political association. See *Leviathan, or the Matter, Forme, and Power of a Commonwealth, Ecclesiasticall and Civill*, ed. Richard Tuck (Cambridge: Cambridge University Press, 1991), chap. 15, p. 107.

restraining the worst consequences of the very free market economies that the liberal movement had earlier helped to legitimate.

Recently, however, two major events have challenged anew the adequacy of existing tools of liberal criticism. The first of these events has been the emergence into view of systematic subordination of people based less on class as such than on race and gender and, in many parts of the world, on religious origin or practice as well. In the United States this type of subordination has become apparent to public view only in recent decades. Prior to the Second World War, black Americans for the most part adopted a stance of resignation in the face of officially sanctioned racial apartheid. During and after the war, and especially during the 1960s, resignation no longer seemed necessary or appropriate, and many white Americans who had been unaware of (or who preferred not to think about) the subordination of their black fellow citizens found it impossible to escape the facts. Since the 1960s, too, the revival of feminism has succeeded in exposing the ideological dodges that sustained the belief that men and women in the United States and elsewhere are equal despite significant differences in their treatment and prospects.

The second event that has challenged existing liberal theories is the collapse, at the end of the 1980s, of the regimes of the former Soviet bloc. On the one hand, the successors to these regimes have in many cases either flirted with or embraced wholeheartedly, if clumsily, the ways of market capitalism. At times these new regimes have appeared to be rushing headlong into the early nineteenth century, a course that might seem to compel them to repeat in some fashion the history of capitalism in its classical phase, with all the horrors to which that mode of organization led. On the other hand, the forces of cultural and national particularism that have emerged throughout the former Soviet bloc appear so strong that they seem destined to lead many of these countries to a future that could prove even more bleak than a repeat of unregulated capitalism at its height would be.

Liberal theories have so far proven less adept at coming to terms with these challenges, with their cultural and social roots, than they have been in the past at responding to problems raised by the state and by the economy. It is true that subordination of people by race or gender is seen as a problem—that is, is seen as *subordination*—because of commitments to freedom and equality that are integral to liberal thought. To an ancien regime aristocrat or a nineteenth-century social Darwinist, subordination would presumably seem natural and unproblematic. Yet familiar liberal theories are poorly equipped to respond to these kinds of subordination. If white Americans move out of their neighborhoods when more than a handful of black Americans move in, and only blacks are interested in buying their vacant houses, the resulting segregation in housing appears to be a product of individual decisions that people should be free to make, according to most liberal theories, even if it happens to be the case that most blacks would prefer to live in integrated neighborhoods.

The challenges posed by these events differ qualitatively from those to which the liberal tradition of political theory has adapted in the past. Although the concepts of individual rights and distributive justice focused on income and wealth remain potent tools of criticism, they are not adequate for the tasks that liberals face today. Liberals insist, correctly, that the most urgent task in most of the countries of Eastern Europe is to establish constitutional governments and the rule of law.[2] Even if we should be fortunate enough to succeed in this task, though, the forces of cultural and racial particularism throughout Eastern Europe will present further problems that may resemble those raised by the persistence of subordination in countries with firmly established constitutional regimes.

Does the liberal tradition have within itself the intellectual resources needed to address these problems and to help guide us toward promising solutions? That is the question I address in this book. My conclusion is that it does. In order to seize control of those resources, however, I argue that we must break with styles of thinking that have tended to predominate within the liberal tradition in the recent past. The standard approaches must be reworked if we are to regain the vigor that will be required to address the new—or at least newly visible—political problems that confront us today.

My focus in this work is on political theory and on the resources that theories make available to us, or fail to make available to us, for political and social criticism. Let us be clear at the outset about what a political theory is: a theory is a particular way of seeing the world. We may compare the product of such a way of seeing with a painting. In a theory, as in a painting, objects or events are arranged in a particular order within a field of vision. Some objects appear in the foreground and at or near the focal point of the picture. Others are shown slightly to one side or in the background. Still other objects or events are represented inconspicuously or marginally. Finally and in a way most importantly, many objects or events are left out of the picture altogether.

Theories arrange perceptions and filter information. They filter out a great deal of information completely and place the pieces of information that manage to make it into the picture in a distinctive order. The order is necessarily hierarchical: only one or a few events or objects can occupy the focal point of a theory. By selecting and arranging information, theories also set agendas, giving us signals about where to look further and conveying messages about the kinds of information that are and are not likely to be worth collecting. The filtering or selection and arrangement of information is an act of

---

[2] As Bruce Ackerman does eloquently in *The Future of Liberal Revolution* (New Haven: Yale University Press, 1992).

power. Political theories are assertions *of* power as well as claims *about* power. Political theories are political acts.

The primordial and most significant act of a political theory is the act of identifying *what counts*, of selecting the items that are to be included in the picture and especially those that are to occupy its foreground. In Jeremy Bentham's classical utilitarian theory, for example, the only things that count in an ultimate sense are pleasure and pain. Determining what counts is only the first step in composing a theory. Once that step has been taken, further questions arise about *how* items of information should be counted and about how they should be "weighed" or "taken into account" in relation to one another. But the initial selection of items for the privilege of inclusion in the picture is the fundamental theoretical act. It determines what the picture will contain, however the items in that picture may be arranged in the end. Theories that make this initial selection lightly and then proceed to lavish attention on discussion of sophisticated methods of counting—including some works rooted in or inspired by the utilitarian tradition—appear shallow.[3]

I shall focus in this work on what counts, that is, on the basic evaluative claims of liberal political theories. I shall begin by taking a partial inventory of theories that have been central to the development of liberal political thought in recent years. I do not consider all the claims, or even all the major claims, asserted by these theories. Instead, I ask two basic questions about each theory: first, according to the theory, what counts? And second, is the theory's selection of the items that are to count convincing? I argue that despite their many strengths, existing liberal theories fail to identify what counts with sufficient perspicacity to guide liberals toward convincing solutions to some of the major political problems we face today. I then go on to propose a revision of liberal theory that takes into account things that are neglected or ignored in existing theories. The heart of my proposal is a suggestion about what we should count, what features we should look for, when we are comparing existing institutions and practices with alternatives.

My proposal is a liberal proposal. It is based on the same fundamental commitments and values that underpin other liberal theories. Despite the shortcomings of these theories, those commitments and values seem to me sound. Suitably interpreted and updated, the liberal tradition of political thought contains the material needed to compose powerful answers to many pressing practical questions that confront us today. In order to find these answers, however, we must give the liberal tradition a fresh look. That is what I do in this book.

[3] I do *not* mean to suggest that the utilitarian tradition of moral and political thought as a whole is shallow. John Stuart Mill, for example, considered himself a utilitarian, but he disagreed with Bentham and James Mill about what counts in moral and political theory, in large part because he seems to have thought more deeply about this question than they had done.

The number of theories that might potentially be examined with these questions in mind is enormous, even if we restrict ourselves to theories within the liberal tradition, broadly construed, and to works published within the past twenty-five years or so. A complete inventory of all these theories could not be taken even in a very long book and is out of the question in a short book like this one. I have, however, selected for close examination a handful of works that seem to me representative of a considerable range of the existing alternatives and especially of the more influential schools of thought within the contemporary liberal tradition. Each of the theories I discuss embodies claims or assumptions that are held in high esteem by many thoughtful people. In effect I have chosen to examine several genres of liberal political theory by considering closely one or a few outstanding examples of each genre, just as one might discuss and compare several schools of painting by selecting one or two representative works from each.

During the past two or three centuries the liberal tradition of political thought has come to play a powerful part in political discourse throughout much of the world, and in some of the most economically developed countries that tradition now occupies a position that might reasonably be described as hegemonic.[4] Theories become powerful by persuading people to perceive the world as those theories represent it. Powerful theories define a world of perception and speech. A theory is powerful when assertions that are consistent with the theory are considered credible and when claims that challenge or are inconsistent with the theory are regarded with suspicion or rejected out of hand. To a substantial degree powerful theories define the way the world really is, because people act on their perceptions to arrange the world to be the way the theory says it is or should be. Beneath the appearance created by a theory's representations, however, the world is never precisely the way a theory represents it to be. There are always items left out of the picture created by a theory. Items that are left out or obscured by a theory's representations are not usually eliminated from reality. Points of view may be made invisible or ignored by the canonical works of a school of thought. Their omission from that canon may make those points of view very difficult to represent and to convey to others, but it does not necessarily extinguish them.

Political theories are reinvigorated when previously unacknowledged or unseen perspectives are forced upon them, when they must take account of things they have been designed *not* to take into account, or when they

[4] For the concept of hegemony, see Antonio Gramsci, *Selections from the Prison Notebooks of Antonio Gramsci* (New York: International Publishers, 1985). Although the liberal tradition is hegemonic in some parts of the world, its hegemony is neither as monolithic nor as secure as Francis Fukuyama has claimed in *The End of History and the Last Man* (New York: Free Press, 1992).

must take things into account in a way different from that to which they are accustomed. That is what liberal political theory must do. To return to a metaphor used previously, I argue that existing liberal theories filter information in the wrong ways. But I also argue that those theories, or at least that tradition of theory, can be modified in ways that will enable it to address important contemporary problems without abandoning its most fundamental commitments.

The realization that theories are selective, that they filter information and shape perceptions in ways that block some kinds of information from entering the picture and suppress some perceptions and points of view, may give rise to a demand for the elimination of selectivity and even for the elimination of theory altogether. "Theory" in this sense may seem to be a medium or instrument that distorts reality or prevents us from grasping it directly and authentically. This suspicion can easily grow into the conviction that theories are *only* more or less disguised attempts to exercise power, that behind all lofty talk and noble ideals there lies nothing but—power.[5]

It would be possible for us to live without political theory. But I do not think we would live better if we were somehow able to eliminate the practice of theorizing about political things from our lives. Political theory is simply the practice of engaging in deliberate reflection on our political and social arrangements. That practice becomes theoretical when it becomes genuinely critical. It becomes genuinely critical when we compare our existing political and social arrangements with alternatives, whether these alternatives are drawn from the real world or from the speculative imagination. Elimination of the practice of political theory would make us *less* able to engage in radical criticism of our current practices and arrangements, not more so.

Political theory consists, most rudimentarily, in the practice of comparing our actual political world with some possible alternative world or worlds. Engagement in this practice naturally leads to speculation about the basis on which comparisons should be drawn. This sort of speculation has been part and parcel of the tradition of political theory at least from Plato onward. One view that was sometimes put forth in antiquity was that political arrangements should be judged primarily by their antiquity or by the likelihood that they would last a long time. Another was that political arrangements should be evaluated by reference to their capacity to produce great and memorable accomplishments, including conquests. A third view that has been widely advocated during the past several centuries is that political and social arrangements should be evaluated on the basis of their capacity to maintain peace and to sustain prosperity. A fourth view, which seems to have arisen

---

[5] Although Michel Foucault never quite falls into this view, he comes close to expressing it in some of his writings. See, for example, *Discipline and Punish: The Birth of the Prison* (New York: Vintage Books, 1979).

in many different ages without ever becoming established as a dominant perspective for very long, is that political arrangements that best sustain the ability of the members of a political community to take part in deliberation and decision making on affairs of common interest are best.

Claims about the basis on which alternative political and social arrangements should be compared are claims about what should count in evaluating those arrangements. We cannot simply compare Athens with Sparta, Judea with Rome, the United States as it actually is at the close of the twentieth century with the United States as it might be with quite different political and social arrangements, without identifying some basis on which to make these comparisons. Claims about what should count in evaluating alternative arrangements are contestable, as are all political claims. But political criticism could hardly occur at all in the absence of these claims.[6]

Even if we were to succeed in banishing claims about what counts in evaluating social arrangements, we would not be able to eliminate the selectivity, the filtering, and the neglect or suppression of some perceptions and points of view that lead some people to object to those claims in the first place. Filtering, sifting through arguments and ideas, and selectivity of perceptions will occur in any case. These processes are integral to the way people think, the way we cope with the world. As Nietzsche has pointed out forcefully, there is *only* perspective seeing, only perspective knowing; knowledge of things "in themselves" or as they "really are," shorn of all particularity of perspective, is impossible.[7] The call for the elimination of filters in our political thinking is as utopian as the demand for the elimination of power in our political lives.

The serious question is not whether we can eliminate filters that lead us to count some things while discounting others in our political criticisms but rather what sorts of filters, what sort of basis for comparison between alternative political arrangements, we would like to adopt. The elimination of claims about what counts in the name of radical criticism is a utopian and self-defeating objective. But the alteration of an existing conception of what

[6] Proponents of the critique of "foundationalism" that became popular among philosophers and political theorists in the 1980s often point out that meaningful social criticism is comparative, that one has to compare the status quo with a plausible alternative in order to establish a persuasive critique. The point is well taken, but antifoundationalists often overlook the fact that comparative social criticism presupposes a *basis* of critical comparison. We cannot compare *X* and *Y* critically without knowing what we are looking for, what we want to take into account in making the comparison. For some examples of the critique of foundationalism, see Michael Walzer, "Philosophy and Democracy," *Political Theory* 9 (1981): 379–99; Don Herzog, *Without Foundations: Justification in Political Theory* (Ithaca: Cornell University Press, 1985); and Richard Rorty, "The Priority of Democracy to Philosophy," in *The Virginia Statute for Religious Freedom*, ed. Merrill D. Peterson and Robert C. Vaughan (Cambridge: Cambridge University Press, 1988), pp. 257–82.

[7] For a fine, clear discussion of Nietzsche's perspectivism, see Tracy B. Strong, "Texts and Pretexts: Reflections on Perspectivism in Nietzsche," *Political Theory* 13 (1985): 164–82.

should count, even if that conception is a powerful or a hegemonic one, though difficult, is *not* a utopian objective.

This question—what should we count when we are considering changes in our political and social arrangements?—motivates my inquiry throughout the pages that follow.

The liberal tradition of political theory has sometimes been depicted as an anticritical, antiradical, and even antipolitical movement, a movement that has sought actively to bring political philosophy to an end.[8] I hope to show that this view is mistaken. Liberal theory is as capable of producing radical criticism today as any school of political theory has been in the past. In order to realize its potential as an effective critical tool, however, liberal theory stands in need of revision and renewal, of a new sense of direction. We need today, as much as at any time in the past, clarity of purpose. John Dewey once argued that "in a complicated and perverse world, action which is not informed with vision, imagination, and reflection, is more likely to increase confusion and conflict than to straighten things out."[9] I have written this book on the premise that the liberal tradition is capable of supplying that vision. It is my aim to show how it can do so.

[8] For a version of the claim that liberalism is antipolitical, see Sheldon S. Wolin, *Politics and Vision* (Boston: Little, Brown, 1960), chap. 9.

[9] "The Need for a Recovery of Philosophy," in John Dewey, *The Middle Works, 1899–1924*, vol. 10, ed. Jo Ann Boydston (Carbondale: Southern Illinois University Press, 1980), p. 46.

CHAPTER ONE

Political Theory and Liberal Values

IMAGINE THAT YOU have been asked to participate in the founding of a new society. One of your tasks is to help select the institutions and practices that will regulate that society's affairs. You do not have to invent those institutions and practices ex nihilo, nor do you have to gather the empirical information on which your decision will be based. That preliminary work has been done for you. Instead, you are presented with a handful of ready-made plans, each of which describes the institutions and practices of a hypothetical but fully operational society. The information provided in the plans is as detailed, roughly, as the information you could acquire about the society of which you are currently a member. In short, although your task is of great significance, it is also narrowly defined. What criteria would you use to make your selection?

In real life this question does not arise, at least not in this bald form. Alternative proposals for political, legal, and social reform arise frequently, but alternative plans for society as a whole do not. Moreover, we generally consider alternative proposals for reform against a background of normative presuppositions. For the most part we focus our critical scrutiny on the reform proposals themselves, not on the norms we use to evaluate those proposals. Sometimes we regard those norms as given, supposing that no critical scrutiny of them is required. At other times we justify norms by appealing to an authority; in the United States some of the documents associated with the country's founding are often favored for this purpose. On other occasions we cite allegedly widespread assumptions or shared understandings as the bases of our criticisms. Most political and social criticism is piecemeal, and most of it also draws on established or allegedly established norms.

All this is probably as it should be. But piecemeal criticism based on existing norms is not the *only* kind of political or social criticism in which we need to engage. Sometimes we are confronted with revolutionary situations brought on by the collapse of a regime or by similarly cataclysmic events. At other times we discover that existing norms conflict with one another, or that the consequences of applying established norms are not those for which we hoped. In these circumstances we must probe more deeply than we are accustomed ordinarily to do. Moreover, even piecemeal criticism and reform based on existing norms presuppose that those norms can be justified by the roles they play in maintaining a good society. We must then consider, more broadly than we usually do, how a good society differs from a bad one. We must confront the problem with which the co-founders of a new society would have to deal.

In this book I consider several liberal political theories. I identify and examine critically each theory's claims about the bases on which we should distinguish between good societies and bad ones (or between better and worse societies). I argue that the existing theories I examine here have defects. I then propose a revised liberal theory that is intended to rectify these defects. The theory I propose is rough and rudimentary, and it will no doubt have to be revised further as well as be developed and refined. Nevertheless, that theory seems to me to take advantage of the strengths of existing liberal theories while avoiding their most serious weaknesses.

The notion of a good society is comparable in some ways to the notion of a healthy individual. One major dissimilarity between these two notions is that the idea of a good society is far more controversial than that of a healthy individual. Suppose, though, that the idea of health were more controversial than it now is. Ordinary people who take a serious interest in their own health and that of others would confront a bewildering variety of recommendations. In the face of seriously conflicting advice from physicians, nutritionists and others claiming specialized knowledge, they might want to review some of the existing conceptions of health held by these specialists and others in order to develop a conception of health for themselves. They might also want to work with others to develop a working definition of health for adoption in contexts affecting many people. For example, they might want to ensure that the ideas about health taught to physicians in medical schools are reasonably consistent with their own. If that task should prove impossible, say because of the resistance of the medical community, then they would at least want to become aware of the discrepancies between their own conceptions of health and those held by that community in order to be forewarned about the basis of the medical advice and treatment they are likely to be given.

My project in this book is similar to that of a person who wants to formulate a usable, working definition of health in the face of conflicting theories of health. The theories I examine in the following pages are like alternative definitions of health for political and social arrangements.

Political Theory and the State

It may be useful here at the outset to specify the scope and purposes of this project a little more precisely. My objective is to compose a satisfactory account of the evaluative or normative bases of political and social criticism.

By political and social criticism I mean criticism of political, economic, cultural, and other institutions and practices that shape a society and determine what the lives of the members of that society will be like. I shall speak of political criticism and social criticism interchangeably. My reason for doing so is to call attention to the fact that criticism of cultural, economic, and social institutions and practices has a political dimension as well as a cultural, economic, or social one. It is not to suggest that I am interested only in criticism that is directed toward *explicitly* political institutions, much less that I am interested only in criticism of that specific political institution we call the "state." In modern societies the state plays an important role in shaping individuals' lives, but it does not play an all-powerful role. I am interested in the full ensemble of political and social arrangements that enable people to do things or that frustrate them and prevent them from doing things.

Similarly, I do not assume that the state is the sole or necessarily the primary agent of reform or change. In some instances the state may be the most appropriate instrument for reforming unhealthy social arrangements to make them healthier. In other circumstances the state may be a poor choice of institutions through which to work for reform. Even if we could formulate a highly precise and full picture of health for a society's political and social arrangements that all the members of that society would agree represents their ideas about a good society better than all known alternatives, it would not follow that the state is the institution best suited to reform existing arrangements to bring them into accord with that picture.

Adam Smith considered the capacity of a society to generate wealth, which he understood to consist of the goods and services that supply the "necessaries and conveniencies" of life to individuals, to be one of the most important determinants of a society's health. But Smith believed that the efforts of the major states of his time to encourage growth in wealth were misconceived because they were based on the errors, as he considered them, of the mercantile doctrine. Further, Smith believed that most efforts by the state to facilitate the generation of wealth would necessarily prove counterproductive. In his view the role of the state in securing the health of a society consists of guaranteeing peace and security to its inhabitants and providing a regime of laws that are impartially conceived and administered. The activities that lead directly to wealth generation are best left to individuals acting independently of the state, though within a framework of laws enforced by it. In Smith's opinion generation of wealth is one of the key aspects of a society's health. Yet he did not think that the state should be the primary agent involved in the creation of wealth.

The existence or acceptance of a standard for comparing and evaluating alternative political and social arrangements does *not* entail acceptance of the need for a centralized and activist state to put those standards into effect.[1] Whether or not a centralized and activist state is a necessary—or even desirable—means of creating and maintaining a good society depends on the content of that standard as well as other factors. Some conceptions of health for political and social arrangements might entail the view that no state, or only a minimal state, can be justified. That is the view Robert Nozick holds.[2] Other views about the bases of social criticism may lead to other conclusions about the appropriate role of the state. My point here is only that if we were to accept the view that a single critical standard applies equally to all societies, that acceptance would not entail the conclusion that a powerful state is needed to enforce that standard.

Political Theory and Democracy

Political and social criticism are activities in which nearly everyone is interested and has engaged in some way. In societies in which they are free to do so without reprisal, people engage in criticism in a spirited and public way. In those societies that do not provide secure protection for freedom of political speech or that actively persecute dissenters, people engage in criticism covertly. The only societies in which the activity of political and social criticism is not widely practiced are those in which repression of dissent is so effective that even covert expressions of dissatisfaction are too dangerous for most people to be willing to risk, and those whose members are unaware that any alternative way of life might be possible—those, that is, in which so little comparative or historical imagination exists that reasoned criticism is impossible.

Although the activities of political and social criticism are nearly universal, the practice of speculating intensively about alternative societies and about the bases of comparison between them is not. This practice has rarely attracted the interest of more than a small handful of people in any society. One reason for this fact is that hard thinking and speculation take time. In most societies relatively few people enjoy the leisure required to engage in these pursuits.

One significant consequence of these facts is that the products of critical

---

[1] Michael Walzer argues in *Spheres of Justice: A Defense of Pluralism and Equality* (New York: Basic Books, 1983) that a "centralized and activist" state would be required to enforce the prescriptions of classical utilitarianism or Rawls's difference principle, and he seems to imply that a powerful state would be required to enforce any general rule of distributive justice (see pp. xv and 14–16). I agree with Walzer that both classical utilitarianism and Rawls's difference principle are problematic, but I think the reason they are problematic is that they emphasize maximization, whether of aggregate utility or of the position of the least advantaged members of society. Nonmaximizing rules do not raise the same kinds of problems. I discuss this problem with the difference principle more fully in chap. 4, sec. IV.

[2] In his *Anarchy, State, and Utopia* (New York: Basic Books, 1974). I examine Nozick's arguments, including his argument on this point, in some detail in chap. 2.

political speculation often have displayed aristocratic sympathies. Political *criticism* is usually a democratic activity, but historically, political *philosophy* has mostly been an aristocratic domain. Yet the historical connection between political philosophy and aristocratic leanings is contingent and sociological, not necessary and conceptual. Political philosophy (or political theory) is not inherently an antidemocratic practice.

Speculation about the bases of social criticism can and should serve a democratic purpose. Arguments about what should count when we compare and choose between alternative social arrangements can help democratic citizens to clarify their thoughts and reasoning. Speculation about alternatives can also be a source of proposals for reform, including radical reform, that can be drawn upon in processes of democratic deliberation.

Jürgen Habermas, a proponent of radical democracy, has suggested that the validity of norms for political and social arrangements can be assessed in part by ascertaining whether those norms incorporate interests that are "generalizable" to all those affected by them.[3] But Habermas has been criticized widely for focusing in his own work on formal or metatheoretical questions regarding the legitimation of norms and for avoiding the kind of substantive discussion of generalizable interests that would give content to his work.[4] The arguments about the bases of social criticism that I shall consider here, including the view I develop in the final two chapters of this book, can be thought of as attempts to give content to this Habermasian effort. In other words, these liberal theories might be regarded as proposed specifications of the generalizable interests we should take into account when we engage in criticism of particular institutions or practices or of our political and social arrangements as a whole. This description of the status of these theories may not in all cases be in accord with their authors' claims, but it is consistent with the approach to these theories that I shall adopt.

Political Theory and Universality

The liberal political theories I discuss in this book, including the rudimentary theory I sketch in chapter five, are intended to be applicable to all societies, or at least to all societies that meet a few well-defined conditions. These theories are universalistic in aspirations.

[3] See his *Legitimation Crisis*, translated by Thomas McCarthy (Boston: Beacon Press, 1975), pp. 104ff.; *Theorie der Gesellschaft oder Sozialtechnologie: Was Leistet die Systemforschung?* with Niklas Luhmann (Frankfurt: Suhrkamp, 1971), pp. 121, 123; and *The Theory of Communicative Action*, vol. 1: *Reason and the Rationalization of Society*, trans. Thomas McCarthy (Boston: Beacon Press, 1981), p. 89.

[4] He has also been criticized, more sharply, for trying to build content into his theory while avoiding the discussion of generalizable interests that would be necessary to justify that content. For a recent example of this line of criticism see David M. Rasmussen, *Reading Habermas* (Oxford: Blackwell, 1990).

The bases of piecemeal social criticism can be explained and defended, at least up to a point, without reference to universalistic claims. For this kind of criticism we can usually appeal to established norms or shared understandings to provide an adequate account of our practical reasoning. But piecemeal criticism is not the only kind of political and social criticism in which we engage or need to engage. Broader sorts of criticism—the kinds of criticism in which we engage in revolutionary situations or in situations in which existing understandings fail to yield a sense of direction clear enough to guide our actions—must be explained by reference to universalistic claims.

Particularistic approaches to social criticism, such as the approach Michael Walzer defends in *Spheres of Justice*, have much to recommend them. Many trenchant criticisms can be formulated by appealing to a society's shared understandings rather than by invoking universalistic claims. The civil rights movement in the United States in the quarter century that followed the Second World War is a prime example of a reform movement that worked as well as it did largely because it could point to serious discrepancies between ideas about the way American society ought to be that were widely shared by both white and black Americans and the reality of American society as it actually was (and to a large extent still is).[5] Moreover, criticisms that appeal to existing norms or shared understandings are likely to be more effective than criticisms that appeal to abstract ideals in which people do not already believe, at least to some degree. However, there are times when existing norms or shared understandings fail to provide needed guidance, or provide the wrong guidance. On these occasions we need to turn to theories that are more universalistic in aspirations than Walzer's approach is.

Walzer does not renounce universalistic claims altogether. He argues that human beings do have some universal rights—rights not to be robbed of life or of liberty—and that for some purposes these rights can lead us to significant practical conclusions.[6] But Walzer also argues that these rights consti-

---

[5] The American civil rights movement can be considered an example of a reform movement rooted in particularistic social criticism, but with two important qualifications. The first is that the relevant understandings were not as widely shared in the American South, where expressions of belief in significant racial differences in capabilities were still commonly expressed in public in the 1960s, as they were in some other parts of the country. The second is that the relevant understandings, such as the view that "all men are created equal," embody universalistic claims.

[6] The argument is developed in Walzer's *Just and Unjust Wars: A Moral Argument with Historical Illustrations* (New York: Basic Books, 1977), esp. chaps. 4 and 8. Walzer reminds the readers of *Spheres of Justice* of his previous use of the idea of universal rights in his preface, p. xv. For an informed and useful discussion of Walzer's views that defends his approach to social criticism, see Glen Stassen, "Michael Walzer's Situated Justice," *Journal of Religious Ethics* *Journal of Religious Ethics* 20, no.4 (Fall 1994).

tute too minimal a basis of criticism for many purposes and that the "effort to produce a complete account of justice or a defense of equality by multiplying rights soon makes a farce of what it multiplies."[7] I agree with Walzer that the strategy of trying to develop a complete account of justice by appealing to rights is not fruitful.[8] However, I also think that human beings have universal or generalizable interests beyond their interests in not being robbed of life or liberty and that we can develop some strong universalistic claims by appealing to those interests without threatening the pluralism Walzer wants to defend.

Like societies, human beings differ from one another in myriad ways. We are young and old, female and male, have different skin, hair, and eye colors, different physical features, different skills. The diversity of human individuals makes it possible for all of us, if we wish, to lead richer lives than we would otherwise be able to have. Yet the diversity of human individuals does not prevent us from applying a single conception of health to all those individuals. A healthy female is not identical to a healthy male; a healthy child is not identical to a healthy adult; but our *single* notion of health is broad enough to encompass those differences. Similarly, a conception of health for political and social arrangements should be both universal and broad enough to accommodate differences. The normative claims that underlie liberal theories are universal claims, as they should be, though the arguments built on those claims should be historically informed and culturally sensitive as well.[9]

I

The theories I consider in this book are *liberal* accounts of the bases of political criticism. The terms *liberal* and *liberalism* are used in a variety of ways. The apparent meanings of these terms have varied so greatly, in fact, that some people have called for their abolition from serious discussion, or at least for a moratorium on their use. I have not followed that advice. I do want to explain, though, what I mean when I call a political theory a liberal theory. In order to do so I shall mention two different ways in which one might define that term.

One way to define a liberal political view would be to identify certain institutional arrangements liberal political theories recommend. These institutional arrangements include a state with an effective constitution, either in

[7] Walzer, *Spheres of Justice*, p. xv.

[8] I argue for this conclusion in chap. 2.

[9] So I endorse Seyla Benhabib's premise that "the crucial insights of the universalist tradition in practical philosophy can be reformulated today without committing oneself to the metaphysical illusions of the Enlightenment," in *Situating the Self: Gender, Community, and Postmodernism in Contemporary Ethics* (New York: Routledge, 1992), p. 4.

written form or inscribed in a common understanding shared by the citizens of that state; a system of legal rules enforced by the state and by a judiciary that has some independence from the electoral and bargaining processes of ordinary political affairs; the existence of an institutionalized distinction between public and private and of effective individual rights; the existence of markets for the exchange of goods and services; and some form of democratic political representation, including protection of political liberties such as freedom of speech and of assembly, a free press, and so forth.

I think that any liberal society would have to possess all these institutions in some form. For my purposes, though, it seems more useful to define liberal political theories as theories that are based on a commitment to certain distinctively liberal values. A liberal would use these values to evaluate political and social institutions. They do not necessarily apply to subjects other than those institutions. For example, a liberal might not want to use these values to determine how a parent should divide her estate between her children or to determine how much, if any, of that estate should go to her children at all. The practice of making bequests would have to take place in a setting defined by institutions that embody these values, but those values need not necessarily determine the actions of a legator or of individuals faced with similar problems of practical reasoning.

Liberal values in the general form in which I shall state them here do not *fully* define the values that a liberal would use to evaluate political and social arrangements. A full statement of those values would be a complete liberal political theory, or at least a complete liberal *normative* theory. Liberal values have to be interpreted, and the differences of interpretation that arise when these values are elaborated into a full theory distinguish different liberal theories from one another. I think that any liberal, though, would consider political and social arrangements that fail to embody these values in some recognizable way unacceptable. In any case, I shall use the word *liberal* to describe theories based on the following commitments or norms.

ONLY INDIVIDUALS COUNT

According to liberal theories, at least as I shall define that class of theories here, the only information that is *directly* relevant for evaluating alternative political and social arrangements is information about their impact on individual human beings.

The liberal view that only individuals count rules out a wide range of possible alternative views. For example, it rules out the view that the military greatness of a state or nation is directly relevant for assessing that state's political and social arrangements. A state's military capacities may be *indirectly* relevant to assessment, of course. If military greatness increases the security of individuals in a society or in some other way improves their lives, then the capacity of a society to achieve that greatness must be counted in its favor. On the other hand, if the organization required to achieve military

greatness damages individuals' lives—say, by subjecting them to stifling reg-
imentation—then that fact weighs against arrangements that promote military greatness. From a liberal point of view, a society's capacity to achieve
military greatness counts for nothing at all on its own account. That capacity
does count, though, through its impact on individuals.

The claim that only individuals count also rules out the view that information about the impact of alternative arrangements on groups or on cultural
artifacts or practices as such is directly relevant to evaluations of those arrangements. Suppose, for example, the members of a society are considering
adoption of a new constitution. The only significant difference between the
proposed constitution and the existing one is that the proposed arrangement
would encourage the preservation of existing ethnic and religious subcultures significantly more than the existing constitution does. From a liberal
perspective, this differential impact of the two alternatives on subcultures is
not in itself a reason to prefer either to the other. What counts from this
perspective is the impact of arrangements on individuals. If the preservation
of existing subcultures can be expected, on the whole, to improve the lives
of the members of that society, then the proposed constitution, which would
encourage that preservation, is superior from a liberal point of view to the
existing constitution, which does not. But if the subcultures in question tend
to harm individuals—say, by encouraging a conception of masculinity that
leads to the subordination of women or by discouraging the acquisition of
knowledge and skills that would enable individuals to lead better lives—
then encouragement or protection of those subcultures should count against
the proposal and in favor of the existing constitution. In a liberal view, what
matters is the impact of arrangements on individuals rather than their impact on cultures or on the preservation of groups as such.

The claim that only individuals should count for the purpose of evaluating
alternative political and social institutions neither entails nor presupposes
the view that individuals are or should be egoistic. The claim that only individuals count embodies a view about the *value* of individuals. Taken by itself, it does not imply a view about the *characters* of individuals. Liberal
theories sometimes *do* make claims about the characters of individuals, but
these claims are not implied by the assumption that only individuals count.

Similarly, neither the claim that only individuals count nor any other key
element of liberal values implies that we must think of individuals, or that
they should think of themselves, as disembodied subjects, abstract persons
shorn of their identities, commitments, traditions, and community ties.[10]

---

[10] Liberalism is associated with the idea of a disembodied subject by Alasdair MacIntyre in *After
Virtue*, 2d ed. (Notre Dame: University of Notre Dame Press, 1984), esp. pp. 29–33, and by
Michael Sandel in *Liberalism and the Limits of Justice* (Cambridge: Cambridge University
Press, 1982). Charles Taylor, who has contributed to this line of argument about liberalism, has
recently reconsidered this characterization; see his *Sources of the Self: The Making of the Mod-
ern Identity* (Cambridge, Mass.: Harvard University Press, 1989), esp. pp. 531–32, n. 60.

This conception of the individual plays only a secondary role even in Kantian versions of liberal political theory, and it plays no role at all in most versions of liberal theory. The persons who count in liberal political theory are real, flesh-and-blood individuals, with families, histories, and views about the ways in which they fit in with other human beings.[11]

The liberal view that only individuals count does not require liberals to be blind to the fact that group membership and shared cultural practices are important to individuals and play a significant role in helping many people to build valuable lives. The cultural heritage of French Canadians, for example, is an important source of identity and meaning in the lives of many Québécois. Nor does this commitment require liberals to ignore the fact that characteristics shared by the members of a group can have other significant effects on those members. Being black in America means having an identity assigned to you by the majority of the members of your society that has nothing to do with your achievements or individual personality. For many black Americans, because of the attitudes of white Americans, the overall impact of this group membership is adverse. The liberal principle that only individuals count does not imply that these effects on individuals should be ignored.

The liberal principle that only individuals count is a claim about the bases of comparison between alternative institutions and practices. It is not a claim about the law or about legislation, at least not directly. From the liberal principle that only individuals count it does not follow that legislation and adjudication must be blind to the existence of groups. Law is a blunt instrument. Ultimately legislation and adjudication should be evaluated by reference to their impact on individuals. In some circumstances, though, legislation or adjudication that recognizes the existence of groups might end up having the most favorable impact on individuals. What counts in the end is that impact, not the specific form legislation happens to take.[12]

Individuals may and often do make plans together, share aspirations and goals, engage in collective projects, and formulate common goals. But the

[11] Nancy L. Rosenblum's *Another Liberalism: Romanticism and the Reconstruction of Liberal Thought* (Cambridge, Mass.: Harvard University Press, 1987) and Will Kymlicka's *Liberalism, Community, and Culture* (Oxford: Clarendon Press, 1989) both respond thoughtfully to criticism of liberal theories for their alleged dependence on the idea of a disembodied subject.

[12] For some discussion of the relevance of groups to adjudication, see Owen M. Fiss, "Coda," *University of Toronto Law Journal* 38 (1988): 229–44; Ernest J. Weinrib, "Adjudication and Public Values: Fiss's Critique of Corrective Justice," ibid., vol. 39 (1989): 1–18; and Cass R. Sunstein, "The Limits of Compensatory Justice," Randy E. Barnett, "Compensation and Rights in the Liberal Conception of Justice," and David Johnston, "Beyond Compensatory Justice?" all in *Compensatory Justice: Nomos XXXIII*, ed. John W. Chapman (New York: New York University Press, 1991), pp. 281–310, 311–29, and 330–54, respectively.

aspirations and hopes associated with these projects and goals are *individuals'* aspirations and hopes. The satisfactions of success and the disappointments of failure are individuals' satisfactions and disappointments. Only individuals can be miserable and can suffer. These are some of the reasons why liberals hold the view that only individuals count.

EVERYBODY COUNTS AS ONE, NOBODY AS MORE THAN ONE

In liberal political theories, individuals are viewed as free and equal persons. The differences between different liberal theories stem from different interpretations of the notions of freedom and equality. All members of the class of liberal theories as I define that class here share some rudimentary assumptions about freedom and equality, however.

Liberal theories assume that all human beings possess whatever features make us worth counting in roughly equal measure with all other human beings. Hobbes argued that it is a law of nature "that every man acknowledge other for his Equal by Nature."[13] Bentham argued that all human beings possess roughly equal capacities for pleasure and pain. For him, this fact entails the conclusion that when we compare alternative institutions or policies, everybody should count as one, nobody for more than one.[14] I shall call this claim the equality stipulation.

Bentham's conception of equality is sometimes held by liberals to be seriously inadequate. But that judgment is based either on a rejection of the reasoning he offers to support his equality stipulation, which emphasizes individuals' capacities for pleasure and pain; or on a rejection of his application of that stipulation, which neglects the separateness of persons; or on both.[15] Liberals accept the equality stipulation itself, though many of them interpret that stipulation differently from Bentham.

The equality stipulation rules out many arguments and claims that have been made in the history of political thought from aristocratic points of view. Hobbes pointed out forcefully that the egalitarian premise of his political theory is incompatible with Aristotelian aristocratic views that were held during his lifetime. The equality stipulation also apparently rules out the Platonic view that the best regime is one in which philosophers

[13] Hobbes, *Leviathan, or the Matter, Forme, and Power of a Commonwealth, Ecclesiastical and Civill*, ed. Richard Tuck (Cambridge: Cambridge University Press, 1991), p. 107.

[14] John Stuart Mill attributes this dictum to Bentham in his "Utilitarianism," in Mill, *"Utilitarianism" and Other Writings* (New York: New American Library, 1974), p. 319. Additional relevant comments occur in Bentham's *Essai sur la Représentation*, written toward the end of 1788 with France in mind. For a useful discussion of this work, see Elie Halévy, *The Growth of Philosophical Radicalism* (London: Faber and Faber, 1972), pp. 147–48.

[15] John Rawls, for example, argues that "utilitarianism does not take seriously the distinction between persons" (*A Theory of Justice* [Cambridge, Mass.: Harvard University Press, 1971], p. 27). Not all forms of utilitarian theory are subject to this criticism, but Bentham's theory is.

rule.[16] And it plainly rules out Nietzsche's view, which is that although only individuals count, some individuals count more than others.[17]

EVERYBODY TO COUNT AS AN AGENT

Liberal theories are based on the view that individuals are free as well as equal beings. Minimally, the claim that we are free means that we possess the capacity to be agents. From a distinctively liberal point of view individuals count equally with one another because we all equally possess the capacity for human agency, not—or at least not only—because we possess roughly equal capacities for pleasure and pain.

By an "agent" I mean a being who is capable of conceiving values and projects, including projects whose fulfillment may not be within the range of that being's immediate experience. This slightly abstruse statement requires some explanation. Suppose you hear a person calling for help and turn to see that she has fallen into a river and is in danger of drowning. Although you have never met the person before, you jump into the river and, with considerable effort and inconvenience to yourself, manage to bring her to shore, thereby saving her life. One way of explaining your action would be to say that you attach value to human life in general, including the lives of people whom you do not personally know. The value of human life to you is independent of your own experience. In other words, you do not attach value to people's lives merely because you expect their existence as living beings to have some impact on you. You simply attach value to the continuation of people's lives, period. In fact, you attach sufficient value to the life of the person who is in danger of drowning that you are willing to experience some inconvenience, and to risk catching a cold, in order to rescue her.

The point of this example is not to suggest that the account of your actions I have offered is the only possible explanation for them. It is not. The point is, rather, that this explanation presupposes that you are an agent. I might

[16] It would be possible to argue that because, according to Plato, philosophers should rule in the interests of the city as a whole, their monopoly on ruling does not mean that in an aristocracy they count as more than other members of the city do. I doubt that this interpretation of the *Republic* is correct. In any case Plato does not seem to hold the most fundamental premise of liberal political theory, which is that only individuals count. To him it seems to be a matter of independent, and in fact overriding, importance that the city should be made safe for the activity of philosophizing, regardless of whether that activity benefits individuals. In this respect his view is similar to the view that societies should be evaluated by their capacity to achieve military greatness.

[17] Nietzsche regarded the liberal egalitarianism I describe here as an expression of a slave morality that is the antithesis of his aristocratic view, which "accepts with a good conscience the sacrifice of untold human beings who, for its sake, must be reduced and lowered to incomplete human beings, to slaves, to instruments." Nietzsche's moral theory is a theory of the *Übermensch*, whose superiority consists in strength of character and in the capacity to create and to live by values. See Friedrich Nietzsche, *Beyond Good and Evil*, trans. Walter Kaufman (New York: Random House, 1966), p. 202.

explain your actions in some other way. For instance, I might argue that you were motivated by an instinct of sympathy that you naturally feel for fellow human beings who are in danger. This latter argument does not presuppose that you are an agent. It presupposes only that you are a sentient being, that is, a being with feelings and sensations to which you are capable of responding. But my initial explanation of your actions assumes more than this. It assumes that you are an agent, a being who is capable of being moved by values that are not *about* your own experiences.

I suppose that agents are beings who are capable of conceiving values and projects that are not about their own experiences, and are capable of acting to realize those values and projects. Agents are of course also capable of conceiving values and projects that *are* about their own experiences. Agents are sentient beings *as well as* agents. Typically, they care about their own experiences as well as other things. But agents are at least *capable* of caring about things that they do not expect to have an impact on their own experiences. In contrast, sentient beings who are not agents are *not* capable of conceiving values and projects that are independent of their own experiences. Both agents and sentient beings who are not agents are presumably capable of attempting to save fellow members of their species who are in danger of drowning. But a description of the reasons for which an agent might act this way would differ from an account of the motives of a sentient being who is not an agent who acts in a similar way.

Although both agents and sentient beings who are not agents may be capable of attempting to save fellow members of their species from drowning, agents are capable of some actions of which sentient beings who are not agents probably are *not* capable. For example, an agent might come to place value on the survival and flourishing of all extant species on the earth and might act in ways that can be explained only on the assumption that she holds that value, a value that is not about her own experiences. Or she might value the preservation of a certain species, such as the bald eagle. She might even value the preservation of that species without particularly valuing the lives of individual members of that species, as long as the species as a whole is assured of survival. It is difficult to imagine a sentient being who is not an agent behaving in ways that would resemble the actions of an agent with this set of values. Being an agent is a prerequisite of being able to make a will to provide for the future of members of one's family. A sentient being who is not an agent would not have the imagination required to conceive the future in the way one must do to make a will. The values of an agent and the motives of a sentient being who is not an agent differ in kind. For example, an agent might desire fervently that other agents of her species colonize Mars, even if she does not care whether she participates in the colonization or not. She might value the colonization of Mars by other agents of her species even if she knows that she will never be able to know whether that objective is achieved. I cannot think of a plausible description of a sentient being who is not an agent with motives similar to those of this fervent supporter of space exploration.

Loren Lomasky has used an apt term to describe human agency. He has described human beings as "project pursuers."[18] Liberal theories, as I shall define that class of theories here, assume that individuals are valuable *qua* agents. Human beings count equally in theories that embody liberal values because they equally are capable of conceiving projects and values and because they equally can claim to have an interest in realizing their projects and values, in bringing their projects to fruition and in seeing their values embodied in the world.

If a liberal theory is a theory according to which all individuals count equally as agents, then Bentham was not a liberal as I define that term here, despite the fact that he accepted the first two of the three liberal principles I have outlined. Bentham held that only individuals count and that all individuals count equally. But he did not view individuals as agents, or if he did, he did not believe that the fact that individuals are agents is important to the way in which we evaluate alternative political and social arrangements. Locke seems to have regarded human beings essentially as agents. So, I think, did John Stuart Mill, whose break with his father and with Bentham within the utilitarian tradition can be seen as revolving largely around his different way of conceiving persons. Marx thought of people as agents, too, though he sometimes seems to reject the first principle of liberal theories as I have described it here, namely, that only individuals count.[19]

Liberal political theories, then, as I define that class of theories here, are theories about the bases on which we should evaluate alternative political and social arrangements that embrace the principles that only individuals count, that all individuals count equally, and that all individuals count as agents.

We might call the view I have just sketched "philosophical liberalism." Philosophical liberalism describes a basis for comparison between alternative institutions and practices. By contrast, we might use the label "institutional liberalism" to describe the view that certain institutions that are generally associated with liberal societies—constitutionalism and the rule of law, a distinction between public and private protected by the

---

[18] Loren E. Lomasky, *Persons, Rights, and the Moral Community* (Oxford: Oxford University Press, 1987).

[19] I say that Marx sometimes *seems* to reject the principle that only individuals count because the concept of class plays such a fundamental role throughout his work. In fact, though, Marx's ethical premises are probably consistent with the basic liberal principles I have outlined here. For an interesting discussion emphasizing individualism in Marx's thought, somewhat idiosyncratically, see Louis Dumont, *From Mandeville to Marx: The Genesis and Triumph of Economic Ideology* (Chicago: University of Chicago Press, 1977).

institution of rights, markets for the exchange of goods, and institutions of representative democracy—are essential to any good society. When I use the term *liberalism* in this book without qualification, I shall mean philosophical liberalism. I have called this book *The IDEA of a Liberal Theory* because I focus on interpretations of philosophical liberalism—on arguments about the basis on which we should compare alternative institutions and practices—rather than on the institutional and policy outcomes of those arguments.

The relation between philosophical liberalism and institutional liberalism is a close and strong one, but it is not a relation of logical entailment or one-to-one correspondence. Philosophical liberalism is democratic in the sense that it incorporates the view that all individuals count equally. But not all theories with liberal foundations reach strongly democratic conclusions about institutions. The argument Robert Nozick makes in *Anarchy, State, and Utopia* is based on a version of philosophical liberalism, but it reaches antidemocratic conclusions about institutions.[20]

Similarly, it is possible to reach conclusions that are recognizable as liberal on the basis of principles or arguments that are not distinctively liberal. Many liberal ideas about political and social institutions evolved historically in close alliance with aristocracy and privilege, not with democracy. But that historical association does not define what liberalism is about today.

It should be clear from the argument so far that as I understand it, liberalism is not neutral toward all possible conceptions of the good life. Liberalism is based on a commitment to a set of values that apply to political and social institutions and practices. Those values are contestable. Historically, they are controversial. Liberal values are incompatible with the aristocratic values of Plato, Aristotle, and Nietzsche because these philosophers deny either that everybody should count as one and only one or that only individuals should count; they are incompatible with the utilitarian theory of Bentham because in that theory individuals figure only as sentient beings and not as agents; and they are incompatible with the view that political institutions should be judged on the basis of their capacity to enable a state or nation to achieve greatness. Liberalism is neutral toward all *reasonable* conceptions of the good life only if we define "reasonable" to mean "compatible with institutions and practices approved by the principles of philosophical liberalism." Many prominent views of the good life for which arguments have been made throughout the history of moral and political philosophy are not compatible with those institutions and practices, at least in the sense that those conceptions of the good life could not flourish within the framework of those institutions.

---

[20] I do not mean to say that the arguments Nozick uses to reach those conclusions are good ones, only that the conclusions he actually draws are antidemocratic. For discussion, see chap. 2.

At the same time, liberalism as I have described it here is relatively capacious. Liberalism is a theory, or more precisely a family of theories, about political and social arrangements. That family of theories does presuppose some things about human beings. It presupposes that we are agents who formulate plans and conceive values and try to realize those plans and values. But liberalism is essentially a view about the bases of political and social criticism, about what counts when we evaluate alternative political and social institutions and practices. When we engage in political and social criticism, we do not necessarily count the same things that we do when we make decisions about our more private lives, such as a decision about how to divide up an estate. If we do count the same things, we do not necessarily count them in the same way or give them the same weight. Liberalism does not seek to prescribe ways of life to individuals except insofar as it prescribes that individuals' ways of life should be compatible with liberal institutions. That constraint is significant, but it leaves a great deal of room for individuals to conceive and to act in accordance with a wide variety of projects and values.[21]

A society in which individuals are free—that is, a society whose institutions and practices embody the view that individuals are agents who conceive values and pursue projects—will allow diverse conceptions of the good life to arise and flourish. Liberal societies embody, and liberal theories presuppose, what I shall call the *assumption of reasonable value pluralism*, the assumption that individuals reasonably conceive different and conflicting values.

The fact that liberal societies embody the assumption of reasonable value pluralism has two consequences that are worth noting here. The first is that liberal societies are by nature societies in which the circumstances of justice prevail. In other words, people will make conflicting claims on resources, even if those resources are relatively abundant. People will have *different* values or conceptions of the good, different projects they wish to pursue. In a society that is pluralistic with regard to values, relations between individuals will to some extent be opaque. Their understanding of one another's particular values will be limited.[22] So even if individuals are not egoistic, they will naturally develop conflicting ideas about many things, including the ways in which their society's resources should be used. These

---

[21] As Charles E. Larmore has put it, liberalism is a philosophy of politics, not a philosophy of man (*Patterns of Moral Complexity* [Cambridge: Cambridge University Press, 1987], pp. 25, 118, 129). In my view Larmore exaggerates the extent to which a liberal society can remain neutral toward controversial conceptions of the good life (see pp. x, 51ff., 69), but his central point about the thrust of liberal political theory is on the mark.

[22] For an excellent discussion emphasizing this aspect of liberal thought, see Jeremy Waldron, "Theoretical Foundations of Liberalism," *Philosophical Quarterly* 37 (1987): 127–50.

conflicting ideas will lead people to make conflicting claims. A liberal society will have to have some means of adjudicating between these conflicting claims.[23]

The second implication of the close relation between liberalism and value pluralism is that diversity in individuals' projects and values—or conceptions of the good—will tend to generate diverse social worlds. Even if it should happen that the same set of conceptions of the good were held by the members of two different liberal societies at a given time, the openness of liberal societies to diversity would tend to pull the two societies in different directions over time. As individuals within the two societies move toward different projects and values, they would begin to act differently in their efforts to pursue those projects and to realize their values. As a result, the two societies would diverge. They would come to be quite different sorts of social worlds, even if both societies remained equally liberal.[24]

II

Any account of the bases of political criticism should satisfy certain general desiderata. Here I want to describe three features I believe any such account or theory ought to have. These desiderata should be met, I think, even by a political theory that rejects one or more of the premises common to liberal theories I have described in the preceding. Their validity is not dependent on the validity of those liberal assumptions. Since this part of my argument may seem dry, I shall keep it as short as possible.

Internal Coherence

A political theory, like any other kind of theory, should be internally coherent. This desideratum seems sufficiently obvious and uncontroversial to make an elaborate explanation unnecessary.

However, one point is worth emphasizing, because it is so easily overlooked. A genuinely coherent theory is a theory that accounts for the things for which it claims to account without appealing to ad hoc considerations. Ad hoc appeals are a sure sign that a theory is defective. If we can show that a theory relies on such appeals to maintain an appearance of plausibil-

---

[23] The circumstances of justice are described in classic statements by David Hume in *A Treatise of Human Nature*, ed. L. A. Selby-Bigge (Oxford: Clarendon Press, 1967), book 2, part 2, sec. 2, and in *An Enquiry Concerning the Principles of Morals*, ed. J. B. Schneewind (Indianapolis: Hackett, 1983), part 1, sec. 3. See also Rawls, *Theory*, pp. 126–30.

[24] Isaiah Berlin has long emphasized the possibility of a plurality of social worlds of roughly equivalent value and the danger of imagining that only one ideal type of social world is possible. For a recent statement, see "The Pursuit of the Ideal," in *The Crooked Timber of Humanity* (New York: Knopf, 1991).

ity, we can be certain that the theory should be either revised or rejected altogether.

The most fundamental act of a political theory is the act of identifying what counts—that is, of selecting those features of a social world that, according to the theory, are significant for the purpose of comparing alternative political and social arrangements. A theory that identifies a given set of features as those that count and then proceeds to draw conclusions for which it cannot account by appealing to those features is incoherent. In other words, when a theory says that certain things count, it cannot then sneak in other things and count them surreptitiously, as it were, in order to make the results of the theory look consistent with its premises. That is the theoretical equivalent of cheating.

Informational Reasonableness

Political theories identify informational bases. When a theory says that X is what counts in comparing alternative institutions or social arrangements, then we must, in order to make use of the theory, find a way to tell whether the alternatives lead to X and, in some cases, how much X they lead to. Suppose, for example, a theory said that the only thing that really counts for the purpose of evaluating alternative political and social arrangements is the amount of wealth they would tend to produce, so that any alternative that would tend to lead to the production of greater wealth is always to be preferred to alternatives that would lead to production of lesser amounts of wealth. In order to make use of this theory to help us evaluate real alternatives, we would have to work out some way of determining approximately how much wealth would be produced by people living in accordance with each alternative. The same observation would apply to a theory that said that the only thing that counts is how much liberty individuals have. In that case we would have to work out some means of measuring liberty, at least in a rough and ready way.

The informational demands of political theories should be reasonable. A theory that requires us to gather information that is unobtainable in principle, or that cannot be obtained without violating some provision of the theory itself, cannot be used in practical reasoning. For example, a theory that says that knowledge of the mental states of all the members of a society is required for the formulation of significant criticism of the institutions or practices of that society imposes unreasonable informational requirements. We cannot expect to be able to obtain that kind of information in the real world. A theory that makes unreasonable informational demands cannot play a serious role in the practice of social criticism. It cannot be used by citizens to compare their institutions and practices with an alternative, because the information needed to make the desired comparison cannot be obtained.

Reasonable demands for information are neither too vague nor too stringent. A theory that makes vague demands for information does not tell us enough about what counts to be a useful tool of social criticism. A theory that makes excessively stringent demands also disqualifies itself as a plausible tool of criticism.

The requirement that a theory's informational demands be reasonable has to be balanced against other desiderata. A theory should preserve the motivation that makes us interested in comparing alternatives in the first place. If a theory does not do this, then it becomes a technical exercise without real attachment to the things that would give it meaning. At the same time, a theory should nevertheless be practical in the sense of being usable for making actual comparisons. If a theory cannot do this, then it risks becoming a mere vehicle for self-expression. To some extent the meaningfulness or relevance of a political theory can pull in a different direction from practicality and usability. I do not know of a good way to describe an optimal balance between these considerations in the abstract, but neither should be ignored.

The requirement that a theory's informational demands be reasonable suggests a significant way in which practical reasoning about political and social arrangements may differ from individuals' reasoning about their own actions and lives. For reasons of accessibility, scale, and the like, the kinds of information on which individuals can draw in order to make decisions about their own actions and lives differ from those on which the members of a society can draw in order to formulate their views and assessments of their political and social institutions. This real disparity between practical reasoning about political and social arrangements and reasoning about individuals' actions and lives can easily be overlooked.

Ordering

A third desideratum for political theories generally is that they should help us to order alternatives. The central purpose of criticism is to promote political and social reform. The objective, in other words, is to substitute better political and social arrangements for worse ones. So an account of the bases of criticism should help us to distinguish between better and worse arrangements. A theory or account of the bases of social criticism would have no point if it did not help us to order alternatives.

How strongly should a political theory order alternatives? I shall call an ordering that enables us to rank-order every member of a set unambiguously so that no two members occupy the same rank a *strong* ordering. Any strong ordering identifies one member of the ordered set as the best of that set. A *moderate* ordering would enable us to rank every member of a set, but some members might share a rank and some rankings might be ambiguous. Moderate orderings rank the members of a set only loosely, enabling us to make some broad distinctions between better and worse members, but not necessarily providing a basis for identifying one member of the set as best. Finally, I shall call an ordering that enables us to rank order the members of a set only very loosely a *weak* ordering.

A theory that yields only a weak ordering would be able to do less than we would like a theory to do. For example, such a theory might be able to support the conclusion that Britain between 1966 and 1979 was a better society than Germany in the years 1933–45. A theory that yields only weak orderings might be of some use, but that usefulness would be limited. Such a theory might, for instance, help us to identify some of the reasons why we hold the views we do hold. In general, though, I think we want political theories to do more than confirm judgments we already make. We want theories to help us *make* judgments, not just to confirm judgments we have already made.

So we would like political theories to yield either strong or moderate orderings. Now it might seem as though a theory that yields strong orderings would, at least in this respect, be preferable to a theory that yields only moderate orderings. If we want theories to help us rank alternatives, would not a theory that produces stronger rankings be preferable to one that yields weaker, that is, only moderate rankings? Oddly perhaps, if the theory in question is liberal in its assumptions, then the answer to this question must be no.

To see why, recall the argument made at the end of section I about the consequences of the assumption of reasonable value pluralism. Liberal institutions allow and encourage the formulation of diverse projects, values, and conceptions of the good. This diversity of individuals' projects and values is bound to generate a plurality of social worlds even among societies that are equally consistent with liberal principles. A strong ordering would be incompatible with the liberal view that a plurality of social worlds of equivalent value is possible. This kind of ordering would be inconsistent with the human condition of plurality and, at bottom, with the assumption that human beings are agents whose political and social institutions should reflect their nature as free and equal beings.

Hence a theory that yields strong orderings would be no more desirable, from a liberal point of view, than a theory that yields only weak orderings. In fact a theory that yields strong orderings might be *less* desirable than one that yields weak orderings. Such a theory would tell us *too much*—too much, that is, to be consistent with the pluralistic implications of liberalism. A liberal political theory should yield moderate orderings, at least when it is used to evaluate alternative societies as a whole.

The conclusion that a liberal political theory should yield orderings of only moderate strength may seem counterintuitive, but it should not be surprising in light of the purposes for which we formulate a theory of this kind. Recall the analogy suggested near the beginning of this chapter between the notion of a good society and that of a healthy individual. A conception of health ranks human beings only roughly and up to a point. It makes few or no significant distinctions among people within the large class of those who are roughly equal in being healthy. The point of a conception of health is not to enable us to rank people per se but to help us to identify those who are ill or unhealthy so that they can receive appropriate nutritional or medical treatment.

Similarly, the point of a conception of political health is to help us to determine when a political community is healthy and when it is unhealthy—when, that is, the political and social institutions and practices that prevail in that community are good ones and when they are not. The notion that a political theory should do more than this—that it should yield strong orderings—is fetishistic. It suggests that in the thinking of its proponent, the business of theory has taken on a life of its own and has become disconnected from the real business of political and social criticism that lends political theory significance, much as Marx claimed that the tradition of German idealism had lost touch with the real world through an overdeveloped division of labor between intellectual pursuits and the productive pursuits that shape human beings' real lives.[25]

A political theory should give a sense of direction to political and social criticism. It should help people to formulate effective, well-conceived criticism, criticism that takes the body politic as a whole into account. If we accept the assumption of reasonable value pluralism, however, we should also accept that political theories based on this assumption will not order all political alternatives, that some issues will *not* be resolvable by appealing to a theory or to some inference from a theory. *Some* issues that arise may not, in fact, be resolvable by any rational means at all.

III

The most significant content of a political theory is the account that theory offers of the bases of political and social criticism, that is, the claims the theory makes about what counts for the purpose of choosing between the status quo and a proposed reform or between alternative reform proposals. But how do we test claims of this sort, other than by determining whether they are coherent, rely on information that we can reasonably expect to be

---

[25] See part 1 of *The German Ideology* in Robert C. Tucker, ed., *The Marx-Engels Reader*, 2d ed. (New York: Norton, 1978), pp. 146–200.

able to obtain, and in fact do what we want them to do, which is to help us to rank alternatives? Presumably, many theories, including theories that lead to sharply conflicting conclusions, can meet these relatively formal tests. We need to know more about how to distinguish between better and worse theories than we can learn by using these tests.

A standard view of the way in which theories should be tested is that the test of a theory consists of a comparison between the content of the theory on the one hand and information about a set of facts that exist independently of the theory on the other. To what information, what set of facts, should we refer to test a theory about the normative bases of political criticism?

The dominant view in political philosophy throughout most of its history was that the adequacy of a political theory is a function of the accuracy with which it represents objective moral norms. This view was based on the assumption that moral norms exist independently of human consciousness and reflection. In principle, according to this view, a normative political theory is tested in much the same way as any explanatory theory would be. The principal task of a normative theory, then, is epistemological: it is to discover moral truths.

This view of the nature of political theory and of moral truth was challenged by Hobbes in the seventeenth century and by Hume and, according to John Rawls, Kant in the eighteenth century.[26] Work in moral philosophy in recent years and in political philosophy since Nietzsche has tended to undermine further the notion of objective moral truth.[27] We cannot say that the existence of objective moral truths has been disproved. But the notion that moral truths exist objectively no longer possesses the general credibility it once had.

The success of the modernist critique of the notion of moral truth has led some to assume that *no* meaningful test of normative claims is possible. According to this view, claims about the normative basis of political and social criticism are fundamentally arbitrary. These claims merely restate the beliefs and prejudices we inevitably acquire in the process of our initiation into a particular culture. We have no more reason for believing that these claims have an objective basis than we do for thinking that the tastes and prefer-

[26] The key text among Hobbes's writings is *The Elements of Law, Natural and Politic*, 2d ed., ed. Ferdinand Tönnies (London: Frank Cass, 1969), part 2, chap. 10, sec. 8. Richard Tuck emphasizes the importance of this part of Hobbes's thinking in his *Hobbes* (Cambridge: Cambridge University Press, 1989). For a statement of Hume's views on this subject, see his *Enquiry*. For Rawls's account of Kant's quite different challenge to the notion of moral truth, see the third of his Dewey Lectures, "Constructivism and Objectivity," in "Kantian Constructivism in Moral Theory," *Journal of Philosophy* 77 (1980): 554–72. A revised form of this lecture appears in Rawls's *Political Liberalism* (New York: Columbia University Press, 1993), pp. 89–129.

[27] Two of the principal works in moral philosophy are John L. Mackie, *Ethics: Inventing Right and Wrong* (Harmondsworth: Penguin, 1977), and Gilbert Harman, *The Nature of Morality* (New York: Oxford University Press, 1977).

ences we happen to have because of the accidents of our experiences and upbringing are objectively valid.

This line of thinking is too hasty. Even if we believe that the idea of objective moral truth should be rejected, it does not follow that no meaningful test of normative claims is possible. An alternative conception of a test for claims about the bases of political and social criticism exists. That conception has been widely discussed in recent years, yet is still not well understood. It has achieved prominence mainly through the work of John Rawls and has been clarified and developed by Norman Daniels. It is called the method of *reflective equilibrium*, or, to be more precise, the method of wide and general reflective equilibrium. I want here to describe the method of reflective equilibrium and to consider whether it can be used to test claims about the bases of political criticism.

Rawls argues that "there is a definite if limited class of facts against which conjectured principles [of justice] can be checked, namely, our considered judgments in reflective equilibrium."[28] So according to the method of reflective equilibrium, we use our considered judgments—Rawls sometimes calls them convictions or intuitions—to test an account of the bases of political criticism (for Rawls a theory of justice is such an account). A successful theory would account for and organize those intuitions or judgments as a whole.[29] As he sees it, an account of the bases of political criticism is a theory of the moral sentiments.[30]

The intuitions or judgments for which a successful theory would account are not just all the intuitions or opinions we happen to have. They are our *considered* judgments, that is, those that we make under conditions favorable to the exercise of our capacities for judgment. Hence opinions formed in haste or in the heat of a moment are not considered judgments. Neither are opinions or intuitions formed on the basis of partial or distorted information. In the idea of reflective equilibrium, the people making judgments are assumed to have the ability to make judgments of this kind and to have the desire to reach sound conclusions.

Further, the notion of reflective equilibrium appeals not to considered judgments as such but to considered judgments in reflective equilibrium. Reflective equilibrium is the state reached by an individual after she has

---

[28] Rawls, *Theory*, p. 51. Rawls's principal discussion of the method of reflective equilibrium in *Theory* occurs on pp. 46–53. He discusses some elements of this method in a much earlier article, "Outline of a Decision Procedure for Ethics," *Philosophical Review* 60 (1951): 177–97. He has elaborated and in some respects modified his arguments in more recent articles, especially those dealing with the notion of overlapping consensus, and in his book, *Political Liberalism*.

[29] "Justification rests upon the entire conception and how it fits in with and organizes our considered judgments in reflective equilibrium" (Rawls, *Theory*, p. 579).

[30] Ibid., pp. 51, 120.

considered the various available theories or accounts of the bases of political criticism as well as any additional accounts or revisions that occur to her and information from her knowledge of human life and from the social sciences. She compares the accounts of the bases of criticism available to her with the intuitions and judgments she possesses at the outset, prior to the process of reflection, giving weight especially to those judgments that seem to her firmest. When she discovers discrepancies between her judgments and the theory that seems to her best to approximate those judgments, she revises either her judgments or the theory to bring them into accord with one another. Typically, then, the process of reaching reflective equilibrium is one of mutual adjustment and adaptation between a set of initial judgments on the one hand and a set of available theories, or the most adequate member of that set, on the other, taking into account information about the ways human life and societies work. During that process it is likely both that the theory that initially seemed to our representative individual best to account for her considered judgments will have changed and that her considered convictions will have been "duly pruned and adjusted."[31] When the individual has achieved a state of affairs in which no further discrepancies between her considered judgments and the most adequate theory of which she knows seem to exist, she has reached reflective equilibrium.

Now the notion of reflective equilibrium, as characterized so far, can be interpreted in different ways. One important difference is between *narrow* and *wide* reflective equilibrium.[32] Narrow reflective equilibrium can be attained when one is presented only with theories that already correspond with one's considered judgments for the most part, so that the discrepancies between the theories considered and the initial judgments of the individual considering them are relatively minor. However, to attain wide reflective equilibrium, one must be presented with "all possible descriptions to which one might plausibly conform one's judgments together with all relevant philosophical arguments for them."[33] Unlike most intuitionist moral philosophers, who rely for the most part on existing intuitions to test moral claims, Rawls argues that we should rely on the wide version of reflective equilibrium, not the narrow one, to test claims about the basis of political criticism. The test of wide reflective equilibrium, unlike that of narrow reflective equi-

[31] Ibid., p. 20.

[32] Rawls distinguishes between these two types of reflective equilibrium, though not by these names, in ibid., p. 49. Rawls first used these terms in "The Independence of Moral Theory," *Proceedings and Addresses of the American Philosophical Association* 48 (1975): 5–22. See also Norman Daniels, "Wide Reflective Equilibrium and Theory Acceptance in Ethics," *Journal of Philosophy* 76 (1979): 256–82; "Moral Theory and the Plasticity of Persons," *The Monist* 62 (1979): 265–87; "Some Methods of Ethics and Linguistics," *Philosophical Studies* 37 (1980): 21–36; and "Reflective Equilibrium and Archimedean Points," *Canadian Journal of Philosophy* 10 (1980): 83–103.

[33] Rawls, *Theory*, p. 49.

librium, holds out the possibility, which Rawls emphasizes several times in *A Theory of Justice*, that the process of achieving reflective equilibrium might lead us to transform our initial views.[34]

Even if an account of the bases of political criticism were to pass the test of wide reflective equilibrium, however, in Rawls's view that would not be sufficient. For the validity of a theory of justice—the form Rawls assumes such an account will take—depends in his view on the ability of that theory to pass the test of *general* as well as wide reflective equilibrium. Wide reflective equilibrium is the state of affairs achieved by an individual when, after considering all possible theories together with all the relevant arguments for them, all the discrepancies between the best of those theories, adjusted in whatever ways are found to be appropriate in the process of reflection, and the individual's considered judgments, duly pruned and adjusted, have been eliminated. Wide and general reflective equilibrium is the state of affairs that would be attained if all the individuals in an association were to agree on a single theory, that is, if the same theory were to be the object of a wide reflective equilibrium achieved by each.

Rawls recognizes, of course, that we are extremely unlikely to attain wide and general reflective equilibrium, strictly defined. For him, wide reflective equilibrium is a state of moral reflection to which individuals can hope to approximate, not a condition they can realistically expect to achieve.[35] Similarly, wide and general reflective equilibrium is a heuristic ideal to which societies can hope to approximate. In fact, in recent years Rawls has tended to refer to the apparently less demanding notion of *overlapping consensus* in lieu of the more demanding idea of wide and general reflective equilibrium.[36] The notion of an overlapping consensus is that of an agreement on principles of justice to regulate the institutions of a more or less just constitutional regime that includes all the reasonable opposing moral, philosophical, and religious doctrines likely to persist and to gain a sizable body of adherents in such a regime over time. The notion of overlapping consensus

---

[34] "The conception of justice, should it be truly effective and publicly recognized as such, seems more likely than its rivals to transform our perspective on the social world . . ." (Rawls, *Theory*, p. 512; see also pp. 52, 451–52). However, Rawls also acknowledges the possibility that the resting point we eventually achieve in reflective equilibrium will be constrained by our initial intuitions: "Perhaps the judgments from which we begin . . . affect the resting point, if any, that we eventually achieve" (ibid., p. 50).

[35] On this point, see Rawls's discussion in ibid., pp. 49–51.

[36] Rawls used the term *overlapping consensus* in *Theory* (pp. 387f.), though not in the sense it has acquired in his more recent work. That sense first appeared clearly in his "Justice as Fairness: Political Not Metaphysical," *Philosophy and Public Affairs* 14 (1985): 223–51. See also Rawls's "The Idea of an Overlapping Consensus," *Oxford Journal of Legal Studies* 7 (1987): 1–25; "The Priority of Right and Ideas of the Good," *Philosophy and Public Affairs* 17 (1988): 251–76; "The Domain of the Political and Overlapping Consensus," *New York University Law Review* 64 (1989): 233–55; and *Political Liberalism*.

is less demanding than that of wide and general reflective equilibrium because it does not incorporate the assumption that the individuals who con-
cur in the consensus must go through a searching and exhaustive process of
reflection in order to test their judgments. If they are able to reach agreement, the fact that they are able to do so seems, according to Rawls's more
recent accounts of the notion of overlapping consensus, to constitute the
principal test of their conclusions.

One major criticism of the idea of reflective equilibrium as a conception
of the way in which normative claims should be tested is that this method
would commit us to a conservative and ethnocentric appeal to received
opinion.[37] The force of this criticism is dependent on the precise way in
which we interpret the idea of reflective equilibrium. If the agreement on
norms or principles envisaged in that idea is to be achieved by narrowing the
range of issues subject to a potential agreement and avoiding the most controversial questions, then the conservatism of the method seems evident. In
fact if we interpret reflective equilibrium in this way, it is difficult to see how
the method of reflective equilibrium could constitute a meaningful *test* of a
theory of the bases of social criticism at all.[38] If, on the other hand, we think
of agreement as something we can *imagine* achieving as a result of confronta-
tion with controversial issues mediated through a comprehensive and thorough process of reflection in which all the members of a society participate,
then the notion of wide and general reflective equilibrium does not seem
inherently conservative or necessarily ethnocentric. In brief, to the extent to
which we emphasize the objective of agreement, especially if we aim for
actual agreement, the method becomes conservative; whereas to the extent
to which we emphasize the process of critical reflection, the method becomes radical.

In reality the obstacles to agreement on basic norms of political criticism
(or public justification) in modern societies, especially liberal societies, are
so great that the usefulness of the idea of agreement is questionable. As I

---

[37] For several different versions of this objection, see Peter Singer, "Sidgwick and Reflective
Equilibrium," *The Monist* 58 (1974): 490–517; R. M. Hare, "Rawls' Theory of Justice," in Nor-
man Daniels, ed., *Reading Rawls* (New York: Basic Books, 1975), pp. 81–107; and G. R. Grice,
"Moral Theories and Received Opinion," *The Aristotelian Society*, supplementary vol. 52
(1978): 2–12. For related criticisms that the method is culturally relativistic, see Steven Lukes,
"An Archimedean Point," *Observer*, 4 June 1972; Lukes, "Relativism: Cognitive and Moral,"
Aristotelian Society, supplementary vol. 48 (1974): 165–88; and Kai Nielsen, "Our Considered
Judgments," *Ratio* 19, no. 1 (June 1977): 39–46. Nielsen adopts a far more favorable view of the
method of reflective equilibrium in his *Equality and Liberty* (Totowa, N.J.: Rowman and Allanheld, 1985), chap. 2.

[38] In his writings beginning in the mid-1980s, Rawls has argued in favor of a "method of avoid-
ance" of controversial and divisive issues as a means of obtaining an agreed basis of public
justification. In my view this strategy is unfortunate. For Rawls's arguments see "Political Not
Metaphysical," esp. sec. 2, and "Overlapping Consensus," esp. sec. 4.

have already noted, liberal societies embody the assumption of reasonable value pluralism. In a society in which diverse values flourish, people will disagree. Much of this disagreement is reasonable and cannot be attributed to the distorting effects of bias, blindness, willfulness, or irrationality. According to Rawls, this "fact of pluralism," as he calls it, renders the notion that the members of a modern democratic society could reach agreement on a comprehensive religious, philosophical, or moral doctrine utopian.[39] Rawls continues to maintain, however, that political philosophy should strive toward societywide agreement on basic norms of political criticism and in fact appears to believe that an actual agreement on norms of this kind is a reasonable objective.

Yet most of the reasons Rawls offers for rejecting the notion of agreement on a comprehensive doctrine apply to the idea of agreement on the bases of political criticism or public justification as well.[40] Rawls cites the fact that the evidence bearing on any comprehensive conception of the good is likely to be conflicting and complex, making evaluation difficult. But the evidence bearing on a proposed theory of the normative bases of political criticism is likely to present similar difficulties. He mentions the fact that even when people agree on the set of factors they consider relevant to a problem, they are likely to assign these factors different weights. The same observation applies to the factors that would have to be considered in framing an account of the bases of political criticism. He discusses the need for reliance on judgment and interpretation; the same reliance is necessary to the framing of a view of the bases of political criticism. He alludes to differences in point of view that stem from diverse life experiences; these differences would affect people's assessments of any proposed theory. He calls attention to the fact that different kinds of normative considerations bear on any given practical question in different ways and may be difficult to weigh in relation to one another: this problem, too, applies to the reasoning that would have to be applied to the problem of designing basic norms of social criticism. Finally, Rawls argues that any set of social institutions can allow only a limited range of values to flourish, so that in choosing any particular set of institutions we are forced to select among cherished values. The selection of a set of basic norms to be used for criticizing political and social institutions involves a similar choice. It follows that different individuals may reasonably incline toward different conclusions about the normative bases of political criticism.

In light of these considerations, it appears that agreement among all the members of a society on an account of the normative bases of political criticism—or on a set of principles to regulate a society's basic structure—would

[39] For these points, see Rawls, "Domain of the Political."
[40] Rawls summarizes these reasons concisely in ibid., p. 237.

be impossible to achieve. Moreover, the difficulty would be greatest in liberal societies, which encourage diversity of belief and allow individuals to pursue a wide range of different ways of life. It might be argued, of course, that the elusiveness of agreement constitutes no decisive objection to the *ideal* of agreement. Ideals do not have to be attainable to serve as useful guides for action. Yet an ideal that is truly implausible is not likely to be a useful guide.

Moreover, in some respects the ideal of agreement is positively *un*attractive. We might not wish to attain consensus on a common point of view from which all conflicting claims about political and social arrangements could be adjudicated[41] even if it were in our power to do so. Agreement on a conception of the bases of political criticism might be desirable *if* we could be virtually certain that our conception was the "right" one, that is, if we knew that it was the best possible conception for that society and was likely to remain the best in perpetuity. But this kind of confidence in a conception of the bases of political criticism cannot be rationally justified. If this kind of confidence cannot be justified, then the objective of agreement cannot be justified, either. In fact we should hope that some lively disagreement on norms of political criticism will remain. Continual disagreement about norms involves the continual generation of alternative normative proposals. While most of these alternatives would probably fail to be rationally persuasive, from time to time a normative proposal might arise that would prove to be rationally stronger than existing norms. In that event those norms should be held open for revision.[42]

I am not arguing that we should abandon the notion of agreement altogether. I do think, though, that we should abandon the objective of securing an actual agreement or common point of view from which to adjudicate claims. The idea of reflective equilibrium can play a useful role in testing proposed accounts of the bases of social criticism if we emphasize the critical and reflective side of that idea and bear in mind that the notion of agreement contained in it is at best a regulative idea, not an objective we should strive to realize, especially not by avoiding difficult or controversial issues.

Appealing to the idea of wide and general reflective equilibrium may help us in a negative way. We may not be able to *confirm* an account of the normative bases of social criticism by referring to this idea, but we may be able to *rule out* some possible accounts by appealing to it. Perhaps, that is,

---

[41] This is how Rawls conceives the purpose of consensus in *Theory*; see p. 5 and compare Rawls's suggestion on p. 243 that "a common understanding of justice as fairness makes a constitutional democracy."

[42] For a forceful argument that a continual competition of ideas is a better route to social problem solving than agreement or consensus, see Charles E. Lindblom, *Inquiry and Change* (New Haven: Yale University Press, 1990).

we will be able to show that some proposed accounts are unacceptable by demonstrating that for some obvious or systematic reason they would not be able to pass the test of wide and general reflective equilibrium even if that test could be met in principle. This use of the notion of reflective equilibrium will not enable us to prove that any account is the best possible one, but it may help us to eliminate some contenders from consideration.[43]

I shall assume in this book that the liberal premises I have outlined above—that only individuals count, that all individuals count equally, and that all individuals count as agents—would pass the test of wide and general reflective equilibrium, if that test could be passed by any theory. I shall not attempt to prove this assumption. Instead, I shall focus my efforts on an attempt to determine how these premises might be elaborated into a fuller account of the normative bases of political criticism. I shall begin by examining, in the next three chapters, some representative works from several different genres of liberal political theory. I shall then, in chapter 5, sketch an alternative to these established versions of liberal theory. My aim is to formulate an account of the normative bases of social criticism that incorporates the strengths of existing liberal theories while avoiding their more serious weaknesses.

Most of my discussion of the method of reflective equilibrium is speculative in any case. I do not think we could carry out completely the test for which that method calls in the case of even one person, let alone many. The number of relevant intuitions and judgments is too great, even if we could bring all those judgments to our consciousness, which we might not be able to do, and the notion that we could consider all possible theories or accounts and all the relevant arguments bearing on them is clearly fanciful. I have discussed the idea of reflective equilibrium mainly because that idea seems to me, when properly construed, to offer a plausible way of thinking about what it would mean to test a theory of the bases of social criticism, not because I think we can carry out tests of this sort in a thoroughgoing manner. In real life we must content ourselves with incomplete scrutiny and partial proof or disproof, with looking at a few proposals from one or a few angles of vision and seeing how they bear up under that partial scrutiny. This, at any rate, is the kind of scrutiny I apply to the theories I consider in this book, to the first of which I shall now turn.

---

[43] This is, roughly, the constructive use Jeremy Waldron suggests for contractarian arguments in his *The Right to Private Property* (Oxford: Oxford University Press, 1988), p. 273. There is also some resemblance between my proposal and T. M. Scanlon's suggestion that an appropriate test of an argument in a contractarian procedure is nonrejectability rather than acceptability; see his "Contactualism and Utilitarianism," in *Utilitarianism and Beyond*, ed. Bernard Williams (Cambridge: Cambridge University Press, 1982), pp. 103–28.

CHAPTER TWO

Rights-Based Liberalism

ONE WAY in which political and social arrangements can embody recognition of individuals equally as agents is to treat those individuals equally as bearers of rights. The idea of individuals as rights-bearers has played a major and well-known role in the liberal tradition from Locke onward. In this chapter I want to explore how far we can take this idea toward a persuasive liberal account of the bases of political and social criticism. I want to suggest that accounts of the bases of social criticism that rely on individual rights to do all or most of their work face substantial difficulties. Briefly, such accounts endorse conclusions that are unacceptable in light of their own normative premises.

It may be useful to put the view I shall consider here into the form of a general principle:

> A set of political and social arrangements is justified to the extent to which it protects the rights of individuals, including their right to transfer rights to others, provided that they do not violate the rights of others.

For convenience I shall call this principle the *Rights-Based Principle* of political criticism.

Some remarks are in order here to flesh out my account of this principle. First, I assume that the individual rights to which the principle refers take priority over all other considerations we might wish to take into account when comparing alternative political and social institutions or practices. The rights are "side-constraints"[1] of a strong sort. In other words, they constrain the range of alternatives from which we may choose in a strict way. Suppose, for example, we were to conclude that a need exists to create a group of young adults to perform some type of national service. Two proposals have been offered, either of which would achieve this objective. The first proposal would conscript people for service, using a lottery to determine arbitrarily who will be required to serve. The second proposal would rely on relatively generous pay incentives and compensation of other sorts to attract enough people without use of conscription. The second proposal would be more expensive than the first. But let us suppose, by hypothesis, that conscription violates individuals' rights. In that case, we would have to adopt the second

---

[1] This is the term Robert Nozick uses to describe these rights in *Anarchy, State, and Utopia* (New York: Basic Books, 1974). See pp. xi, 28–42, 293.

proposal, despite its far greater expense, in order to avoid violating people's rights. Avoiding violations of rights takes priority over all other considerations involved in our choice between the two proposals.

Second, I assume that the Rights-Based Principle is designed to do most of the real work of accounting for the bases of social criticism. The Principle does not entail that protection of individuals' rights is the only thing that can be taken into consideration in comparing alternatives. If, for example, we need to choose between two proposals for raising revenue for government expenditures, neither of which violates individuals' rights, then we may take into account the proposals' likely effects on economic activity as well as any other effects we happen to consider important. In general, though, I assume that the rights protected by the Rights-Based Principle are sufficiently extensive that the Principle can be expected to have a significant bearing on most decisions we will have to make about institutions or policies.

Although my interest in this chapter is in the general idea of individual rights as a basis for social criticism, it will be helpful to focus on one or two actual theories that make use of this idea. Robert Nozick's rights-based theory is an appropriate choice because it is a virtually pure case of an argument from the Rights-Based Principle of political criticism. According to Nozick, the key fact that must be considered in deciding how to organize a state, and in fact in deciding whether there should be any state at all, as well as in making decisions about the allocation of property and about the many legal and policy issues that have an impact on that allocation, is that "individuals have rights." Nozick continues: "So strong and far-reaching are these rights that they raise the question of what, if anything, the state and its officials may do. How much room do individual rights leave for the state?"[2] Nozick does not qualify the rights that individuals have by allowing exceptions or modifications of any kind. His theory is a pure deontological theory—one, that is, in which our duty to respect others' rights takes priority over all other considerations, including considerations of material welfare and all utilitarian concerns.

One possible drawback to the selection of Nozick's theory for close scrutiny is that it is incomplete. The relative incompleteness of Nozick's theory is often cited as one of that theory's greatest failings.[3] Anticipating this objec-

---

[2] Ibid., p. ix.

[3] Not, however, by Jeremy Waldron, who considers the incompleteness of Nozick's theory at least defensible and at best a virtue, at least for his purposes. I follow Waldron's discussion of this point in his *The Right to Private Property* (Oxford: Oxford University Press, 1988), pp. 254–56. For two examples of criticism of Nozick on this point, both cited by Waldron, see Robert Paul Wolff, "Nozick's Derivation of the Minimal State," in *Reading Nozick: Essays on "Anarchy, State, and Utopia,"* ed. Jeffrey Paul (Totowa, N.J.: Rowman and Littlefield, 1981), p. 101; and James Griffin, "Towards a Substantive Theory of Rights," in *Utility and Rights*, ed. Raymond G. Frey (Oxford: Blackwell, 1985), pp. 137–38.

tion, however, Nozick argues that it is unreasonable to demand that new theories should be presented only when they are complete: "What more does one need or can one have, in order to begin progressing toward a better theory, than a sketch of a plausible alternative view, which from its very different perspective highlights the inadequacies of the best existing well-worked-out theory?"[4] In fact, Nozick finds the usual manner of presenting philosophical work in the form of a seemingly impregnable fortress, a final product that purports to be the last word on the subject, puzzling.[5] Nozick believes that it is a virtue for philosophers to be candid about the weaknesses and lacunas in their work. Likewise, he believes that it is no vice for philosophers to present work with lacunas, as long as that work at least illuminates the shortcomings of existing theories or has something else of interest to say.

This argument seems fair enough to me. Moreover, Nozick's combination of attempted argumentative rigor together with his relative candor about the points at which his theory remains undeveloped makes his work particularly useful for my purposes. I am interested in this work principally in the *bases* of political and social criticism rather than in a particular substantive *conclusion* about political and social arrangements. Nozick's approach offers an opportunity to focus on the Rights-Based Principle of political criticism itself, relatively (though not completely) free of the distractions that would be caused by a theory more bent on presenting the appearance of a complete structure than Nozick's theory is.

Nozick's theory is a *natural rights* theory. Nozick assumes that individual rights derive ultimately from a primordial right of self-ownership that individuals possess by virtue of their natures as human beings. But this natural rights view is not the only form the Rights-Based Principle of political criticism may assume. An alternative to the assumption that individuals' rights are rooted in nature is the view that rights are (or can usefully be regarded as) the products of an agreement or convention among individuals. This *contractarian* approach has been adopted by many writers since the early 1970s, including John Rawls, James Buchanan, and David P. Gauthier.[6]

I shall discuss Buchanan's contractarian version of the Rights-Based Principle in addition to, though more briefly than, Nozick's natural rights version. Buchanan's arguments seem more suitable for my purposes in this chapter than Rawls's for two reasons. First, though Rawls does use a con-

---

[4] Nozick, *Anarchy*, p. 230.

[5] Ibid., p. xii.

[6] Rawls, *A Theory of Justice* (Cambridge, Mass.: Harvard University Press, 1971); James Buchanan, *The Limits of Liberty: Between Anarchy and Leviathan* (Chicago: University of Chicago Press, 1975); and David P. Gauthier, *Morals by Agreement* (Oxford: Oxford University Press, 1986). Another example is Jan Narveson, *The Libertarian Idea* (Philadelphia: Temple University Press, 1988).

tractarian procedure to derive rights, his arguments do not really make use of the Rights-Based Principle of political criticism. True, Rawls's theory does include the proposition that individuals have rights that take priority over all other considerations for the purpose of comparing alternative institutions. But these rights play a limited, though crucial, role in Rawls's theory as a whole. For Rawls, only a few quite *basic* individual rights take priority over other considerations. His scheme of rights does important work in his theory, but it does not do most of the work, for much of which other considerations (described in his second principle of justice) come into play. Second, I discuss Rawls's theory extensively in chapter 4. That theory is sufficiently distinctive, and sufficiently important, to merit the fuller discussion that can be given to it in a chapter of its own.

Buchanan's theory also seems more suitable than Gauthier's for my purposes because of the former theory's comparative simplicity. Gauthier's theory is more sophisticated in many ways than Buchanan's, and it deals with some problems more convincingly than Buchanan's earlier argument does. But Gauthier's contractarian approach does not differ significantly from Buchanan's in those fundamentals that are relevant to my inquiry. The issues on which I shall focus are issues about those fundamentals, which can be dealt with straightforwardly through a discussion of Buchanan's simpler formulation.

Two further observations are in order before we proceed. First, although both Nozick and Buchanan are libertarians, the relation between the Rights-Based Principle of political criticism and libertarian conclusions is not as close as might be assumed. The Rights-Based Principle can be used to support nonlibertarian conclusions as well as libertarian ones. At the same time, libertarian conclusions, such as the conclusion that a minimal state is the most extensive state that can be justified, can be supported on grounds other than those expressed in the Rights-Based Principle. Hayek's consequentialist libertarianism is an example of an approach that is not rights-based yet leads to libertarian conclusions about the permissible extent of state power.[7] I do not deal with his arguments because my objective is to probe how far the idea of individuals as rights-bearers can take us toward an account of the bases of social criticism, not to determine whether libertarian conclusions about the permissible extent of state power are sound.[8]

Second, one objection that is sometimes alleged against rights-based lib-

---

[7] See Friedrich A. Hayek, *The Constitution of Liberty* (Chicago: University of Chicago Press, 1960).

[8] Douglas B. Rasmussen's and Douglas J. Den Uyl's *Liberty and Nature: An Aristotelian Defense of Liberal Order* (La Salle: Open Court, 1991) comes closer to endorsing the Rights-Based Principle of political criticism than Hayek does and would be a worthy alternative to Nozick for a discussion of the kind I offer here. But Nozick's theory still embodies the rights-based view in a purer form than Rasmussen's and Den Uyl's theory.

eral views is that in emphasizing individuals' *rights*, these views neglect *responsibilities*. This objection is typically misconceived, or at least misstated. It would be more accurate to say that advocates of rights-based liberalism adopt a distinctive view of responsibility. For rights-based liberals, individuals are responsible, in a very strong sense, for themselves and for their own lives. Nozick, for example, argues that one of the great weaknesses of Rawls's theory of justice is that it denigrates "a person's autonomy and prime responsibility for his actions . . . One doubts that the unexalted picture of human beings Rawls' theory presupposes and rests upon can be made to fit together with the view of human dignity it is designed to lead to and embody."[9] Individuals are also responsible in a strong sense, on this view, for fulfilling their commitments to other persons. The real objection that might be made to rights-based liberal theories like Nozick's is that those theories assume that the only responsibilities individuals have toward others are those that they have accepted explicitly by obligating themselves to others. This objection raises serious and complex issues that I shall not explore here. My point is only that rights-based liberalism leads to a distinctive view about responsibility; it does not avoid the issue.

I

The general contours of Nozick's theory are so well known that I want here only to mention a few of its main ideas. Nozick's point of departure is the claim that individuals have rights. These rights are natural rights: they are not derived from an agreement or convention, and individuals can be deprived of them only by consenting voluntarily to transfer them away. The basic right is one of self-ownership. Individuals can also acquire rights to other things, which Nozick calls generally *holdings*.

Nozick uses the idea of individuals as the bearers of rights over holdings to develop a partial theory of justice, which he calls the Entitlement Theory, and to formulate an argument about the sort of state that can be justified. The completed Entitlement Theory would consist of three parts: a Principle of Justice in Acquisition (PJA), a Principle of Justice in Transfer (PJT), and a Principle of the Rectification of Justice in Holdings (PRJ). Nozick focuses most of his attention on the formulation of a PJT and on elaborating the implications of that principle. He does not formulate a PJA for his Entitlement Theory, and his discussion of a PRJ is relatively brief. These aspects of the theory he leaves to be elaborated later.

Nozick begins his argument about the state by pointing out that the fundamental question of political philosophy is not how the state should be organized but whether there should be any state at all. He then develops the

---

[9] Nozick, *Anarchy*, p. 214.

idea of an anarchical state of nature organized entirely through the voluntary actions and transactions of individuals. He argues that by transferring certain of their rights, individuals in this state of nature may form mutual protection associations to help guarantee their security and the security of their holdings. On close inspection, the characteristics of a mutual protection association under certain conditions turn out to be identical to those of a minimal state, that is, a state limited to the functions of protecting its citizens against violence, theft, and fraud and to enforcing contracts. According to Nozick, a minimal state may be justified, then, since this kind of state can arise through legitimate transfers of rights.

Nozick goes on to consider whether a more-than-minimal state constructed for the purpose of realizing a conception of distributive justice can be justified. He argues that no "end-state principle or distributional patterned principle of justice"—that is, no principle that stipulates a pattern of holdings other than one that would be generated by the voluntary actions and transactions of individuals with one another—can be justified, because such a pattern could be achieved only through "continuous interference with people's lives,"[10] interference that would violate people's rights. According to Nozick, since no patterned principle of distributive justice can be maintained without violating individuals' rights, no more-than-minimal state designed to maintain a pattern of this sort can be justified. The "minimal state is the most extensive state that can be justified. Any state more extensive violates people's rights."[11]

The claim that individuals have rights that impose strict constraints on justifiable social arrangements plays such a central role in Nozick's theory that it is worth asking what reason he can offer for making this claim. Nozick develops his rationale for the claim that individuals have rights only briefly, so briefly, in fact, that he has been accused of failing to explain the moral basis of rights.[12] But the explanation Nozick does offer is important.

Nozick's response focuses on the notion that human beings are agents.[13] We possess, he asserts, rationality, free will, and moral agency, as well as the ability to regulate and guide our lives in accordance with some overall conception or plan of life that we choose to accept. But why, he asks rhetorically, should the fact that we possess these capabilities constitute a reason for the conclusion that individuals have rights? Why should we not be free to interfere with other people's shaping of their own lives? Nozick conjectures that the answer to this question has something to do with the elusive notion of the meaning of life: "A person's shaping his life in accordance with some

[10] Ibid., p. 163.

[11] Ibid., p. 149.

[12] For this line of criticism, see Thomas Nagel, "Libertarianism without Foundations," in *Reading Nozick*, ed. Jeffery Paul, pp. 191–205.

[13] See Nozick, *Anarchy*, pp. 48–51 and the fragmentary comments on pp. 30–31, 214, and 273.

overall plan is his way of giving meaning to his life; only a being with the capacity to so shape his life can have or strive for a meaningful life."[14] It appears, then, that rights exist—that is, that we are constrained from interfering with individuals and with the holdings to which they are entitled without their consent—because to violate those rights would disturb or harm the ability of individuals to give meaning to their lives.

Despite its brevity, this response at least shows that for Nozick, individuals count as agents. But do all individuals count *equally* in Nozick's theory? It is easy to assume that they do not. After all, one of the best-known facts about Nozick's theory is that it purports to justify *inequality* in holdings. For Nozick, though, that inequality in holdings is a direct result of acceptance of human beings' equality as agents, that is, as beings who are capable of shaping their own lives in accordance with their own designs. Not interfering with individuals' efforts to shape their own lives means, among other things, not preventing them from transferring rights to holdings in ways that are likely to give rise to unequal holdings. In Nozick's theory, everybody counts as one and nobody counts as more than one, but the things to be counted are individuals' activities as agents, not holdings.

This rationale lends Nozick's rights-based account of the bases of political criticism considerable appeal from a liberal point of view. For it suggests that he takes seriously not only the premises that only individuals count and that all individuals should count equally, in some recognizable sense, but also the claim that individuals should be considered as agents, that is, as beings whose capacity for conceiving and acting to realize values and projects is of great intrinsic value. The Rights-Based Principle of political criticism, or at least Nozick's version of it, is on its face a genuinely liberal principle, one that incorporates recognition of the basic values that make liberalism itself an appealing view.

I want now to proceed to an assessment of Nozick's theory. My main interest is in the claims Nozick makes about the bases of political and social criticism rather than in his conclusions about property and the minimal state. Of course, the conclusions to which a theory leads are relevant to assessment of that theory's premises. If an account of the bases of social criticism has unacceptable implications, then that account must be flawed. Conceivably, though, Nozick's account of the bases of criticism could be sound even if his conclusions about property and the minimal state are not, because the reasoning he uses to reach those conclusions may be erroneous. In any case, Nozick's claims about the bases of criticism constitute an interpretation of liberal principles. I want to see whether that interpretation is sound or at least promising.

I shall focus on some of the implications of Nozick's Principle of Justice in

---

[14] Ibid., p. 50.

Transfer (PJT) for two reasons. First, the PJT is the only part of his theory that Nozick develops in a relatively full way. He does not develop a PJA, though he points out that such a principle would be needed to complete his theory, and his discussion of a PRJ is fragmentary compared to his discussion of the PJT. It seems both fair to Nozick and most useful for my own purposes to concentrate on the part of his theory he develops most fully. Second, Jeremy Waldron has already formulated a cogent critique of the general idea of a PJA.[15] Any criticism I might make of that aspect of Nozick's theory would likely borrow heavily from Waldron's argument. Nozick's PJT has been criticized too, of course, and to some extent my discussion will necessarily cover ground that has been traveled before, though from a different vantage point.[16] But I know of no systematic critique of the idea of a PJT comparable to Waldron's critique of the idea of a PJA or to the critique of Nozick's PJT that I shall offer here.

II

As we have seen, Nozick believes that it is possible to reach significant conclusions about the permissible extent of state power and about distributive justice on the basis of his Entitlement Theory of Justice, even without working out the substance of that theory fully. It is surprising, though, that in addition to failing to formulate a PJA for his theory, Nozick also fails to offer an explicit account of the PJT on which he relies. In general, however, it appears that for Nozick individuals are entitled to transfer to others *any* rights they wish, whether by way of gift or by way of exchange, for any reason they wish. Further, Nozick clearly assumes that the rights acquired by the recipient in such a transfer are identical to the rights transferred by the giver or transferor. For Nozick, rights are not diminished by the act of transfer.

I shall discuss three difficulties with Nozick's theory, all of which relate to the practice of transferring rights. I argue that in these three cases, Nozick's version of the Rights-Based Principle of political criticism leads to conclusions that are unacceptable in light of Nozick's own premises. My conclusion is that although Nozick's premises are compatible with the tenets of philosophical liberalism, his version, at least, of the Rights-Based Principle is an inadequate account of the bases of political criticism.

The first difficulty can be explained easily. According to Nozick, "Someone may choose (or permit another) to do to himself *anything*, unless he has

---

[15] Waldron, *The Right to Private Property*, chap. 7.

[16] See especially Samuel Scheffler's "Natural Rights, Equality, and the Minimal State," in *Reading Nozick*, ed. Jeffrey Paul, pp. 148–68. Scheffler does not focus on Nozick's PJT and in fact mentions Nozick's entitlement theory as a whole only in passing, but in spirit his critique is close to mine.

acquired an obligation to some third party not to do or allow it."[17] Specifically, in his view a person has the right to transfer to any other person of his choosing any right he pleases. In a "free system" individuals would be allowed to make any commitments whatsoever they choose to make and to transfer any rights they might choose to transfer, as long as they are not constrained by previous commitments. If they choose, they may even sell themselves into (or otherwise commit themselves to) slavery. Likewise, they would be allowed to commit themselves never to enter into a transaction that would result in their enslavement.[18] Nozick's point is that individuals should be entitled in all circumstances to choose whether to commit themselves and whether to transfer any right they please, subject only to whatever constraints on their actions they have voluntarily accepted in the past. This choice should not be constrained on the basis of any preconception about what is good and what is harmful for a person, and it should not be made for individuals by legal or social arrangements that limit their freedom to choose.

The obvious objection to this view is that it legitimates the possibility that individuals might sell themselves into slavery. Even if it seems unlikely that many individuals would deliberately and explicitly agree to their own enslavement at a stroke, it is quite plausible to suppose that they might transfer away rights in bits and pieces through a series of transactions whose cumulative result would be their virtual enslavement. Yet the conviction that slavery in any form, including the voluntary enslavement of which Nozick's theory approves, is wrong appears to be among the firmest of all our considered judgments.

Moreover, matters are made worse when we consider Nozick's claims about the way in which we should distinguish between voluntary and nonvoluntary transfers of rights. According to Nozick, a person's actions are not rendered nonvoluntary merely because that person faces severely limited alternatives.[19] The crucial factor is how the person's alternatives came to be limited. If a person's alternatives are limited by facts of nature, then the person's actions are voluntary. Similarly, if a person's alternatives are limited because of things others have done, and if those others have acted within their rights, then the person's actions remain voluntary, even if his alternatives are severely constrained. If, for example, a person is stranded on a desert island, then that person's actions are voluntary, even if he is faced with a simple choice between working very hard for a slim chance of survival and death. Likewise, if others act within their rights in a way that leaves a person with only two alternatives from which to choose, one of which is to accept slavery in return for subsistence while the other is death, the per-

---

[17] Nozick, *Anarchy*, p. 58.

[18] Ibid., p. 331.

[19] Ibid., pp. 262ff. Nozick's discussion here also has further implications, which I take up in secs. III and IV of this chapter.

son's acceptance of enslavement would, according to Nozick's account, be voluntary.

This implication constitutes a strong objection to Nozick's theory. Whether that objection is decisive is unclear. Nozick might argue that in fact the likelihood that anyone would enslave himself, or that anyone would find himself in a position of having to choose between enslavement and death, is minuscule. He might claim further that given the (alleged) fact that this likelihood is extremely small, the advantages of his view outweigh its disadvantages. He does after all squarely acknowledge the fact that his theory would legitimate voluntary enslavement. Presumably he thinks that a good reason exists for us to accept this prima facie unattractive consequence. (Nozick does not argue that the fact that his theory legitimates voluntary enslavement constitutes a reason in that theory's favor.) The fact that a theory has *some* undesirable consequences does not in itself demonstrate that the theory is unacceptable.

I do not know whether Nozick would adopt this line of argument or not; the fact is that even though he is forthright about acknowledging that his theory would legitimate "voluntary" enslavement, he does not even discuss the at least prima facie objection to the theory to which this implication leads. I am in any event less sanguine about the facts than a proponent of this line of argument would appear to be. On a worldwide basis, slavery is far from obsolete. Even in the many states in which slavery is outlawed, conditions of slavery or near-slavery are not unusual. In the United States, for example, some migrant workers and prostitutes live in conditions of near-slavery.

Nevertheless, I assume that a theory has to be judged, finally, on the basis of its capacity to account for our considered intuitions and judgments *as a whole*. The fact that a theory conflicts with one or two of those judgments, even firm ones like the judgment that slavery is wrong, or that its acceptance would require us to transform one or two of our judgments, is not a sufficient reason to justify its rejection if the theory has other advantages that outweigh this powerful mark against it. It is conceivable that a theory of the type Nozick develops could have such advantages. Accordingly, let us consider some of the other implications of Nozick's theory.

III

Voluntary enslavement is a possible *first-party* effect of the practice of transferring rights in accordance with the PJT as Nozick conceives it. That practice also has a variety of *third-party* effects, which in the jargon of economic theory are usually called externalities. I want now to consider some of the things Nozick has to say about the third-party effects of the practice of transferring rights.

Nozick's general line of argument about third-party effects of transactions runs along the following lines. Transactions between two parties A and B sometimes have effects on the position of a third party C. If those effects violate C's rights, then either the actions that lead to them may be prohibited or the parties who impose them may be required to compensate C for the violation. Nozick suggests that whether an action should be prohibited depends on whether compensation requirements would deter potential violators.[20] If those effects do not violate C's rights, however, then neither compensation for nor prohibition of the actions in question is justified. If the action leaves C worse off than she was before, then so much the worse for C. If the action leaves C better off, as could conceivably happen, then so much the better for her.

Let us consider two examples of transactions having third-party effects that Nozick offers in his book. In the first example, Nozick asks us to imagine that there are twenty-six women and twenty-six men, each of whom wishes to marry.[21] All members of each sex rank all members of the opposite sex in the same order of desirability for marriage, from A to Z in descending preferential order for the members of one sex and from A′ to Z′ for the others. A and A′ marry. B, who would have preferred to marry A′, then marries B′. C, who would have preferred to marry either A′ or B′, then marries C′, and so on down the line. Z would have preferred to marry any other member of the opposite sex, from A′ to Y′, to marrying Z′, but prefers marrying Z′ to not marrying at all, and Z′ feels the same way about Z. So Z and Z′ marry.

Nozick assumes that all twenty-six women and twenty-six men have the right to marry whomever they choose. He argues that the fact that the alternatives open to Z and Z′ are severely limited does not make their choices any less voluntary than are the choices of A and A′, both of whom have a large number of potential marriage partners from whom they may choose.[22] He offers the following general rule to apply to cases of this sort: "A person's choice among differing degrees of unpalatable alternatives is not rendered nonvoluntary by the fact that others voluntarily chose and acted within their rights in a way that did not provide him with a more palatable alternative."[23] Nozick's point is that even though Z and Z′ may be in a worse position after

---

[20] Ibid., p. 69.

[21] Ibid., p. 263.

[22] G. A. Cohen, who discusses this example in his "Robert Nozick and Wilt Chamberlain: How Patterns Preserve Liberty," in *Justice and Economic Distribution*, ed. John Arthur and William H. Shaw (Englewood Cliffs, N.J.: Prentice-Hall, 1978), pp. 246–62, suggests that Nozick's point is that the transactions between A through Y and A′ through Y′ do not reduce freedom for Z and Z′ (see his p. 257). Cohen argues that this point is false. But Cohen reaches this conclusion by assuming a conception of freedom that is different from the negative concept of liberty Nozick appears to accept. Moreover, although Nozick is interested in freedom, his argument is centrally about *rights* as distinct from freedom. Nozick's point is that A through Y and A′ through Y′ have an inviolable right to act as they choose to do and that they do not violate the rights of Z and Z′ in doing so. Nozick claims that his theory protects rights, not that it maximizes freedom.

[23] Nozick, *Anarchy*, pp. 263–64.

the marriages of A and A′ through Y and Y′ than they would have been in had those marriages not taken place, Z and Z′ act voluntarily because their rights were not violated by the marriages that preceded theirs. Z and Z′ are owed nothing by the others to compensate for the fact that they face limited alternatives, since compensation is called for only when individuals' rights are violated. The others had the right to act as they did.

Nozick applies the same line of reasoning to a second example, which deals with market exchanges between workers and owners of capital. Here is what he says: "Z is faced with working or starving; the choices and actions of all other persons do not add up to providing Z with some other option. (He may have various options about what job to take.) Does Z choose to work voluntarily? (Does someone on a desert island who must work to survive?) Z does choose voluntarily if the other individuals A through Y each acted voluntarily and within their rights."[24]

It is clear from Nozick's discussion that Z is in a worse position than he would have been in if the choices and actions of other individuals had not left him with a more limited range of alternatives than he would have had if those actions had not taken place. But Z's actions are still voluntary, according to Nozick, because his rights have not been violated. Moreover, Z's actions would still be voluntary, and his rights would still be intact, according to Nozick, even if the choices and actions of others left him more severely limited alternatives than those that Nozick's example identifies. Suppose, for example, the choices and actions of others leave Z with only two alternatives: to accept an offer of indentured servitude in return for the basic means of subsistence or to die. (This is the case to which I alluded in section II.) Even in this case, Nozick's PJT implies that Z's actions are voluntary and that Z retains his rights in full.

Nozick might agree that Z is in an unfortunate position. But Nozick's theory says that we should treat Z's misfortune as if that misfortune had been caused by a natural disaster or by Z's being marooned on a desert island. Since Z's misfortune does not result from a violation of Z's rights, his misfortune should not be considered an occasion for criticism of the social arrangements that gave rise to it, even though, by assumption, it would be within our power to alter those arrangements in a way that would mitigate Z's misfortune—or that of a migrant worker or a prostitute who has accepted indentured servitude.

In leading to this conclusion, Nozick's rights-based account of the bases of social criticism appears to have lost touch with the rationale Nozick himself offers to justify that approach. Nozick explains the moral basis of rights by pointing out that human beings have the capacity to shape their own lives in accordance with an overall plan. By conducting our lives in this way, he suggests, we are able to give meaning to our lives. Individuals have rights in

[24] Ibid., p. 263.

order to protect their ability to give meaning to their lives. Yet a person in
Z's position is not able to shape his own life in accordance with an overall
plan. He has two alternatives: to accept indentured servitude or to die. The
terms of servitude constitute a "plan" that is ready-made for the individual.
They provide little scope for an individual to strive for a meaningful life.

Nozick's labor market example derives some of its prima facie plausibility
from the analogy he draws between it and his marriage example. But in fact
the two cases are quite dissimilar, especially when we consider the fact that
the reasoning used in the labor market example would justify the extreme
consequence of indentured servitude as well as the milder consequence, on
which Nozick focuses, of forcing people to work. Being deprived of the opportunity to marry the partner of one's dreams can be considered a misfortune, perhaps, but a deprivation of this sort need not prevent a person from
shaping his life in accordance with an overall plan or from having a meaningful life. The deprivation resulting from one's consent to an arrangement of
indentured servitude or enslavement is another matter. This latter kind of
deprivation can and typically does prevent people from shaping their lives
in accordance with an overall plan. Yet Nozick's rights-based theory is no
more equipped to justify criticism of indentured servitude that is voluntary
by his standards than it is to justify criticism of the practice of marriage. Of
course, not all transactions that worsen the positions of third parties should
be prohibited or regarded as occasions for claims of compensation by those
third parties. For if we were to accept the position that all such transactions
create grounds for claims for compensation, competitive markets would become impossible. The difficulty with Nozick's approach to this issue is that
it denies that any such transactions create grounds for compensation unless
those transactions violate third parties' rights. And in Nozick's view, those
rights do not include a right not to be put in a position of having to choose
between slavery and death.

IV

The fact that Nozick's natural rights interpretation of the Rights-Based Principle leads him to approve of the practice of voluntary enslavement and to
offer reasoning about the effects of voluntary transactions on third parties
that purports to justify the imposition by some human beings of misfortunes
like that suffered by the hapless Z upon other human beings weighs heavily
against his natural rights account of the bases of social criticism. Even
greater difficulties come into view, however, when we consider closely the
line of reasoning Nozick offers to support his own principal conclusion about
political and social arrangements, namely that no state more extensive than
the minimal state can be justified.

Nozick's argument that a "minimal state, limited to the narrow functions of protection against force, theft, fraud, enforcement of contracts and so on"[25] can be justified begins, as we have seen, by postulating a hypothetical state of nature in which all individuals enjoy perfect freedom to do whatever they wish, including transfer any rights they choose to others, provided they do not violate the rights of others.[26] Nozick argues that in such a state of freedom individuals may take advantage of the right to transfer their rights to others to form mutual protection associations designed to help them enforce their rights. Over time a dominant protective association may emerge. The dominant protective association proves to be identical to the minimal state.

Having established that his rights-based theory enables us to justify a minimal state, Nozick goes on in part 2 of his book to ask whether a state more extensive than the minimal state can be justified. The argument for a more-than-minimal state that occupies his attention is that such a state is necessary in order to achieve some kind of equality or distributive justice that would not necessarily result from voluntary transactions among individuals alone. Nozick argues that no such aim is legitimate because "no end-state principle or distributional patterned principle of justice can be continuously realized without continuous interference with people's lives."[27] In his view, any attempt to implement a preconceived principle of distributive justice would violate individuals' rights.[28]

In order to assess Nozick's argument accurately on its own terms, three aspects of that argument, all of which we have discussed at least briefly already, must be emphasized:

First, according to Nozick individuals have the right to transfer any of their rights they choose to others, as long as they do not violate the rights of others in doing so.

Second, the right of individuals to transfer rights to others (or for that matter to do anything else they wish) cannot be restricted for the purpose of preventing those individuals from harming themselves, even if the harm takes the form of their enslavement. The sole purpose for which individuals can be prevented from transferring their rights is to prevent them from violating others' rights.

Third, as we have seen, the right of individuals to transfer rights to others cannot be restricted merely because the position of some third party or parties might be worsened as a result of the contemplated transfer or transaction, even if that third party is left in a position of having to choose between slavery and death. We would have to show that someone's rights are violated to be able to justify any restriction on the right to transfer rights. As the case of Z makes clear, it is

---

[25] Ibid., p. ix; cf. pp. 26, 272.
[26] Ibid., pp. 10ff.
[27] Ibid., p. 163.
[28] See ibid., pp. 149, 297.

permissible to impose serious misfortunes upon third parties as a result of others' transfers of rights, as long as those transfers do not violate that third party's rights.

In the penultimate chapter of his book, Nozick considers whether there might not be "some way to *continue* our story of the origin of the (minimal) state from the state of nature to arrive, via only legitimate steps which violate no one's rights, at something more closely resembling a modern state" (by which Nozick means a state with considerably greater powers than those necessary to protect its members against violence, theft, and fraud and to enforce contracts).[29] He then sketches a series of steps, in each of which individuals legitimately transfer rights, leading to the system of government he calls *demoktesis*. *Demoktesis* arises through the sale by individuals of shares in themselves. In its final form, as Nozick envisages it, "each person owns exactly one share in each right over every other person, including himself."[30] In the end the shareholders establish the system of "one shareholder, one vote."[31] This result, Nozick argues, "is recognizable as a modern state, with its vast panoply of powers over its citizens. Indeed, we have arrived at a *democratic* state" characterized by "ownership of the people, by the people, and for the people."[32]

Nozick suggests that the position of persons in a *demoktesis*, and in a democratic state, resembles that of slaves. He acknowledges that for the most part the members of that state would not be *completely* enslaved. According to the scenario he sketches, when individuals sell rights in themselves, they limit those rights. Nevertheless, if the democratic collectivity has bought up all the rights that individuals have sold, then those individuals are subject to the collectivity's desires in a way that is likely to make them feel oppressed.[33]

This result may be unfortunate. As Nozick himself admits, however, the state of quasi-slavery he calls *demoktesis* is consistent with the principles of his own theory. By his own hypothesis, that state arises through a series of legitimate transfers of rights. We cannot justifiably forbid individuals to transfer their rights in order to prevent those individuals from doing harm to themselves, even if that harm takes the form of their own enslavement. If the standard we must use to evaluate political and social arrangements is the degree of protection they provide for rights, including the right of individuals to transfer their rights to others, and if we interpret the content of individuals' rights via Nozick's conception of the natural right of self-ownership, then there seems to be no legitimate ground for criticism of *demoktesis*, despite Nozick's efforts to portray that state as an unpleasant one.

[29] Ibid., p. 276.
[30] Ibid., p. 285.
[31] Ibid., pp. 286–87.
[32] Ibid., p. 290.
[33] Ibid., p. 283. See also Nozick's "Tale of the Slave" on pp. 290–92.

Suppose a new generation of individuals arises within our imagined democratic state and, at maturity, the individuals in that generation refuse to accept the terms of membership offered to them?[34] We may assume that these malcontents retain all their rights, since they have been minors up to this point and have not been in a position to transfer any of those rights away. The current members of the democratic state cannot legitimately force these individuals to join their political community, since those individuals retain their natural rights of self-ownership, including the right *not* to transfer to others any rights that they do not wish to yield. At the same time, the democrats need not cater to the young upstarts by offering the latter an alternative more attractive to them. The only alternative they *must* offer to the malcontents is the possibility of exiting from the community altogether. The democrats violate no one's rights by restricting the malcontents to the alternatives of either accepting membership on the democrats' terms or departing from the community altogether; the malcontents' natural rights of self-ownership do not entitle them to a greater range of choices than this stark either-or. In effect they are in the position of third parties whose rights are not violated by the voluntary actions of other individuals acting within their rights, even if those voluntary actions leave the malcontents in a worse position than they would have occupied if those actions had not taken place.

Nozick's sketch is a cautionary tale designed to show how undesirable democratic states with extensive powers are. Yet his own account of the bases of social criticism, which accords priority to individual rights over all other factors, ensures that we will have no basis on which to criticize such a state. If the members of that state have acted within their rights at every step, and if they have allowed the young the opportunity to exit at maturity with their natural rights of self-ownership intact as an alternative to accepting membership, then by the criteria expressed in Nozick's own theory, the democratic state with extensive powers that results from their actions is as just as the minimal state he favors.

Nozick does argue that even if a *demoktesis* is not necessarily unjust, some of its members may find it "intolerable."[35] But Nozick's theory does not identify tolerability as a factor that should be considered in evaluating political and social arrangements. Of course, that theory does not prohibit us from considering tolerability, either. It does, however, rule out the use of claims about tolerability (or intolerability) as the basis of an argument for limiting individual rights. The heart of Nozick's theory is the claim that individual rights take priority over all other considerations that we might wish to take into account in comparing alternative social arrangements or policies. An individual who has voluntarily agreed to his own enslavement may later come to find that enslavement intolerable. Unless that individual can per-

---

[34] Nozick considers this scenario in ibid., pp. 287–90.
[35] Ibid., p. 283.

suade the person to whom he has enslaved himself to restore his rights voluntarily, however, Nozick's theory allows the enslaved individual no way out
of his misery. The slave has an absolute duty to respect the rights of the
person to whom he is enslaved, rights the slave has previously transferred to
his enslaver or to some third party who has in turn transferred those rights
to his enslaver. The slave's rights are not violated by this arrangement, since
the slave voluntarily transferred those rights to someone else.

Similarly, if a democratic state with despotic powers arises by a series of
legitimate steps, then it violates no one's rights. Further, the members of
such a state have no right to alter the arrangement that subjects them to
democratic despotism, no matter how intolerable that subjection might be,
unless they can secure the agreement of *everyone* whose rights would be
affected by the change. In the scenario Nozick envisages, individuals own
shares in one another. Individuals in whom shares are owned by others
cannot rightfully regain those shares unless those now entitled to them agree
voluntarily to transfer them. Any member of the *demos* may refuse to transfer her rights over others. As a practical matter it could prove impossible to
abolish a *demoktesis* in a manner that would be accepted as legitimate on the
terms established by Nozick's theory once such a regime is in place, even if
that regime is intolerable to many of its members. Within the framework of
his rights-based theory, Nozick's claim of intolerability is strictly an ad hoc
appeal.[36]

Nozick himself points out that the "very extensive domination of some
persons by others" characteristic of a *demoktesis* "itself is not unjust."[37] Is
there a flaw, then, in the derivation of this more-than-minimal state? For
Nozick, it might be argued, the flaw is that a *demoktesis* would require actual
universal consent in every generation. As we have just seen, though, it is
plausible to suppose that the required consent would be (or has been) given,
particularly if potential new members' only alternative to consent is to exit
from their political community altogether.

---

[36] In the closing paragraphs of his chapter sketching the hypothetical history of a *demoktesis*,
Nozick asks: "How should hypothetical histories affect our current judgment of the institutional
structure of a society?" (ibid., p. 293). Nozick suggests in response to his question that under
some circumstances, hypothetical histories are irrelevant. If the actual history of an existing
society is unjust, then "institutional structures closer to the rights individuals possess in virtue
of the moral side constraints will be more just than institutional structures more distant"
(p. 294).

The problem with this response is that we have no way of knowing what substantive rights
individuals possess by virtue of the moral side constraints. Nozick's theory is a historical theory.
The rights individuals would possess under a legitimate despotism are as consistent with the
moral side constraints *as Nozick construes them* as would be the rights of individuals in anarchy.
In light of this fact, the rule for judging institutional structures that Nozick proposes in this
passage seems virtually meaningless.

[37] Ibid., p. 283.

One might argue that even if it is not implausible to suppose that universal consent to a despotic state has been or might be given, it is *unlikely* that it would be. But this argument misses the point. For Nozick's theory tells us that if people *were* to consent to a state that turns out to be intolerable for many of them by transferring away the rights that give that state its despotic powers, then they are morally bound to abide by their commitments. The fact that they find that state intolerable cannot be helped—not, that is, within the framework of Nozick's theory. This result seems unacceptable. Moreover, it appears to be inconsistent with the rationale behind Nozick's rights-based theory of political criticism, which rests upon the idea of individuals as beings who are capable of shaping their lives in accordance with an overall plan that gives meaning to those lives. The flaw is in Nozick's account of the bases of political criticism, which focuses so exclusively on rights that it loses sight of the purposes that give rights their point.

In fact Nozick's theory appears to be compatible with a wide range of possible conclusions about political and social arrangements. That theory tells us to evaluate current states of affairs by examining how those states of affairs came into being. If the only means of evaluating a given distribution of goods is to discover the genesis of that distribution, then the only means of evaluating political institutions must likewise be to ascertain how those institutions came into being. If individuals have the right to transfer to others any right they choose, then they have the right together to create any set of political institutions they choose. Despite appearances and his own claims, then, Nozick's premises are relatively indeterminate. A reasonable argument could be made from those premises for virtually any set of political and social arrangements that one might happen to prefer.

At least two strategies exist by means of which Nozick's theory might be revised to support a more determinate conclusion. One would be to abandon the historical approach to evaluation that he prefers in favor of what he calls an end-result or end-state approach to evaluation. The danger of this strategy from Nozick's point of view, of course, is that its adoption for the purpose of evaluating political institutions would legitimate adoption of an end-state approach to the evaluation of current distributions of goods as well. Nozick wants to avoid an end-state approach to evaluation of current distributions of goods because he believes that approach entails continual interference by the state with individuals' rights.

An alternative strategy that Nozick might adopt to enable his theory to produce more determinate conclusions would be to abandon his view that individuals have the right to do to themselves anything they choose, including the right to transfer to others any rights they choose. This gambit would allow a rights-based theorist to argue that some states are unjustified because public authorities in those states act as if they possessed rights that no individual could possibly have transferred to them. The difficulty with this view from Nozick's viewpoint is that it would open the door to restrictions on individuals' rights to do whatever they want providing they do not violate the rights of others.

In any case Nozick's natural rights interpretation of the Rights-Based Principle of political criticism seems unsatisfactory. The theory Nozick develops on the basis of that interpretation could be used to justify enslavement that would be voluntary only in the thinnest sense, imposition of severe misfortunes on third parties without their consent, and democratic despotism. It has these consequences mainly because it relies on a conception of rights so rigid that if we were to take that conception seriously, as Nozick asks us to do, we would have to ignore the destructive effects those rights would have, under plausible conditions, on individuals' abilities to shape their lives in ways intended to give meaning to them.

V

An alternative to the natural rights approach to determining the content of individuals' rights that is consistent with the Rights-Based Principle of political criticism is to proceed as if rights were the products of an agreement or convention among individuals each of whom seeks to further his own advantage. This contractarian approach has been developed by James Buchanan and others. Buchanan does not argue that individuals' rights are the product of an *actual* agreement. He suggests, though, that we can generate an account of the content of individual rights by imagining the terms of a hypothetical agreement about rights that would be likely to win acceptance by individuals who desire to avoid the harmful effects of anarchical conflict.

Buchanan asks us to imagine a world consisting of two persons, each of whom possesses a share of the one and only scarce good that exists in their world. They do not produce this good, which falls down on them like manna from heaven, nor can they benefit from trade with one another, since only one scarce good exists. Nevertheless, each may stand to gain from predatory efforts to acquire a portion of the other's share of that good. Similarly, each has an incentive to invest in efforts to defend against predation. The eventual result of their interaction will be that each establishes a mix of investments in predatory and defensive actions that results in a distribution of the one scarce good in their world that Buchanan calls the "natural distribution."[38]

Both individuals in this imaginary world stand to benefit from a cessation of predatory and defensive activities. Both therefore have an interest in negotiating an agreement to bring their hostilities to an end. They must, however, find terms on which both parties can agree and discover a means for

---

[38] Buchanan, *Limits*, p. 24. Buchanan's concept of the natural distribution is drawn from Winston Bush (see ibid., p. 183, n. 9).

guaranteeing that those terms will be adhered to. In the scenario Buchanan describes, these tasks give rise to a four-stage sequence of contractual agreements. The first stage is a *disarmament contract* that establishes the limits on behavior that enable individuals to leave the predatory state of nature and found a society. The basis for this agreement is the status quo current at the time of the agreement—that is, the natural distribution of goods established by the mix of predatory and defensive activities in which the parties have engaged up to the time of the agreement. The second stage is (in Buchanan's lexicon) the *constitutional contract*. This stage establishes the parties' rights of ownership over resources, including human capacities as well as nonhuman resources. At this stage the hypothetical de facto distribution of goods established through the parties' predatory and defensive efforts is transformed into a legitimate distribution by virtue of its acceptance by the parties involved. The third and fourth stages constitute what Buchanan calls a *postconstitutional contract*. In the first postconstitutional stage the parties establish a *protective* state to enforce the rights on which they agreed in the constitutional contract. In the second, they establish a *productive* state to provide public goods.

Buchanan's contractarian argument may appear to be conservatively biased, since it assumes that individuals' rights are based on a status quo. In fact, however, Buchanan envisages a constitutional contract that is subject to continuous renegotiation. His concept of the natural distribution is supplemented by the concept of "renegotiation expectations."[39] Renegotiation expectations are the expectations that individuals form at any given time when they ask themselves how their current positions in the distribution of goods compare with those they might expect to secure if the terms of the constitutional contract were renegotiated at that time. Buchanan's premises are individualistic and, like Nozick's theory, his theory is inegalitarian in its implications for property holdings. But his theory is not conservative in the sense of necessarily working in favor of the existing order of things.

In fact Buchanan suggests that the concept of renegotiation expectations gives his theory real evaluative bite. "This approach," he argues, "offers a means of evaluating social rules, legal structure, and property rights."[40] The evaluative questions we ask about these matters "can only be answered through an evaluation of the existing structure, *as if* it were the outcome of a current contract, or one that is continuously renegotiated."[41] The basis of evaluation for Buchanan is the congruence or lack of congruence between the actual distribution of rights that obtains at a given time and the distribution that would be expected to result if the constitutional contract were renegotiated at that time. Buchanan argues that if the disparity between these

[39] Ibid., p. 75.
[40] Ibid.
[41] Ibid.

two distributions is great, then people can be expected to be relatively un-willing to comply with existing rules and the time may be ripe for a contrac-tual change in the status quo.

The apparent implications of Buchanan's contractarian approach to rights differ significantly from the substantive conclusions Nozick attempts to de-fend. In Nozick's view the only state that can be justified is a minimal or protective state whose sole purpose is to protect individuals' rights from violation by others. Buchanan agrees with Nozick on the importance of pro-tection for individuals' rights. However, whereas for Nozick the ultimate source of rights is a primordial right of self-ownership, for Buchanan that source is an agreement among contracting parties reached in order to help them satisfy wants. On Buchanan's view, the narrowly protective state Nozick favors would frustrate individuals' wants unnecessarily through fail-ure to provide sufficient public goods and through inadequate protection against "public bads," including pollution.[42] There is no bar on Buchanan's view that might prevent the members of a society from arranging for the provision of public goods and the prevention of public bads. In the scenario Buchanan sketches, these arrangements are the subject of a postconstitu-tional contract that establishes a productive state.[43]

Let us now consider some difficulties with Buchanan's contractarian ver-sion of rights-based political criticism.

VI

The first significant difficulty with Buchanan's contractarian theory is that like Nozick's theory, it legitimizes slavery under some circumstances. The reason is that in Buchanan's theory rights derive from an agreement that establishes ownership over resources *including human capacities*. A person whose place in the natural distribution leaves him in a poor bargaining posi-tion might find himself compelled to accept the status of slavery or of some degree of indentured servitude as the price demanded by others to secure their agreement to cease hostilities. Buchanan explicitly recognizes this pos-sibility as an acceptable outcome of a constitutional contract. According to him a "contract of slavery would, as other contracts, define individual rights, and, to the extent that this assignment is mutually accepted, mutual gains may be secured from the consequent reduction in defense and predation

---

[42] Nozick's theory would enable property owners to protect themselves from pollution, but Nozick does not provide an account of a way in which pollution of unowned things could be prevented or regulated, and in fact it seems unlikely that it could be, consistently with the basic principles of Nozick's theory. For Nozick's own comments on pollution, see *Anarchy*, pp. 79–81.

[43] It has been argued that very few truly public goods exist. "The idea that there are lots and lots of public goods . . . is a Leftist illusion" (Jan Narveson, *The Libertarian Idea*, p. 196). It would be interesting to know Buchanan's response to the claim that he is a propagator of this illusion.

effort."[44] As in the case of Nozick's theory, this implication constitutes a powerful objection to Buchanan's argument, since it conflicts with the evidently well-founded conviction that slavery is wrong. Even if we set this objection aside, however, other serious difficulties with Buchanan's approach arise.

A second difficulty has to do with the informational requirements of Buchanan's theory. The key concept of that theory for evaluative purposes is the concept of the natural distribution. The natural distribution forms the basis of individuals' renegotiation expectations, which in turn provides those individuals with a standard for criticism of prevailing social arrangements. Yet it seems that that distribution would be impossible to ascertain, even approximately.

Buchanan suggests that the qualities that would contribute to determining the natural distribution might include physical strength, cajolery, and stealth, among others.[45] As his discussion makes clear, however, his list of these qualities is quite indefinite. The reason for this vagueness is that we have no way of identifying the qualities that would be most likely to prevail in a predatory situation that could hypothetically result from the breakdown of an existing social order. Presumably brute physical strength would confer some comparative advantage, but would that advantage be greater or less than that which would result from a capacity for strategic planning or from keen eyesight? Perhaps a talent for deception would prove decisive over all others, but perhaps not.

Moreover, even if we were able to draw up a plausible list of qualities and the respective contributions they would make to a person's comparative advantage in a hypothetical predatory situation, we would still be unable to determine the magnitudes of many individuals' endowments of some of these qualities. Physical strength, sharpness of vision, and other purely physical qualities could be measured, but a person's capacity for cunning, ruthlessness, and other qualities that have to do with character may not appear from that person's conduct in everyday life and in many cases could not be determined accurately in the absence of actual conflict.

The difficulties of estimating the natural distribution and individuals' renegotiation expectations are compounded by the fact that some individuals would probably form coalitions.[46] No reasonable means of predicting the likely membership and comparative strength of potential coalitions exists, nor does such a means seem likely to be within our reach in the foreseeable future. In many real-life instances it is extremely difficult to predict the outcome of prospective battles even when we possess considerable informa-

[44] Buchanan, *Limits*, p. 60.
[45] Ibid., p. 24. See also p. 81.
[46] As Buchanan suggests they would. See ibid., p. 110.

tion about the size and membership of coalitions, their skill and combat readiness, the armaments available to them, and so forth. In the case of hypothetical predatory activities that must be imagined without most of this information at hand, no meaningful estimate of the outcome of those activities is possible.

The informational requirements of Nozick's theory of entitlements raise difficulties for that approach, too.[47] In the case of that theory, though, these difficulties can be circumvented. Nozick himself acknowledges that in the absence of reliable historical records we must fall back on the art of estimation to rectify past injustices in the acquisition and transfer of holdings. Once that rectification has occurred, however, Nozick's theory could be applied with considerable accuracy. The informational difficulty with Nozick's theory stems from a lack of historical records; once we get past that difficulty, the problem need not recur. In the case of Buchanan's theory, though, the informational problem arises because that theory identifies as normatively significant a hypothetical situation that may never actually arise. Moreover, the theory postulates that constitutional contracting should be viewed as a continuing process. If we were to accept Buchanan's approach, the informational demands that approach would impose would constitute a continuing and insoluble problem.[48]

Even if a means of ascertaining the natural distribution and hence of assigning renegotiation expectations to individuals were available to us, a third difficulty would still arise. The problem, which has been pointed out by David Gauthier,[49] is that it does not seem credible to assume that rational individuals would accept the natural distribution as a basis on which to determine the allocation of rights. Acceptance of this arrangement would constitute agreement by all individuals to allow all others to enjoy in the future the fruits of predatory activities they have pursued in the past. If predatory activities were prohibited by mutual agreement, however, then the victims of past predatory activities would no longer have a reason to allow their former oppressors to enjoy the spoils of their previous behavior. The relatively weak would have no reason to cede advantages to the relatively strong when they know that the strong will not be able to make use of their strengths for predatory purposes. Buchanan's argument assumes that victims of extortion—for that is in effect what the relatively disadvan-

---

[47] Nozick himself discusses these difficulties briefly in *Anarchy*, p. 231. For some further discussion, see Lawrence Davis, "Nozick's Entitlement Theory," in *Reading Nozick*, ed. Jeffery Paul, pp. 344–54; and Robert E. Litan, "On Rectification in Nozick's Minimal State," *Political Theory* 5 (1977): 233–46.

[48] Equally great if not greater informational difficulties are raised by the more complex version of the contractarian argument David Gauthier works out in *Morals by Agreement*. For a trenchant critique of Gauthier's version of this argument that emphasizes these difficulties, see David Braybrooke, "Social Contract Theory's Fanciest Flight," *Ethics* 97 (1987): 750–64.

[49] Gauthier, *Morals by Agreement*, pp. 194ff.

taged individuals in his bargaining scenario are—would be willing to allow the extortionists to keep their violently or coercively obtained goods even when the former extortionists are no longer in a position to make effective threats.

A fourth and most decisive difficulty with Buchanan's contractarian interpretation of the Rights-Based Principle is that the theory to which that interpretation leads does not support conclusions that seem acceptable, even to Buchanan. Buchanan argues for a "reconstruction of the basic constitutional order"[50] based on a recognition both of market failures and of governmental failures. In his view this reconstruction would "redefine individual rights and reduce the scope for collectively determined coercive activity."[51] Buchanan believes that individual freedom can best be protected by limiting strictly those constraints that are imposed with the backing of the coercive power of the state. He argues that if state activity were subject to legitimation through a series of contractual agreements among individuals of the kind he envisages, then the scope of that activity would be limited to well-defined protective and productive tasks. "The operation of an unconstrained collectivity could scarcely emerge from rational constitutional contracting among persons."[52]

Buchanan's reasoning is defective. As we have seen, the bargaining positions of individuals in the natural distribution as he describes it depend on the resources that those individuals would be able to command in a predatory situation, including any advantages they might gain from forming coalitions as well as from their intrinsic capacities and skills. If a coalition were to establish control over a sufficiently large share of the available resources to achieve a dominant bargaining position, then there would be nothing to prevent that coalition from demanding the right to maintain a state designed to serve the coalition's purposes, whatever they might be, without limitations on the scope of state authority of the kind Buchanan wishes to prescribe. If other participants in the bargaining refuse to accept the dominant coalition's terms, then that coalition could continue to engage in overt predatory activity until its opponents could be persuaded to submit. The outcome of a bargain concluded within this scenario might well include an *expansion* rather than a reduction of the scope of "collectively determined coercive activity" from present levels.[53] Buchanan's suggestion that the scope of coercive state activity in the United States in recent years has been

---

[50] Buchanan, *Limits*, p. 167.

[51] Ibid., p. 179.

[52] Ibid., p. 50.

[53] David Braybrooke cogently criticizes David Gauthier's version of the contractarian theory on the similar ground, among others, that his theory fails to guarantee the results Gauthier envisages. For this critique see Braybrooke's "Gauthier's Foundations for Ethics under the Test of Application," in *Contractarianism and Rational Choice: Essays on David Gauthier's "Morals by Agreement"*, ed. Peter Vallentyne (Cambridge: Cambridge University Press, 1991), pp. 56–70.

excessive may be correct.[54] But the contractarian theory on which Buchanan claims to rely for the purpose of evaluating social arrangements does not provide a basis for that suggestion.[55] In fact the theory might, under plausible conditions, authorize despotism, a result that would be incompatible with liberal principles and with Buchanan's own intentions.

Although Buchanan's contractarian interpretation of the Rights-Based Principle of political criticism differs in many significant respects from Nozick's natural rights view, then, his interpretation has weaknesses similar to those from which Nozick's theory suffers. Buchanan tells us that his "natural proclivity as an economist is to place ultimate value on process or procedure, and by implication to define as 'good' that which emerges from agreement among free men, independently of intrinsic evaluation of the outcome itself."[56] Like Nozick, Buchanan attempts to avoid normative presuppositions about the preferences individuals ought to have or about the things individuals ought to be allowed to do with or to themselves. Individuals should be allowed to act on their own individual values, whatever these may happen to be, provided they do not violate others' rights. Further, Buchanan wishes to avoid normative assumptions about the distribution of goods. In his view goods should be distributed among individuals as a result of the actions of those individuals themselves. We cannot prescribe a pattern in advance to which that distribution should conform. If we cannot prescribe a pattern to which the distribution of goods should conform, however, we cannot prescribe a pattern that would limit the scope of state power, either. Power must be distributed as a result of the actions of individuals rather than in accordance with a pattern prescribed in advance. We have no basis for maintaining that the distribution to which those actions lead would have to result in a state limited to certain protective and productive tasks or, for that matter, for drawing any definite conclusions about the political and social arrangements that would emerge from hypothetical constitutional contracting.

---

[54] "Few who observe the far-flung operation of the executive arm of the United States government along with the ubiquitousness of the federal judiciary could interpret the activities of either of these institutions as falling within meaningful restrictions of the enforcer" (Buchanan, *Limits*, p. 163).

[55] Buchanan argues that "a fundamental shift in preferences has occurred at least for some individuals and groups, a shift toward individual freedom and away from constraints" (ibid., p. 128). If we assume that as an empirical matter this observation is accurate, then it would appear to support Buchanan's views about the scope of state power, at least to the extent that we are willing to accept current preferences as authoritative. But Buchanan also admits that many people "are likely to exhibit personal preferences for collective action" rather than for "individual freedom" (ibid., p. 160). Even by his own testimony, then, the outcome of an approach to evaluation that places as much weight on individual preferences as Buchanan does appears highly problematical.

[56] Ibid., p. 167.

Like the natural rights approach, then, the contractarian version of the Rights-Based Principle fails to do the most important work for which it was designed. That view could be used to justify slavery, which seems incompatible with liberal principles and with some of the strongest considered convictions about justice we have. It could be used to justify despotism, which is incompatible both with liberal principles and with Buchanan's own intentions. We cannot define as "good" that which would emerge from agreement among free men in a hypothetical situation of the type Buchanan proposes, because we cannot determine even approximately the substance of that agreement. Buchanan's attempt to account for the bases of political criticism by reference to a hypothetical convention or contract specifying the content of individual rights seems to lead to a dead end.

VII

The arguments I have offered in the preceding do not amount to a refutation of the Rights-Based Principle of political criticism. In fact, a strict refutation of that principle as a whole may not be feasible. For although the Rights-Based Principle identifies the degree to which political and social arrangements protect individual rights as the crucial factor to be considered in comparing alternative arrangements, the principle itself does not specify the content of those rights which are to be protected. Different versions of the principle specify the content of those rights in different ways. Presumably there could be an indefinite number of versions of the principle, one for each precise description of the rights covered by it. A strict refutation of the Rights-Based Principle would consist of a refutation of every one of these versions, a task that may be impossible to accomplish in practice.

Nevertheless, the arguments made here against Nozick's pure natural rights version of the Rights-Based Principle and against Buchanan's pure contractarian theory of rights constitute a strong case against the view that either of these rather stark versions is acceptable as an account of the normative bases of political criticism. Even here, I cannot claim to have *disproved* either Nozick's or Buchanan's view in a strict sense. But that is because theories that attempt to account for the normative bases of political criticism *cannot* be proved or disproved in a strict sense. The measure of a theory of this kind is the degree of success it could be expected to attain in accounting for and organizing our considered judgments. That is a probabilistic test, which by its nature leaves room for dispute and for differences of interpretation. I think, though, that the potentially despotic implications of these theories place them into a class of views that would have very little chance of passing that test, if we could carry it out in the real world.

Even if Nozick's and Buchanan's theories are ruled out, however, it might turn out that some other version of the Rights-Based Principle would be able to pass the test of reflective equilibrium. One example of a more promising approach to political criticism that makes use of a style of argument that seems to be at least roughly in line with the Rights-Based Principle is Ronald Dworkin's use of the notion of rights as trumps.[57] Most of the arguments Dworkin tries to make with this approach are more plausible than either Buchanan's or Nozick's theory. But that is at least partly because rights do not occupy the position of strict priority over other considerations in Dworkin's approach that they do in Nozick's and Buchanan's. According to Dworkin, it follows from the concept of a right that rights must take priority over some social goals.[58] But few rights, if any, take priority over *all* social goals. And the reason for that, I suggest, is that rights do not do the real work—by which I mean the work of describing or accounting for the bases of political criticism—in Dworkin's approach. The real work in that approach is done by the view that human beings should have the resources they need to give meaning to their lives. Rights for Dworkin are an important *tool* of political and social criticism, but they do not define the real *basis* of that criticism.

Locke might be considered another example of a theorist who relies on the Rights-Based Principle of political criticism. But Locke, like Dworkin and unlike Nozick and Buchanan, never loses sight of the *purpose* of rights.[59] Locke's description of that purpose, which focuses on the subsistence and preservation of human beings, is less expansive than Dworkin's, but that description, rather than the more specific rights he derives from it, constitutes the core of his account of the bases of political criticism.[60]

These observations suggest that approaches that identify protection of rights as such as the basis of political criticism in the way that I have assumed the Rights-Based Principle does are likely to be problematical if and to the extent that they neglect the purposes and significance of rights, as both Nozick and Buchanan do. Rights exist for reasons. They derive their value from those reasons. So it is unlikely that we will be able to formulate a persuasive account of the bases of political criticism in the form of the Rights-Based Principle unless our description of the content of the rights

[57] For one relatively full statement, among many, of Dworkin's idea of rights as trumps, see his *Taking Rights Seriously* (Cambridge, Mass.: Harvard University Press, 1978), chap. 4, pp. 82ff. Dworkin uses this approach in many of his writings; see generally his remaining essays in *Taking Rights Seriously* and the essays in his *A Matter of Principle* (Cambridge, Mass.: Harvard University Press, 1985). In his more recent work, *Life's Dominion: An Argument about Abortion, Euthanasia, and Individual Freedom* (New York: Knopf, 1993), Dworkin relies less heavily on rights claims than in most of his earlier writings.

[58] Dworkin, *Taking Rights Seriously*, p. 92.

[59] Though Locke's account of property rights is defective. See Waldron's excellent discussion in *The Right to Private Property*, chap. 6.

[60] See, in addition to Waldron's chapter (chap. 6) on Locke in *The Right to Private Property*, Alan Ryan, *Property and Political Theory* (Oxford: Blackwell, 1984), chap. 1.

protected by that principle is really a statement of the purposes rights are supposed to serve.[61]

Rights-based liberal views call attention to the fact that individual rights play a role of great importance in the institutional structure of liberal societies. Despite the fact that his theory is subject to serious and well-founded criticisms, there is a ring of truth to Nozick's underlying point that a theory which takes seriously the notion that human beings are agents capable of conceiving values and projects must accept the consequence that unequal holdings are likely to result from the actions individuals take to realize those values and to pursue their projects. Nozick's theory fails, as does Buchanan's, because it takes this insight to extremes, locking onto it in a way that leads Nozick to lose sight of the reasons that give rights their value. But the shortsightedness of Nozick's view should not blind *us* to the fact that individual rights are, in all likelihood, indispensable in any society that operates in accordance with liberal principles. Rights cannot bear the entire weight of an account of the bases of political and social criticism. But rights *are* integral to any society in which human beings are recognized as agents.

The strongest form of refutation that is possible in political theory is the proposal of a more plausible alternative theory or at least, as Nozick suggests, a sketch of a plausible alternative view. So far I have considered only two theories and have rejected both. Is a stronger theory available? That is the question to which I shall now turn.

---

[61] For two examples of arguments that make use of the concept of rights in roughly this way, see Henry Shue, *Basic Rights: Subsistence, Affluence, and U.S. Foreign Policy* (Princeton: Princeton University Press, 1980); and Jeremy Waldron, *Liberal Rights: Collected Papers, 1981–1991* (Cambridge: Cambridge University Press, 1993).

CHAPTER THREE

Perfectionist Liberalism

RIGHTS ARE VALUABLE because human beings are agents. That is, we are creatures who are capable of conceiving and of trying to bring to fruition projects and values, including projects and values that are not designed simply to affect our own experiences. In this chapter I want to consider a strand of liberal thought that develops the concept of human agency into a normative conception of the person and places that conception at the center of an account of the bases of political criticism.

The idea that a normative conception of persons might play the key role in an account of the bases of political criticism is one of the oldest organizing assumptions in political philosophy. The pioneer of this approach was Plato, who was the first writer to develop a comprehensive or synoptic theory linking forms of political regime to distinct types of character and arranging these types in a hierarchical order running from best to worst.[1] This approach has played a role in the arguments of diverse political thinkers since Plato. Here, for example, is Max Weber in one of his well-known methodological essays: "Only one thing is indisputable: every type of social order, without exception, must, if one wishes to *evaluate* it, be examined with reference to the opportunities which it affords to *certain types of persons* to rise to positions of superiority through the operation of the various objective and subjective selective factors."[2] Although Weber's contention that there can be no dispute about this approach to evaluation was mistaken, his statement is at least indicative of its enduring appeal.

The strand of thought I examine in this chapter focuses on a liberal conception of the person. Statements of such a conception have played an important role in the development of the liberal tradition since its inception. Locke, for instance, argues that "the forebearance of a too hasty compliance

---

[1] Plato, *Republic*, trans. Richard W. Sterling and William C. Scott (New York: Norton, 1985), books 8–9. The best regime, in Plato's view, is an aristocracy or regime of rule by the best and wisest members of the political community, which supports a life of philosophical contemplation for the few; the worst is a tyrannical regime, to which there corresponds a tyrannical man, who is portrayed memorably in *Republic*, book 9.

[2] "The Meaning of 'Ethical Neutrality' in Sociology and Economics," in Max Weber, *The Methodology of the Social Sciences*, trans. Edward A. Shils and Henry A. Finch (New York: Free Press, 1949), p. 27 (emphasis in original). Note that both Plato and Weber focus on the types of persons who rise to positions of superiority.

with our desires, the moderation and restraint of our Passions, so that our Understandings may be *free* to examine, and reason unbiassed give its judgment, being that, whereon a right direction of our conduct to true Happiness depends; 'tis on this we should employ our chief care and endeavours."[3] Only when we obey our rational judgments rather than our unexamined desires, Locke insists, are we truly free.[4] The provisions for civil government Locke describes in his *Second Treatise of Government* are designed to protect freedom in this sense of reflective self-direction.[5]

A similar conception of the person informs Kant's political thought. In his essay on the enlightenment, for example, he declares that "nature has cherished, within its hard shell, the germ of the inclination and need for free *thought*. This free thought gradually acts upon the mind of the people and they gradually become more capable of acting in freedom."[6] Kant's essay is an exhortation to cultivate the capacity to act in freedom by applying the courage and determination required to use one's own intelligence rather than relying on the guidance of others. As this capacity matures, he hopes, governments will gradually come to treat "man, who is now more than a machine," with the dignity that creature deserves.[7]

One of the most celebrated statements of this conception of the person was made by John Stuart Mill: "He who lets the world, or his own portion of it, choose his plan of life for him, has no need of any other faculty than the ape-like one of imitation. He who chooses his plan for himself, employs all his faculties . . . It really is of importance, not only what men do, but also what manner of men they are that do it. Among the works of man, which human life is rightly employed in perfecting and beautifying, the first in importance surely is man himself."[8] While Mill's statement emphasizes individuality whereas Locke's and Kant's statements do not, all three writers share a commitment to the view that human beings live best when they live a life of reflective self-direction.

Mill's statement makes explicit a claim that is less clearly developed by Locke and Kant, namely, that the perfection of our capacities as agents capable of shaping our own lives by pursuing projects and attempting to realize values that we conceive for ourselves is a task of first importance for human

---

[3] John Locke, *An Essay Concerning Human Understanding*, ed. Peter H. Nidditch (Oxford: Oxford University Press, 1975), book 2, chap. 21, sec. 53, p. 268 (emphasis in original).

[4] Ibid., sec. 47, pp. 263–64.

[5] For a lucid discussion of Locke's conception of the person, see Rogers M. Smith, *Liberalism and American Constitutional Law* (Cambridge, Mass.: Harvard University Press, 1985), pp. 26ff.

[6] Immanuel Kant, "What Is Enlightenment?" in *The Philosophy of Kant*, ed. Carl J. Friedrich (New York: Random House, 1949), pp. 132–39 (emphasis in original).

[7] For a discussion and critique of Kant's conception of the person, see Larmore, *Patterns of Moral Complexity* (Cambridge: Cambridge University Press, 1987), pp. 77ff.

[8] Mill, *On Liberty*, ed. David Spitz (New York: Norton, 1975), chap. 3, p. 56.

beings. A person who has perfected these capacities, or who has at least developed them to a high degree, is often called an *autonomous* individual.

Perfectionist liberalism holds that human beings should be autonomous individuals. This claim can be used to support a diverse array of prescriptions for political and social arrangements. For example, Rasmussen and Den Uyl argue from the premise that self-directedness or autonomy is the first in importance among all final ends for individuals to the conclusion that political and social arrangements should assume a libertarian form.[9] In contrast, many other authors argue that paternalistic measures that are incompatible with libertarian conclusions are necessary in order to help individuals become autonomous.[10]

My purpose in this chapter is to examine critically the perfectionist claim about the *bases* of political and social criticism rather than consider the diverse, and in some cases contradictory, arguments that have been made about the practical implications of perfectionist premises. This purpose does not, of course, preclude discussion of some of the possible practical implications of perfectionist liberalism. Indeed, one way of testing claims about the normative bases of social criticism is to identify practical implications that would follow from criticism made from the normative vantage point from which these claims are made to see whether those implications can be reconciled with our considered judgments. My immediate objective, though, is to see how far the perfectionist approach can take us toward an account of the bases of social criticism, that is, toward an account of what we should count when we are comparing the merits and flaws of existing institutions or practices with those of some proposed alternative to or revision of those practices.

As before, it may prove worthwhile to state the claim I intend to consider here in a general form:

> A set of political and social arrangements is good to the extent to which it protects and promotes a life of autonomy for all members of the society to which those arrangements apply.

I shall label this claim the *Autonomy Principle* of political criticism. The question I shall try to answer in this chapter, then, is, How far can the Autonomy Principle take us toward a persuasive account of the bases of political and social criticism?

---

[9] Rasmussen and Den Uyl, *Liberty and Nature: An Aristotelian Defense of Liberal Order* (La Salle: Open Court, 1991). For their claims about autonomy, see pp. 70–75.

[10] For an example of this line of argument, see Robert Young, *Personal Autonomy: Beyond Negative and Positive Liberty* (London: Croom Helm, 1986); and for some additional discussion along similar lines, see John Kleinig, *Paternalism* (Totowa, N.J.: Rowman and Allanheld, 1984), and Joel Feinberg, *Harm to Self*, vol. 3 of *The Moral Limits of the Criminal Law* (Oxford: Oxford University Press, 1986).

I

The term *autonomy* has a wide range of meanings,[11] and the concept of individual autonomy has been a subject of intense discussion and debate in recent years.[12] So my first task is to define the concept of autonomy with some precision. In fact, it will be useful for my purposes to distinguish three different types of autonomy. These three types do not, needless to say, exhaust the possibilities, but they do describe the possible understandings of autonomy that are most relevant for my inquiry.

First, a person might be considered autonomous when she is capable of conceiving and acting on (or attempting to realize) projects and values including, at least potentially, projects and values that are about things other than that being's own experiences. Understood in this way, the concept of an autonomous individual is identical to the concept of an agent. Since I want to distinguish this type of autonomy from two others, both of which might reasonably be identified by the same word, I shall call this type of autonomy *agency* or *autonomy$_1$*.

As I have suggested earlier,[13] one way of distinguishing between an agent and a sentient being who is not autonomous$_1$ (or is not an agent) is to point out that an explanation of the actions of an agent would take a different form from an explanation of the actions of a sentient being who is not an agent. For example, if a sentient being who is not an agent were to jump into a river to rescue a fellow creature from drowning, we would try to explain that being's actions by suggesting that the nonautonomous$_1$ being was moved by natural or instinctive feelings of sympathy for its endangered fellow creature. We would not say that the nonautonomous$_1$ being values human life (supposing for a moment that the endangered creature is a human being), because we would not ascribe to the nonautonomous$_1$ being the capacity to *value* things in the ordinary sense. But if an *agent* were to jump into a river to save a fellow creature from drowning, we would be inclined to say that that individual did what she did because she values human life. At least, we

---

[11] Joel Feinberg distinguishes many of these meanings in a useful discussion in his *Harm to Self*, chap. 18. Feinberg doubts that the term has a single, coherent meaning.

[12] John Christman's "Constructing the Inner Citadel: Recent Work on Autonomy," *Ethics* 99 (1988): 109–24 is a useful survey of much of the recent literature. Two excellent and for my purposes important works not included in this survey are Joseph Raz's *The Morality of Freedom* (Oxford: Oxford University Press, 1986) and Stanley I. Benn's *A Theory of Freedom* (Cambridge: Cambridge University Press, 1988). Two useful collections of essays bearing on the topic are Christman's *The Inner Citadel: Essays on Individual Autonomy* (New York: Oxford University Press, 1989) and Thomas C. Heller, Morton Sosna, and David E. Wellbery, eds., *Reconstructing Individualism: Autonomy, Individuality, and the Self in Western Thought* (Stanford: Stanford University Press, 1986). See also Gerald Dworkin's *The Theory and Practice of Autonomy* (Cambridge: Cambridge University Press, 1988).

[13] In chap. 1, sec. I.

would assume that this is the most plausible explanation of the bare facts presented if the endangered human being and the individual who saves him were strangers to each other before they were brought together by the threatened drowning.

I do not know whether any nonautonomous$_1$ beings would attempt to rescue a stranger in the circumstances envisaged in this illustration, but it is possible that strong feelings of sympathy would drive some nonautonomous$_1$ beings to attempt this sort of act. However, nonautonomous$_1$ beings are incapable of doing some things that agents (autonomous$_1$ human beings) do routinely. For example, an agent can take an interest in the sorts of lives her children will have after her death and can take actions to affect those lives. She might make a will to ensure that her children will have certain financial resources in the event of her death, or to appoint a guardian. These kinds of actions are impossible for nonautonomous$_1$ beings not merely because they do not have the institution of property and others like it, but because (we suppose) they do not have the kind of imagination that is necessary to envisage their children's future lives. They are, we assume, incapable of formulating projects and conceiving values.

Of course, an agent can take an interest in states of the world that will arise after her death other than her children's well-being. She might take an interest in founding a dynasty, as John D. Rockefeller did, or in doing other things that will be likely to cause her name to be known to people long after her death. Agents have emotions that nonautonomous$_1$ beings do not experience. We assume, for instance, that nonautonomous$_1$ beings are not capable of ambition of the sort Rockefeller evidently had.

The capacity to become an agent is not difficult to develop. Ordinarily, it seems, human beings become agents in due course without deliberate training or tutelage, much as human beings seem to develop the capacity for linguistic competence in due course without special training. However, people are not born with autonomy$_1$ any more than they are born with linguistic competence. They are born only with the capacity to develop autonomy$_1$. Although the conditions required to become an agent are not particularly stringent, *some* conditions are required to become an agent, just as some conditions are required to develop the capacity to use a natural language.

A second way of thinking of autonomy is to suppose that a person is autonomous when she has an effective sense of justice. I shall call this type of autonomy *moral autonomy* or, at times, *autonomy$_2$*. The Kantian idea of moral autonomy is a species of this genus, but it is only a species. The concept of moral autonomy is broader than Kant's specific theory of moral autonomy.

To have a sense of justice is to recognize that other human beings are agents like yourself, with projects and values of their own, projects and values that may impose limits on the things you can do in pursuit of your own projects and values. A person who has a sense of justice realizes that she may have to restrain her own actions and claims on other people and resources in recognition of the fact that other people have claims of their own.

The mark of a person who lacks moral autonomy is an inability to think of other human beings as anything other than objects that are available to be used for that person's own purposes. Suppose, for example, that you are an ambitious businesswoman who is determined to achieve great financial success within a large established firm. (The fact that you are ambitious shows that you are an agent with a project to pursue.) If you lack a sense of justice, or if you allow the strength of your ambition to overcome your relatively weak sense of justice, you will do whatever it takes to achieve the success you crave. You might try to make the work of others with whom you are competing for advancement more difficult or to denigrate your competitors in the eyes of your superiors. You might think of ways to sabotage their work or them so as to remove them from the path toward advancement that you wish to carve. Whatever specific means you adopt, your lack of a sense of justice will be evident in your unscrupulousness. As far as you are concerned, your competitors, and your superiors, too, are mere obstacles to your advancement or means to that goal.

Here is another example. Suppose you are a young male in your teens or early twenties. You are unemployed and spend much of your time hanging out on the streets with some other young men whose life circumstances are similar to yours. You and your buddies decide to form a gang, mainly to attain some kind of solidarity and to distract your attention from the fact that you have nothing more constructive to do, that your life is not going anywhere, rather than for any specific activity. One evening you decide to have a meeting in a vacant lot. In the midst of your meeting two teenage girls happen to walk onto the lot on their way home after a party. Motivated by the anger you share with your buddies and accustomed to thinking of girls as sexual objects, you help grab the girls and participate in a sexual assault on them. Afterward, you boast about the assault. When you are caught several days later, you feel no guilt and express no remorse for your actions.

Both these examples describe individuals who lack a sense of justice, or who have such a weak sense of justice that they are not deterred by it from acting ruthlessly or viciously toward other people, or who have such a narrow sense of justice that they do not consider their victims to be agents who deserve to be recognized as such. When we describe a person as "depraved," we usually mean that that person lacks moral autonomy, that he has failed to develop his capacity for a sense of justice.

A person who has the capacity for moral autonomy (or autonomy$_2$) does not necessarily succeed at all times in recognizing other human beings as agents with claims of their own that deserve recognition. As far as I know, all human beings fail to treat other human beings as agents from time to time. Having the *capacity* for autonomy$_2$ is not the same thing as *acting* autonomously$_2$ all the time. However, a person who has the capacity for autonomy$_2$ will demonstrate that capacity in at least some of her actions by limiting her claims on people or resources or by exercising restraint in her actions in recognition of the fact that other human beings are agents with their own projects, values, and claims.

Notice that it is possible to take an interest in other human beings without having a sense of justice. It would be possible, for example, for the ruthless businesswoman to take an interest in her children's future well-being. It would also be possible for her to seek to found a dynasty, like the one John D. Rockefeller founded. In fact, it would be possible for her to take an interest in saving human beings from famine, or in saving bald eagles from extinction. These projects and motives presuppose that the businesswoman has *values*. But they do not presuppose that she has a *sense of justice*, that is, a developed capacity to recognize other human beings as agents with projects and values of their own.

Like agency, moral autonomy is probably acquired, normally, without a great deal of deliberate instruction or training. But moral autonomy does not appear to be universal among human beings. Some people seem to have only a *weak* sense of justice. That is, their sense of justice is easily defeated by their other values and projects. Others have only a very *narrow* sense of justice; they are able to recognize only the members of a small set of people as agents with claims that deserve to be recognized. Still others may have no sense of justice at all. Presumably all or nearly all human beings are born with the capacity to develop moral autonomy, but some conditions are evidently required to develop that capacity into moral autonomy, just as some conditions, including a significant amount of exposure to other human beings who use speech, are required for a person to develop the capacity for linguistic competence.

Autonomy$_2$ presupposes autonomy$_1$. In other words, one cannot have a sense of justice without being an agent. For in order to recognize others as agents with claims that deserve recognition, one has to be an agent oneself, to understand what a "claim" is. However, not all agents are necessarily morally autonomous. One can have ambitions, plans, and projects—and values, too—without having a sense of justice. The businesswoman and the smoldering young man I described above are agents, but neither has a sense of justice or, if they do, they have a weak or narrow one. Hegel's discussion of *Herrschaft* and *Knechtschaft* (lordship and bondage, or master and slave) in his *Phenomenology of Spirit* describes the interaction between one agent who fails to recognize another human being as an agent (the "master") and another agent who is the object of the master's designs (the "slave").[14]

---

[14] Georg W. F. Hegel, *Phänomenologie des Geistes* (Hamburg: Felix Meiner, 1952), pp. 141–50.

The concepts of agency and moral autonomy correspond approximately to the two features that, according to John Rawls, define the notion of a moral person.[15] Rawls asserts that moral persons are distinguished by two features: first, they are capable of having a conception of the good; and second, they are capable of having a sense of justice. To have a conception of the good means to have plans you wish to follow, projects you wish to pursue, or values you wish to realize. To have a sense of justice means to recognize that other individuals are agents who have claims that deserve to be recognized and respected, where that recognition and respect entails that you are willing to limit your own actions and claims for the sake of allowing other agents to pursue their projects.

A third type of autonomy is achieved when a person autonomously chooses his own projects and values. A person who has attained the ability to do this may be variously described as an agent of self-authorship, a self-defining subject, a self-fashioning individual, or a subject of free and conscious self-creation. An agent is a being who is capable of conceiving and striving to realize projects and values. A person who is autonomous in this third sense, though, actively chooses the projects and values he wishes to pursue. I shall identify this concept of autonomy with the terms *personal autonomy* and *autonomy$_3$*.

The notion of an individual who is self-defining or self-fashioning, or who is an agent of self-authorship or a subject of free and conscious self-creation, may seem to imply the view that individuals who have achieved personal autonomy invent their characters, or at least their values and projects, ex nihilo. That view is not credible and is not intended by most advocates of the ideal of personal autonomy. In this respect the term *reflective self-direction* is less misleading than some of these alternatives. As a matter of necessity, individuals base most of their values and ambitions on the values and ambitions that they see others adopt. The difference between a person who has achieved personal autonomy and one who has not is that the autonomous$_3$ individual subjects those values and projects to critical appraisal and fashions them into a relatively consistent and coherent whole.

Perhaps an example of a life that is *not* a life of personal autonomy will help to make the concept of personal autonomy clear. Suppose a young man (we will call him Michael) is born and raised in a relatively provincial town of medium size. He attends public schools in his neighborhood and goes on to a local college, where he studies to become a pharmacist. After graduation, he marries a girlfriend whom he has known through most of his years

---

[15] See Rawls's accounts of the idea of moral personality in *A Theory of Justice* (Cambridge, Mass.: Harvard University Press, 1971), pp. 505ff., and in "Kantian Constructivism," pp. 524ff. The idea of moral personality plays a smaller role in Rawls's arguments in *Theory* than in his later works, but his definition of that idea in these works does not differ significantly from his earlier account.

in school and goes into a business run by his father, which consists of a small local chain of pharmacies. He and his wife have children, whom they raise in much the same way as other people from their town with backgrounds similar to theirs.

Michael is an agent. He has things he wants to accomplish and values by which he tries to live. He also has a sense of justice. He recognizes that other people have their own values and plans. For the most part, he treats other people in accordance with this recognition by exercising self-restraint in the means he uses to pursue his ends and allowing other people to pursue their own objectives. However, Michael never gives serious consideration to any pattern of life other than the one he actually pursues. It never occurs to him to leave his home town or to take up a different career. He never seriously questions his fundamental values, which are similar to the values of most of the other people he knows. For him, large questions about how he might go about living his life differently never arise. One might say he falls into a pattern of life. He is intelligent and he makes choices, but the choices he makes are mainly about the particulars of his life, the means he wants to adopt to pursue that life, rather than about his fundamental values or about his way of life as a whole. Nothing in his life ever calls seriously into question either his sense of identity or his basic values. In short, Michael is not personally autonomous; he has not attained autonomy$_3$.

Contrast Michael's life with that of Marie. Marie is born in the same town as Michael. Unlike him, though, Marie demonstrates a persistently inquisitive bent from an early age. She is not content to accept the ways to which her family and friends are accustomed, but seeks continually to experiment with, or at least to know about, alternative ways of doing things. Marie goes to a college several hundred miles from her home town and meets people there from many different states and several countries. She is exposed at least partially to a variety of cultures, including many that were completely unknown to her previously. Through this exposure she learns that people's values vary far more radically than she had ever realized before. As a result, she is no longer able simply to accept a way of life in the way Michael does. She cannot just fall into a pattern of life. Instead, she must make choices about the sort of life she wants to live, the sort of person she wants to be, and the kinds of values to which she will try to adhere. She develops a habit of critically appraising alternative values and alternative paths of life. She has acquired personal autonomy.

Like moral autonomy, personal autonomy presupposes autonomy$_1$. In other words, to be the kind of person who engages in critical self-appraisal and reflective self-direction, one has first to be an agent, a being who is capable of conceiving and pursuing projects and values. However, the relation between personal autonomy and moral autonomy is less direct. A person could be morally autonomous without being in the habit of subjecting her own values and projects to critical appraisal. Similarly, while it is impossible to attain personal autonomy without first being an agent, it *is* possible to be personally autonomous without being morally autonomous. The habits of critical self-appraisal and reflective self-direction would have no point if the person who develops these habits has no values or projects to appraise in the first place. But these habits do not presuppose a sense of justice. As Joseph Raz, one of the foremost advocates of the ideal of personal autonomy in recent years, points out, "Personal autonomy, which is a particular ideal of individual well-being, should not be confused with the only very indirectly related notion of moral autonomy."[16]

Now, with the distinctions between these different types of autonomy in hand, we are in a position to formulate our question—how far can the Autonomy Principle take us toward an account of the bases of social criticism?—in a more precise way. Let us break the question into two main parts. First, which, if any, of these types of autonomy—agency, moral autonomy, and personal autonomy—must a good society protect and promote for all its members? Second, assuming that a good society should protect and promote autonomy in at least one of these senses, how far does this fact take us toward a persuasive account of the bases of social criticism? How much of the work needed to develop a persuasive account of the normative bases of social criticism does the idea of individual autonomy do?

Perfectionist liberalism, as I shall interpret that strand of liberal theory here, holds that a good society would protect and promote autonomy of all three types. John Stuart Mill, one of the principal advocates of the perfectionist view, contrasts the character of a person "who lets the world, or his own portion of it, choose his plan of life for him" with that of a person "who chooses his plan for himself."[17] This contrast emphasizes the idea of personal autonomy, but Mill, who was provoked to write *On Liberty* by a feeling that people in his own society did too little independent, critical thinking, assumed that people should be morally autonomous, too. He did not emphasize the importance of a sense of justice in *On Liberty* because he did not believe that the members of his society generally failed to have an effective sense of justice or, if he did believe this, he did not write *On Liberty* to address this problem. In Mill's view, though, individuals in a good society would be both morally autonomous and personally autonomous.

Similarly, Joseph Raz, one of the most prominent proponents of the perfectionist view today, holds that in a good society individuals would be both personally autonomous and have a sense of justice. In his view "personal

---

[16] Raz, *Morality*, p. 370, n. 2. Raz takes moral autonomy to refer to "a doctrine about the nature of morality" and may interpret that concept more narrowly than I do. Nevertheless, his point that moral autonomy and personal autonomy are distinct things is essentially the same as mine.

[17] Mill, *On Liberty*, p. 56.

autonomy [is] an essential ingredient of the good life." He suggests a "principle of autonomy," which he describes as "the principle requiring people to secure the conditions of autonomy for all people." He views this principle as "one of the most important moral principles." Summarizing the main features of his view, Raz argues that "one may not pursue any goal by means which infringe people's autonomy unless such action is justified by the need to protect or promote the autonomy of those people or of others."[18] Again, Raz's principal work on this topic is mainly about personal autonomy, not moral autonomy. Nevertheless, Raz believes that a sense of justice is part of personal autonomy in the sense that a person who is personally autonomous would want to avoid doing things that are unjust. I shall call the combination of all three types of autonomy—agency, moral autonomy, and personal autonomy—*strong autonomy.*

Perfectionist liberalism holds that strong autonomy is *necessary,* though not *sufficient,* for a good life. The notion of self-development plays a key role in Mill's thought, but that notion is connected with and justified in part by the idea of moral progress.[19] As Mill sees it, individuals who are autonomous are likely to make better choices and to do better things than individuals who are not. Though he considered himself a utilitarian, he believed that the value of different "pleasures" or mental states should be measured by competent, knowledgeable judges, not by people who lack the power to distinguish between qualitatively different pleasures.[20] Mill thought that in a good society all individuals should be personally autonomous—capable of critically appraising and choosing between alternative projects and values—so that all individuals could make competent judgments about the value of things for themselves.

Similarly, Raz regards the principle of autonomy as an important *part* of a moral doctrine, not as the whole of that doctrine. Though Raz is not a utilitarian, he, like Mill, assumes that intrinsically good and bad things exist. For him, at least one reason why personal autonomy is a good thing is that it enables us to choose, and to do, good things rather than bad ones. In Raz's view a good society must do more than promote autonomy. A good society must promote autonomy—strong autonomy—and other things as well.

In the remainder of this chapter I shall examine critically the perfectionist view that a good society must protect and promote strong autonomy, that is, autonomy in all three of the senses I have distinguished above. I do *not* examine Mill's theory, or Raz's, as a whole. Both theories have many attrac-

---

[18] Raz, *Morality,* pp. 408, 415, 425.

[19] As Alan Ryan puts it, "Mill's concern with self-development and moral progress is a strand in his philosophy to which almost everything else is subordinate" (*The Philosophy of John Stuart Mill,* 2d ed. [Basingstoke, Hampshire: MacMillan, 1987], p. 255).

[20] For a good recent account of Mill's theory that emphasizes his interest in individuals' capacities as judges of value, see Wendy Donner, *The Liberal Self: John Stuart Mill's Moral and Political Philosophy* (Ithaca: Cornell University Press, 1991).

tive features. My aim is only to consider their perfectionist claim that the individuals in a good society would necessarily be strongly autonomous.

Raz and other perfectionist liberals, like Nozick and rights-based liberals, hold that individuals ultimately should be able to build and to shape their own lives in accordance with plans in a way that will make those lives meaningful and worthwhile. Unlike the rights-based approach to liberal theory advocated by Nozick, though, perfectionist liberalism is rooted in the insight that individuals are not born with the skills required to shape their lives into meaningful wholes. A normal individual may be born with the capacities to become an agent and to be morally and personally autonomous, but those capacities must be developed to enable individuals to have autonomous, meaningful, worthwhile lives.

The strength of this insight seems clear. For plainly, individuals are *not* born with the skills required to attain the various types of autonomy that liberals emphasize. If strong autonomy is essential for a good life, as Raz contends, then the perfectionist thesis should be affirmed. What we must ask ourselves, then, is whether it is necessary to develop the capacities for personal autonomy and for a sense of justice as well as the more rudimentary capacity for agency for human beings to have good lives. If it is, then it seems to follow that a good society would have to secure the conditions needed for all its members to become agents, to acquire a sense of justice, and to develop personal autonomy. Let us consider each of these types of autonomy in turn.

II

Any good society would secure the conditions required for all its members to become agents, that is, to be autonomous in the rudimentary sense of being capable of formulating projects and conceiving values and striving to realize those projects and values. For without these capabilities, it would be impossible for a person to lead a meaningful life. Few claims about a society's political and social arrangements could be more devastating than the claim that those arrangements fail to secure the conditions necessary for individuals to lead meaningful lives. But an individual who lacked the attributes of an agent would be unable to lead a meaningful life.

The idea of agency appears to be central to the concept of a *person*. Human beings share many attributes with some other animal species. Both humans and animals have mental attributes—that is, it seems to make sense to describe some animals as conscious beings, beings who have mental states. Both humans and animals are also sentient beings. Animals, like humans, can experience enjoyment and suffering. Similarly, some animals have desires and motives, as humans do, and can experience a range of emotions. Further, humans are not alone in the ability to make choices, which they share with some animal species. The members of some species even appear to deliberate and to make decisions based on their prior experiences. At least some animals are capable of learning. Only humans, however, appear to conceive projects and values, especially projects and values that are not focused on their own immediate experience.

The idea of agency is broader than the idea of freedom of the will, which Harry Frankfurt takes to be a key attribute of persons.[21] Frankfurt's argument hinges on a distinction between first-order desires and second-order desires. First-order desires, as he describes them, are desires in the ordinary sense. A desire for food, for example, or for warmth is a first-order desire. So is a desire to see a movie, to go hang gliding, or to have a conversation. When we think of desires or wants, most of the time we have in mind first-order desires. In contrast, second-order desires are desires about one's own first-order desires. For example, a person might wish he did *not* desire foods that are rich in fat, like meat and ice cream, which are bad for his health. Or he might desire to be free of the desire to go hang gliding, since he thinks the exhilaration he experiences while doing it is not worth the expense and danger involved. If he did not have these desires, he would not have to struggle against them to prevent himself from doing things of which he does not approve, nor would he find himself, from time to time, giving in to unwelcome desires and later regretting the fact that he has done so. A person might also desire to have some desires that he does not have. He might, for instance, want to have a desire to go to church on Sunday mornings, since he often misses church services and usually feels guilty afterward; or he might want to have a desire to read and study more often, since he considers himself lazy and is worried that without that desire, he will not do as well in college as he hopes. Frankfurt calls second-order desires that one actually wants to be effective second-order volitions.[22]

According to Frankfurt, the key to being a person is the capacity to form second-order volitions. Frankfurt contrasts persons with "wantons." Wantons, he explains, are beings who have first-order desires but do not form second-order volitions. Wantons may desire food, warmth, and many other things. According to Frankfurt, though, the essential characteristic of a wanton is that he does not care about his will. In other words, it does not occur to a wanton to want to be moved by the desires he actually has or to want to be moved by other desires that he does not have. But persons do care about their wills. The essential attribute of a person, in fact, is the capacity to become critically aware of one's will and to form second-order volitions.

<hr/>

[21] See his classic article "Freedom of the Will and the Concept of a Person," *Journal of Philosophy* 68 (1971): 5–20.

[22] As Frankfurt points out, it is possible for a person to have a second-order desire that he does not want to become effective—that is, to wish to have a desire without wishing to act on that desire. This point plays a relatively minor role in Frankfurt's argument, however, and has no significant bearing on my discussion.

Persons, unlike wantons, possess the capacity for reflective self-evaluation and freedom of the will.

Frankfurt is right to say that only persons are capable of reflective self-evaluation and freedom of the will, but his claim that the capacity to form second-order volitions is the key attribute of persons is too narrowly drawn. In fact the distinguishing attribute of persons seems to be the capacity to be an agent, that is, to use one's imagination to conceive projects that are not by nature bounded by the limits of one's own experience. Although animals of many species are conscious, and some are capable of deliberation and at least some rudimentary forms of reasoning, no animal species, so far as we can tell, possesses the capacity for imagination or the ability to create new things with which humans are endowed by virtue of our imaginative capacities.

The human capacity for imagination is the basis for our ability to formulate projects. *Projects* are integral to people's everyday experiences. A project can be as simple as a plan to go bicycling or swimming on the weekend. A project of this sort can be imagined and thought out in advance. The idea of carrying it out can be evoked as a source of pleasure both before and after the event (assuming that it actually takes place). A plan to build a house is a more complex project, as is a plan to make a career for oneself in a given field of work. Projects of all sorts, however, have in common the fact that they can be created in the imagination in advance and relived in the imagination after they have taken place. A proposal for political or social reform is a project.

The capacity to form second-order volitions is simply the capacity to engage in a project of a particular sort. Just as a person can imagine a bicycling expedition or a house, a person can imagine herself or some particular attribute of herself, such as her body or her character or her desires. A person can, therefore, imagine herself as the subject of a project. For a person to form second-order volitions is for her to formulate a project about her desires or some of her desires. Although it is correct, then, to say that only persons are capable of reflective self-evaluation, the claim that the capacity to form second-order volitions is the key attribute of persons is too narrow. The key attribute of *persons* is the capacity to formulate projects. Projects about one's own desires are only one type of project, one example, albeit a very important one, of the wide range of things humans uniquely are able to do by virtue of their imaginative capacity to formulate projects.[23]

---

[23] If this argument is correct, then the line Frankfurt draws between persons and wantons is drawn in the wrong place. For according to Frankfurt, beings who have no second-order volitions are not really persons at all; they are wantons and cannot, therefore, be persons (see "Freedom of the Will," p. 86). On Frankfurt's account, the class of wantons includes all nonhuman animals that have desires, all very young children, and perhaps some adult human beings. Moreover, Frankfurt suggests that adult human beings may be more or less wanton. So according to Frankfurt's definition, many human beings are not persons, or are persons at some times, but not others.

A human being who is incapable of formulating projects and conceiving values would be truly animallike, or as animallike as a human being could be. Such a creature could be moved only by desires about its own experiences. Though it might be capable of experiencing sympathy with other creatures, it would not be capable of empathy, that is, of imaginatively thinking itself into the position or circumstances of another being. It would be incapable of making even simple plans. John Stuart Mill's caustic remark that classical utilitarianism as conceived by Bentham and his father was a doctrine "worthy only of swine"[24] appears to be based on the view that that doctrine does not sufficiently identify the attributes that distinguish a human being from a creature of this extremely limited sort.

Human beings seem to develop their capacities to formulate projects and to conceive values in a way that is roughly similar to the way in which they develop their capacities to become competent speakers of a language. Deliberate training in the ordinary sense does not usually seem to be required. However, even human beings who appear to possess normal physical and mental capacities do not necessarily develop the capacity to become competent speakers. Feral children, who grow up with little or no contact with other humans and are not exposed regularly to linguistic performances, fail to develop the capacity to use language. Feral children who grow to adulthood without significant human contact actually seem to lose that capacity. By the time they become adults, it is too late for them to begin to learn how to be competent linguistic performers; by that time their capacity to do so has been irretrievably lost. Linguistic competence is a skill that must be developed at the appropriate stage of life. Similarly, although the capacity to formulate projects and conceive values does not seem to require deliberate training, it probably *is* a skill that, if left uncultivated for a sufficiently long time, can be lost irrevocably.[25]

The social conditions required to develop the skills characteristic of agents have not been studied extensively and are not well understood. However, if the analogy with linguistic competence holds up, it is likely that in order to develop those skills, human beings must be raised in an environment in which other human beings formulate projects and carry them out

[24] Mill, *The Collected Works of John Stuart Mill*, 33 vols., ed. John M. Robson (Toronto: University of Toronto Press, 1963–90), vol. 10, p. 210.

[25] For discussion of the acquisition of language in the context of individual human growth and maturation, see Eric H. Lenneberg, *Biological Foundations of Language* (Malabar, Fla.: Krieger, 1984), esp. chap. 4. The principal body of scholarship relevant to development of the capacity to formulate projects and values is the literature within the cognitive-developmental approach to socialization pioneered by George Herbert Mead and Jean Piaget, among others. For a somewhat dated but still useful overview of much of this work see Lawrence Kohlberg, "Stage and Sequence: The Cognitive-Developmental Approach to Socialization," in *Handbook of Socialization Theory and Research*, ed. David A. Goslin (Chicago: Rand McNally, 1969), pp. 347–480.

and in which others conceive values, express them in some way, and adhere to them to a substantial and evident degree. Circumstances that make this kind of performance difficult or impossible for fully developed human beings probably also stunt children's capacities for agency. For example, in an environment of extreme uncertainty or danger, elaborate or long-term projects may not seem worth pursuing, and the predominant value may be self-defense. If adults do not evidently pursue projects of these sorts or conceive and adhere to more capacious values, it will not even occur to children to think of formulating them. If children reach adulthood without having learned to formulate complex or long-term projects or to conceive capacious values, they will probably be unable to learn to do so as adults.[26]

Social conditions approximating these prevail in some communities and neighborhoods in the United States. What is most remarkable about the people who live through these conditions is the tenacity with which they struggle to acquire the skill of formulating complex projects and the capacity to conceive values to which they can adhere despite appallingly discouraging conditions. I can imagine no more serious indictment of a society that makes a show of being civilized than the claim that it permits the perpetuation of conditions that work inexorably against the efforts of some of its own members to develop the attributes that are essential to being a person.

III

Must a good society secure the conditions required for all its members to become morally autonomous? Perhaps if we were asking whether moral autonomy is necessary for a good life for an isolated, asocial individual, the answer would be "no, if a good life for such a creature is possible at all." But we are not asking about the conditions an isolated human being would require to live well in isolation from other human beings. Our question is about the normative bases for criticism of political and social arrangements, that is, for arrangements intended to regulate the ways in which human beings interact in a society together. It would be a trenchant criticism of a society's political and social arrangements to say that those arrangements fail to lead its members—all or nearly all of them—to acquire autonomy$_2$, that is, to develop an effective sense of justice. The notion of a sense of justice may

---

[26] The term *industry* was widely used in the seventeenth century and earlier to denote both the capacity to formulate complex plans and the actions required to carry them out. Both Hobbes and Locke use the term in this sense. Hobbes's claim that in a condition in which "the life of man [is] solitary, poore, nasty, brutish, and short" there "is no place for Industry; because the fruit thereof is uncertain" (*Leviathan, or the Matter, Forme, and Power of a Commonwealth, Ecclesiastical and Civill*, ed. Richard Tuck [Cambridge: Cambridge University Press, 1991], chap. 13, p. 89) evokes a condition similar to the kind of environment I have in mind, with similar consequences.

not be integral to the concept of a person, but some degree of moral autonomy does seem to be necessary for human beings to have good lives in any kind of political association.

All political associations are characterized by what Hume calls the circumstances of justice. We do not, as Hume put it, find ourselves bestowed with "such profuse *abundance* of all *external* conveniencies, that, without any uncertainty in the event, without any care or industry on our part, every individual finds himself fully provided with whatever his most voracious appetites can want, or luxurious imagination wish or desire."[27] On the contrary, typically goods are scarce in relation to human wants. Hume traced this fact in part to human "*selfishness* and *limited generosity*."[28] But it is important to recognize that the circumstances of justice are virtually certain to arise in any human society, whether its individual members are selfish or not. For unless all those individuals share a single conception of the good—a single vision of the way in which they want their own lives to work out in relation to the lives of all the other members of their society—disagreements about the use of resources will arise, and goods will be scarce in relation to wants.

To illustrate this point, suppose that you and I are both members of a single society. Both of us have modest wants for ourselves, and we both take considerable interest in the well-being and circumstances of our fellow citizens. However, we do not take the same *degree* of interest in the same *group* of citizens. You are particularly anxious that in our society, the special discomforts and inconveniences usually associated with being physically handicapped should be alleviated as far as possible, and in fact eliminated if possible. By contrast, I think that a more urgent task than alleviation of the plight of handicapped citizens is improvement in the quality of education for children, which I think is currently deplorable. Our society is relatively wealthy, but we do not have sufficient resources both to bring the circumstances of the handicapped to parity with those of citizens who are not handicapped and to provide the children in our society with the high quality of education I believe they deserve. Our wants for ourselves are modest, but the claims we believe should be made on our society's resources on behalf of others are not. Because we would like to see our society's resources used in different ways, our relations are characterized by the circumstances of justice.

In the circumstances of justice, people disagree with one another about the allocation of resources. These disagreements may be resolved in either of two ways. First, individuals may choose to accept allocations that fail to meet their claims fully. For example, I may agree to accept the fact that

---

[27] David Hume, *An Enquiry Concerning the Principles of Morals*, ed. J. B. Schneewind (Indianapolis: Hackett, 1983), sec. 3, part 1, p. 21. See also Hume's *A Treatise of Human Nature*, ed. L. A. Selby-Bigge (Oxford: Clarendon Press, 1967), book 3, part 2, sec. 2, pp. 484–501.

[28] Hume, *Treatise*, p. 494.

children in our society will not be taught Japanese in elementary school, despite the fact that I think it would be highly desirable for them to begin learning Japanese as early as possible. I do not need to abandon my goal of securing the resources needed for children to learn Japanese in elementary school, but I do decide to live without the realization of that goal at least for the present. At the same time, you agree to accept that handicapped adults who are unable to drive an automobile will not all be provided with specially equipped cars and drivers. Without these special chauffeur-driven vehicles, handicapped people will be less mobile than people who have full use of their limbs, so your goal of equalizing the circumstances of the handicapped and those who are not handicapped will have to go unfulfilled for now. Neither of us gets all of what we want. But since we know that our society has insufficient resources for both of us to get what we want and since each of us believes that the other's claims are made in good faith (though I think you place far too much emphasis on the needs of the handicapped in comparison with those of children), we agree to accept less than we want for now. Of course, we do not agree that we will not push for more in the next year's budget.

The second way in which our disagreements can be resolved is by force. If we cannot agree to accept a solution that fails to satisfy the claims we think should be satisfied in full, and our society does not have sufficient resources to satisfy all the claims all of us make, whether for ourselves or on behalf of others, then our disagreement will lead to a struggle that must be resolved by force. The resolution may be achieved through a fight between us, or it may be imposed coercively by a third party on both of us.

The modern state is, among other things, an institution through which solutions to disagreements are imposed coercively upon citizens who are unable to agree to solutions among themselves without the state's coercive involvement. Since Hobbes and especially since Max Weber, the coercive element has been regarded as central to the state's role in modern society; sometimes coercive power has been considered the defining feature of the state.[29] Yet both Hobbes and Weber recognized that states that depend too heavily on coercion to maintain their authority and to resolve disputes rest on weak foundations. That is why Hobbes insisted that one of the first duties of a ruler is to make sure that its authority is recognized as legitimate. For without that recognition, according to Hobbes, the rights of sovereignty (and the authority of rulers) "cannot be maintained by any Civill Law, or terrour of legall punishment."[30]

The capacity for moral autonomy—for a sense of justice—is the capacity

---

[29] "Today . . . we have to say that a state is a human community that (successfully) claims the *monopoly of the legitimate use of physical force* within a given territory" (Max Weber, "Politics as a Vocation," in *From Max Weber: Essays in Sociology*, ed. H. H. Gerth and C. Wright Mills [New York: Oxford University Press, 1958], p. 78).

[30] Hobbes, *Leviathan*, chap. 30, p. 232.

to understand that other human beings are agents with their own projects and values and to accept limits in recognition of their claims on the things you can do to advance your own projects and values. Individuals who lack this capacity would be unable to resolve disagreements without the use of force or the threat of force. Coercion and the application of force would be the only means available to resolve disputes and to maintain peace. Peace would always be fragile, since all those who fail to triumph completely in every dispute in which they are involved would regard an imposed solution as a hostile act against them. In short, life in a political society whose members do not have a sense of justice would be filled with hostility, smoldering resentment, and fear, or worse. It would be the sort of life that calls into question any professed advantages of society over continual civil war.

A life lived in fear, hostility, and resentment is not a life that can be shaped by an individual in accordance with her own designs. It is not a life of meaningful endeavors and worthwhile pursuits. It is not a good life. A good society is a society whose members have an opportunity to make something meaningful and worthwhile of their lives. In a society whose members lack a sense of justice, however, this kind of life would be impossible. No society whose members lack a sense of justice could be a good society.

It is probably rare for human beings to grow to maturity in any society without developing some sense of justice. But the quality of life in a society depends heavily on the strength and breadth of its members' capacities for moral autonomy, not just on whether they have developed *some* sense of justice. A society whose members possess a sense of justice that is narrow or weak cannot be a good society.

Like the imaginative capacities that enable human beings to become agents, the skills that constitute individual moral autonomy seem to be acquired in a way that parallels approximately the acquisition of linguistic competence.[31] Ordinarily, relatively little tutelage or deliberate training seems to be required. Nevertheless, social conditions can facilitate or hinder the acquisition of a robust sense of justice. If children perceive that justice

---

[31] Jean Piaget's *The Moral Judgment of the Child* (New York: Free Press, 1965), which was first published in the early 1930s, is a classic work on the acquisition of these skills. For a brief, lucid overview of Piaget's views, see John H. Flavell, *The Developmental Psychology of Jean Piaget* (New York: Van Nostrand, 1962), pp. 290–97. See also the more recent work by Lawrence Kohlberg, especially "Stage and Sequence"; "Moral Stages and Moralization: The Cognitive-Developmental Approach," in *Moral Development and Behavior: Theory, Research, and Social Issues*, ed. T. Lickona (New York: Holt, Rinehart, and Winston, 1976); and *The Philosophy of Moral Development* (San Francisco: Harper and Row, 1981). Kohlberg's work has been criticized vigorously in recent years, most notably by Carol Gilligan in *In a Different Voice: Psychological Theory and Women's Development* (Cambridge, Mass.: Harvard University Press, 1982). Gilligan's critique is highly controversial. Moreover, that critique focuses more on the implicit teleology in Kohlberg's theory of moral stages than on his claims about the process of acquiring the skills of moral autonomy.

is usually returned with justice and that the relations between adults are characterized generally by reciprocity, then they are likely to develop a reasonably robust sense of justice. If, however, they see that justice is returned with injustice and that the relations between adults are manifestly unequal or lack reciprocity, then children are likely to develop a relatively weak sense of justice.

IV

A good society would secure the conditions required for all its members to develop the skills characteristic of agents and to acquire a sense of justice, that is, to become morally autonomous, since in a society whose members lack these skills, individuals would find it difficult or impossible to lead meaningful, worthwhile lives. $Autonomy_1$, or agency, and $autonomy_2$, or moral autonomy, are essential ingredients of any good life for human beings in association with others. But is $autonomy_3$, or personal autonomy, also essential? Would it be a telling criticism of a society's political and social arrangements to say that they fail to lead its members to choose their own projects and values in an autonomous way?

To help us consider this question, let us go back to Michael, the pharmacist. Michael, recall, is an agent, with projects he strives to pursue and values to which he tries to adhere. He also has a sense of justice, since he treats other human beings as agents and recognizes, through the restraint he exercises in pursuit of his own projects, that others have projects and claims of their own. Yet Michael is not personally autonomous. He falls into a pattern of life instead of giving serious consideration to alternative abodes, careers, or ways of life. He never seriously questions his own identity or his fundamental values.

Does Michael's life lack an attribute that is essential to a good life for human beings in association with others? Such an attribute need not be essential for *Michael's* good considered apart from the good of other human beings. Moral autonomy, for instance, is essential for a good life for human beings in association with others largely because we all have a reason of great importance to want all the *other* members of our society to have a sense of justice. An attribute may be essential for a good life for human beings in association with others without being essential to the person whose attribute it is. The question, then, is whether personal autonomy—the developed capacity and inclination to appraise one's own projects and values in a critical way in comparison with alternatives—is an essential ingredient of the good life either for Michael's own good or for Michael to be the sort of person with whom others can live in a good human association.

I shall begin by identifying some arguments culled from the literature bearing on the idea of autonomy that support the conclusion that personal autonomy *is* an essential ingredient of the good life, or at least that personal autonomy is a highly valuable attribute. John Stuart Mill touches on nearly all these arguments at some point, though he does not develop all of them as fully as some other authors have done.[32] I shall discuss each of the arguments on this list briefly. I shall then list and discuss some counterarguments. Finally, I shall draw the conclusion that seems to flow most plausibly from a consideration of all these arguments.

One argument in favor of the view that the capacity and inclination to appraise one's own projects and values critically is essential to a good life is that this capacity is necessary for individuals to measure the value of things, either in general or specifically for themselves, to distinguish good things from bad ones and to discriminate between those alternatives that are more worthwhile and those that are less so. This argument is central to John Stuart Mill's case for the ideal of self-development. In Mill's utilitarian view, judgments of utility are the appropriate evaluative basis for all our practical reasoning. Mill believed, however, that accurate judgments of value can be made only by competent moral agents, by human beings who have reached a certain level of self-development. Attainment of personal autonomy is a distinguishing feature of the level of self-development a person has to reach to be a competent moral agent. So personal autonomy, in Mill's view, is essential for a good life in the sense that it is essential for individuals to discover the ways of life that are best for them.[33]

It might be claimed that Mill's emphasis on self-development has elitist implications. Mill's writings do contain elitist as well as egalitarian tendencies, but his emphasis on self-development and personal autonomy as such does not entail elitist conclusions. The view that human beings are capable of making accurate practical judgments only if they are competent moral agents can be taken to imply either of two conclusions. On the one hand, one might argue that, given this view, the task of making practical judgments—of participating in deliberations and in decision making on matters of practical importance—should be allocated to those who have attained the necessary competence. On the other hand, one might conclude that every effort should be made to enable every adult member of a society to acquire the

[32] Despite the fact that he is one of the foremost contemporary champions of the ideal of personal autonomy, Raz offers very little by way of argument for that ideal. His work is devoted mainly to developing the implications, as he sees them, of the ideal of personal autonomy rather than to defending that ideal from criticism. Stanley Benn's *A Theory of Freedom* contains argument in favor of the ideal of personal autonomy, much of which develops themes touched on by Mill. See also Christman's collection *The Inner Citadel*, which contains excepts both from works that defend the ideal of personal autonomy and from works that criticize that ideal, and the essays in Heller et al.'s *Reconstructing Individualism*, most of which are either critical of or seek to reformulate the ideal of personal autonomy.

[33] John Gray emphasizes this line of argument in his reconstruction of Mill's view of autonomy in *Mill on Liberty: A Defence* (London: Routledge and Kegan Paul, 1983), pp. 70–86.

requisite competence. Although Mill sometimes resorted to elitist solutions to practical problems, he regarded the latter solution as the optimal one toward which societies should tend ultimately.

Mill offers a second argument for the view that personal autonomy contributes significantly to a good life in *On Liberty*. There he suggests that whereas people who are incapable or disinclined to appraise their own projects and values critically tend to cling to institutions and practices that are familiar even when those practices work badly, individuals who are personally autonomous are willing to engage in experimentation, to try out new social institutions and practices as well as other unfamiliar things. This penchant for experimentation is an essential ingredient in the process of social and moral discovery and invention. Mill believed in the possibility and the value of moral and social progress; in fact the idea of moral progress stands at the center of his entire practical philosophy. Without personal autonomy and experimentation, however, he believed that progress would not occur.

A third argument in favor of the view that personal autonomy is an essential ingredient of a good life is that this form of autonomy helps individuals to formulate projects and values that are better for them than those to which they would otherwise adhere. This argument is really an elaboration of the first two arguments. The argument suggests that if our Michael were capable of considering, and inclined to consider, alternative paths of life seriously instead of simply falling into a way of life without bothering to think about whether an alternative might be better for him, he might well discover that some alternatives would be better than the projects and values he unthinkingly adopts. Michael would then have a better life than the one for which, in our illustration, he actually settles. His life might be better in the sense that he would be a more just person or a more moral person, or it might be better in the sense that he would be able to attain higher pleasures than those that he would otherwise be able to reach, or his life might be better in some other sense.

A fourth argument in favor of personal autonomy is that to become personally autonomous is to develop a capacity for critical self-appraisal or reflective self-evaluation (or reflective self-direction) that is important to personhood and may even be the defining feature of personhood. Once again, Mill touches on this argument. In Mill's view, the development of our capacities as human beings, especially those capacities that enable us to attain the higher pleasures, is intrinsically good. Since we are capable of becoming personally autonomous, we ought to do so, in the sense that we have a duty, at least to ourselves, to do so.

A fifth argument, which is closely related to the fourth, is that a life of personal autonomy—of choosing one's own projects and values in an autonomous way—is more in keeping with the essential nature and dignity of human beings than is a life that falls short of personal autonomy. On this view the human capacity for critical self-appraisal or reflective self-evaluation is a kind of *telos* for human nature, an end or goal toward which human beings naturally strive or should strive. Not to pursue that goal is to fail to realize oneself as a human being; it is to fail to become fully human. Significant traces of this argument can again be found in Mill, whose ideal self may have been modeled in part after Pericles, whom Mill studied as a boy. This ideal self was, for Mill, self-developing and self-perfecting. It has dimensions of perfection that are social in nature, such as tolerance, a capacity for dialogue manifest in articulateness and in the skill of listening, and in a penchant for participation and for responsiveness. Mill's version of this ideal was democratic and participatory in tendency, but not all versions are. Both Aristotle and Nietzsche offer perfectionist arguments for personal autonomy that are teleological in nature, but their arguments are aristocratic and (to different degrees) exclusionist.

A sixth argument for personal autonomy—for the view, that is, that an essential element in a good life is the developed capacity and inclination to choose one's own projects and values in an autonomous way rather than simply accept projects and values that are readily available from one's elders and peers—focuses on the social consequences of that attribute. This argument is that in promoting personal autonomy, we promote the practice of social criticism, thereby helping to make our societies better and more just. The practice of social criticism helps us to distinguish the things about our society that are better from those that are worse. If personal autonomy encourages this practice, then it may have salutary consequences for society that go well beyond its benefits to the person who is personally autonomous.

Perhaps, for example, Michael once flirted with the idea of joining the Ku Klux Klan. Since as we have sketched him, Michael is not the sort of person to consider alternatives to his own way of life seriously, we may suppose that he did not consider membership in the Klan seriously. Suppose, however, that he had done so. Suppose further that Michael is personally autonomous—that he has a strong inclination to investigate alternatives to his own way of life and to consider them in a genuinely serious way. He might then have discovered that members of the Klan adhere to unjust, indefensible values, that they are racists and antiegalitarians who pose a danger to their victims and to those who might be persuaded to join them. If Michael had done these things, he might have decided to raise his voice against the Klan. By being an autonomous person he would be contributing to the practice of social criticism. Michael would have become a social critic, at least on a small scale. Even if Michael had joined the Klan, his (bad) example might have been instructive to many of the rest of us by demonstrating to us in a vivid way the sort of life we should *not* choose to lead. A similar claim might be made about Germans in the years 1933–45. Perhaps if Germans during that period had been more autonomous, they would have been more critical of the Nazi regime and less willing to tolerate its injustices.

Each of these points constitutes a serious argument that should not be dismissed easily or lightly. Cumulatively, they make up a strong case for the view that personal autonomy is an attribute of great value. The question, though, is whether they constitute a solid case for the view that personal autonomy is an essential ingredient in a good human life in association with others. Some counterpoints weigh against that conclusion.

First, it might be argued that it is misguided to suppose that the developed capacity for critical self-appraisal enables us to be competent agents who can measure the value of things. For this notion seems to presuppose that the goodness of things is inherent in those things and that our task as agents is to *discover* the goodness (or badness) that is already in things. This assumption fails to take seriously the fact that human beings hold a plurality of conceptions of the good. In reality, human beings value different things in markedly different ways. I think that, all things considered, the provision of an excellent education for children is far more important—has greater value—than the achievement for handicapped people of parity in capabilities with those who are not handicapped, whereas you value parity for the handicapped more than you do excellence in education for children. (Actually, you consider my view that excellence in education requires the teaching of Japanese to schoolchildren a bit fanatical.) We do not disagree about the facts. We just value things differently. It is a mistake, then, to suppose that we could discover the "correct" value of these things by becoming more competent agents. Whatever else the developed capacity for critical self-appraisal might do for us, it will not enable us to measure the value of things correctly, because there is no such thing as the correct value of things.

This rebuttal of the first argument for personal autonomy suggests that Mill's claim that only competent agents can measure the value of things rests on an obsolete objectivist conception of value. Perhaps, though, Mill just means that personal autonomy enables people to discover things that are best *for them*. What is best for one person may not be best for another. So people may value things differently and still find that personal autonomy helps them discover what is best for them. But this line of argument still assumes that what is best for one person is a matter of objective fact, something that *exists* to be discovered. The goodness of things may be relative to persons and yet be an objective good at the same time. Mill's argument seems to presuppose at least that for each individual, certain things are objectively best while others are objectively of lesser value. This argument still seems to presuppose an objectivist conception of value that, since Nietzsche, seems untenable.

It might also be argued, in response to the second line of reasoning in favor of personal autonomy, that Mill's apparent view that the penchant for experimentation is always—or at least usually—a good thing is flawed. One possible difficulty with this view is that Mill's underlying faith in moral and social progress cannot be sustained. According to this view, human morality and society may get better over time in some respects, but a long-run tendency toward improvement of the sort in which Mill believed simply does not exist. Experimentation, on this view, is likely to lead to random variation in human social arrangements, not to their improvement.

Another difficulty with Mill's claims for experimentation is that even if a long-run tendency toward improvement or progress does exist, the "costs" of experimentation to human beings may be far higher than Mill himself acknowledges. People may discover or invent new social forms that improve over established or better-known practices through experimentation. On the other hand, many of their inventions may turn out to be worse than established ways. Mill might rejoinder that in that case, the experiment can be abandoned. But this rejoinder neglects the fact that social experiments can go badly wrong, sometimes ruining people's lives. Perhaps if I had made a serious effort to try out the communal life with which I flirted when I had just become an adult, the result would have been a tangle of commitments and illegitimate children that would have seriously damaged my life and the lives of the others involved in the experiment, including the children. The point is that Mill just does not seem to consider seriously enough the fact that experiments have consequences that are not always beneficial.

It might be argued that Mill need only establish that the *overall* consequences of experimentation are, on balance, good. This claim is consistent with the claim that *some* of those consequences are not good at all. This is a plausible claim, but its force still really depends on whether one thinks the long-run tendencies of human affairs lead toward improvement or toward decline. In a century that has seen total war and totalitarian despotism, the correct view of this long-run tendency is not clear.

Third, it could reasonably be argued that personal autonomy does not, in general, help individuals to formulate better projects and values than those to which they would otherwise adhere. Joel Feinberg, a prominent student and proponent of the idea of autonomy, concedes that the projects and values of an autonomous person are not necessarily better than those of a nonautonomous one. "No further analysis," he writes, "can be expected to rule out as impossible a selfish but autonomous person; a cold, mean, unloving but autonomous person; or a ruthless, or cruel autonomous person."[34]

Sometimes, at least, personal autonomy might lead individuals to formulate *worse* projects and values. Nietzsche was a vigorous advocate of a perfectionist morality according to which the marks of superiority are

---

[34] Joel Feinberg, *Harm to Self*, chap. 18, p. 45.

strength of character and the capacity of a human being to create values and to live by his own creations. These marks are characteristic of a person who has developed his capacity for personal autonomy to a high degree. But Nietzsche argued that attainment of this type of autonomy would lead the *Übermenschen*, the "higher men," who achieve it to feel "contempt for the cowardly, the anxious, the petty, those intent on narrow utility"[35] and to distinguish sharply between the superior class of men to which they belong and the class of inferior, slavish people who constitute the great mass of humanity. Nietzsche's perfectionist morality was an aristocratic and exclusionist morality whose adherents would disdain the claim that human beings are of equal worth in any sense. These aristocratic values, values that endorse an attitude of contempt for most human beings, are the values Nietzsche believed would be held by people who achieve personal autonomy.

Fourth, the claim that development of the capacity for personal autonomy is crucial to personhood appears to be misguided. As we have seen, Harry Frankfurt has argued that the key to being a person is the capacity to form second-order volitions and to engage in reflective self-evaluation. But that argument is mistaken and is dependent on Frankfurt's willingness to draw the class of persons so narrowly that many human beings are excluded from it. A more plausible view of the key to being a person is that it consists of the imaginative capacity to formulate projects and values. These projects and values may, but need not, include projects and values about the self, for which reflective self-evaluation is required.

The claim that a life of personal autonomy is more in keeping with the essential nature or dignity of human beings than is a life that "falls short" of personal autonomy, which underpins the fifth argument in favor of personal autonomy, is highly contestable. A life in keeping with the essential nature and dignity of human beings is a life in which people formulate projects and values through which they try to create meaningful and worthwhile lives for themselves. Whether or not they choose their projects and values through a process of critical appraisal is far less important than whether they are able to make meaningful, worthwhile lives for themselves by pursuing those projects and trying to adhere to their values.

The fact is that some people just do not want to be personally autonomous. From the viewpoint of a strong advocate of personal autonomy, this want may appear to be a "mere" heteronomous desire that fails to reflect fully the person's true capacities. I do not think, though, that we should be quick to dismiss a person's values simply because those values do not lead him to wish to be personally autonomous. For this lack of desire to be in the

[35] Nietzsche, *Beyond Good and Evil*, trans. Walter Kaufman (New York: Random House, 1966), pp. 204–5.

habit of critically appraising alternative values and alternative paths of life may itself be integral to a person's project or conception of himself as a person. To dismiss the values of a person who does not wish to be personally autonomous would be to fail to take seriously the project for himself the person wishes to pursue.

James Griffin claims that autonomy is valuable to everyone. He also qualifies this claim by suggesting that some people might be made so anxious by being autonomous that it would be better for them not to be autonomous.[36] This argument seems plausible. But if Griffin's argument is correct, then it would be erroneous to suppose that a society's political and social arrangements should be criticized for failing to lead all its members to develop the attributes of personal autonomy. It would be implausible to argue that a person might be a better person if she lacked the imaginative skills required to be an agent. It is entirely plausible, though, to suppose that some people may be better people or lead better lives without the developed capacity and inclination to appraise their own projects and values critically in comparison with alternatives than they would with that developed capacity. Some people may be able to lead better lives without these attributes than with them.

Sixth and finally, while it may be true that personal autonomy tends to lead individuals to become social critics who will push their society to become better and more just or to set examples—even if these are bad examples—from which others can learn, it does not follow that measures to promote personal autonomy will tend to make a society better or more just. If it should turn out that measures to promote personal autonomy would not make that society better or more just, then the claim that a society's social arrangements fail to do things to lead their members to be personally autonomous is not a criticism of those arrangements.

Measures to promote personal autonomy may not make a society better because those measures may have effects other than the promotion of autonomy. Isaiah Berlin identifies one possible effect of this sort in his famous critique of the notion of positive freedom.[37] Berlin distinguishes between negative freedom, which circumscribes an area within which individuals are or should be allowed to do as they wish without interference from other persons, and positive freedom, which derives from the wish on the part of the individual to be his own master. He argues that although positive freedom derives from the "wish to be a subject, not an object; to be moved by reasons, by conscious purposes, which are my own, not by causes which affect me, as it were from outside," the notion of positive freedom constitutes an invitation to those who identify freedom with resistance to and control

---

[36] James Griffin, *Well-Being: Its Meaning, Measurement, and Moral Significance* (Oxford: Clarendon Press, 1986), p. 58; cf. pp. 82, 114, 137, 145, 236.

[37] Berlin, "Two Concepts of Liberty," in *Four Essays on Liberty* (Oxford: Oxford University Press, 1969), pp. 118–72.

over desires—in short, with rational self-direction—and who are likely to accept the view that for each individual there is "one unique pattern which alone fulfills the claims of reason."[38] According to Berlin, this view may lead to despotic paternalism, which is "an insult to my conception of myself as a human being, determined to make my own life in accordance with my own (not necessarily rational or benevolent) purposes, and, above all, entitled to be recognized as such by others."[39] Berlin concludes that individual freedom in the negative sense, as distinct from individual autonomy, should be an important, though not necessarily the sole or dominant, "criterion of social action."[40]

Although Berlin does not distinguish among different types of autonomy, the target of his argument is autonomy$_3$, or personal autonomy, as I have called it. Personal autonomy is the type of autonomy that emphasizes the wish to be moved by reasons that are my own rather than by causes that affect me from outside. His critique does not apply to autonomy$_1$ or autonomy$_2$. There can be no insult to a person's conception of himself as a human being in social arrangements designed to enable individuals to develop the imaginative capacities to formulate plans and values. Social arrangements that *fail* to do this are an insult to humanity. Nor do social arrangements that encourage individuals to acquire a sense of justice insult human nature, since the aim of those arrangements is to help make it possible for all individuals to pursue projects and adhere to values of their own.

It might be argued that the despotic paternalism of which Berlin warns would arise only from institutions or practices to promote autonomy$_3$ or personal autonomy that are badly designed. Perhaps. But in rejoinder, it could be argued that some social objectives are more likely to lead in practice to badly designed institutions or projects than others. Berlin's underlying point is that the difference between the capacity to appraise one's own projects and values in a critical way—the value of which he does not deny—and rational self-direction of the sort that invites despotic paternalism is difficult to get right even conceptually and may be impossible to get right in practice.

Even if we set Berlin's objection aside, despotic paternalism is not the only likely unwanted effect of efforts to promote personal autonomy. It could be that social arrangements that tend to encourage personal autonomy would also lead to a good deal of anomie, thereby—perversely—undermining rather than strengthening individuals' capacities to be effective agents.

To see why, consider Michael one last time. Suppose that instead of going to a local college and devoting most of his studies to courses needed for his career as a pharmacist, Michael goes away to the more academic liberal arts

---

[38] Ibid., pp. 131, 136, 147.
[39] Ibid., p. 157.
[40] Ibid., p. 169.

college Marie attends. There he is exposed to people from a variety of backgrounds and cultures and to academic subjects, including literature and philosophy, that stretch his imagination far beyond the bounds within which his thoughts moved before. He reads Coleridge and Emerson, Hegel and Nietzsche. He experiments with relationships that he had not realized were possible.

What sort of life does Michael have after college? Imagine two alternatives. In the first, Michael goes into a profession and lives a life of far greater self-awareness and knowledge of the world than he would have had if he had remained in his hometown and become a pharmacist. He subscribes to interesting and provocative publications and asks probing questions about social affairs. He sets more complex and challenging projects for himself than he would have done, and his values, though not fundamentally different from those to which he adhered when he was younger, are more nuanced and are developed with greater sensitivity. Michael is a more autonomous person than he would have been had he not gone away to the college he ended up attending.

There is a second alternative. Instead of leading him to enter a profession and live a life of wide-ranging interests in and knowledge of the world, Michael's college experience leaves him disoriented. His exposure to philosophy leads him to conclude that the values with which he was raised are groundless, that they are mere expressions of local prejudices that cannot be rationally justified. Michael comes to believe that the views he held prior to his college experience were the products of an excessively sheltered life. He develops a taste for critical self-examination and for revelatory experiences. Yet these experiences and introspections do not enable him to construct a consistent and coherent system of beliefs and values of his own. Instead they lead toward disintegration and disorientation from which Michael never fully recovers. Michael loses confidence in himself and, along with his self-confidence, loses his ability to be an effective agent.

These alternative scenarios are speculative. They have no evidentiary force. Yet the second scenario does not seem less plausible than the first. The effect of a mind-broadening experience on Michael might be to lead him to become more autonomous, or it might be to lead him to become more anomic.

What inferences can we draw from this collection of arguments bearing on the claim that personal autonomy is an essential ingredient of the good life for human beings in association with others? Notice that all the arguments against that claim that are not merely refutations of arguments in its favor raise objections to social arrangements or conditions or policies designed to promote personal autonomy. They do not raise objections to personal autonomy itself. These objections are of two types. The first type of objection suggests that measures intended to promote personal autonomy may actually have the unintended consequence of diminishing, rather than enhancing, individuals' abilities to be effective agents. This type of objection constitutes a valid reason for exercising caution in formulating such measures, but it does not seem to constitute a reason for rejecting the entire idea that social arrangements should tend to foster personal autonomy. The second type of objection points out that measures to promote personal autonomy sometimes conflict with the projects and values people already have, projects that, as Berlin points out, may not seem rational or benevolent to an advocate of strong autonomy but that nevertheless express objectives to which real people aspire.

This second type of objection raises deep difficulties concerning the validity of projects and values formulated on a basis of incomplete information or through processes that involve cognitive distortion. I cannot resolve those difficulties here.[41] However, it seems, on balance, that *some* degree of ability to appraise or reappraise one's projects and values critically is essential to a good life for human being in association with others. This ability seems necessary to enable individuals to formulate projects and values they can effectively pursue, projects and values that are neither too extravagant nor too modest. A person whose projects are too extravagant in relation to the share of resources he can reasonably expect to enjoy would be frustrated consistently by the failure of his projects. A person whose projects are too modest would make less of his life than he would be capable of making. In either case, the person in question would be a less effective agent than he might be. Moreover, a person who is wholly unable to reappraise his projects and values would probably be incapable of having an effective sense of justice— or being morally autonomous—as well. For in order to restrain his actions and claims in recognition of the fact that other human beings are agents with their own projects, values, and claims, a person must be able to appraise his projects and values in a critical way. Moral autonomy and personal autonomy are conceptually distinct. But in order to be morally autonomous, a person must possess and use, to some degree, the skills that are constitutive of personal autonomy. The relation between moral autonomy and personal autonomy is indirect, but a real relation between these two attributes exists.

In short, a good society would enable and encourage its members to acquire some degree of skill at appraising and re-appraising their own projects and values. Precisely what degree of skill is required is difficult to say. In fact, a full answer to this question is probably impossible in the absence of information about the particular society in question. I do not think, however, that we should accept the view, which some perfectionist liberals appear to hold, that the more personally autonomous the members of a society are—

---

[41] For some interesting discussion of this topic, though, see Jon Elster, *Sour Grapes: Studies in the Subversion of Rationality* (Cambridge: Cambridge University Press, 1983).

the more able and inclined they are to appraise their own projects and values critically—the better that society is. I suggest as a general rule of thumb that a society should promote conditions that foster personal autonomy insofar as—only insofar as—those conditions can be expected to contribute to individuals' capacities to be effective agents. In my view, the value of personal autonomy, like that of moral autonomy, derives from the role that attribute plays in enabling individuals to be effective agents. Personal autonomy is valuable to the extent that it contributes to this end rather than as an end in itself.

V

If the arguments presented in the preceding are correct, then the *full* perfectionist view—the view that a set of political and social arrangements is good to the extent that it protects and promotes a life of autonomy for all members of the society to which those arrangements apply, where by a life of autonomy we mean a life of agency, of moral autonomy, and of personal autonomy—is mistaken in part. Nevertheless, the greater part of that view is on target. Perfectionist liberalism rightly calls attention to the fact that individuals must develop some capacities to become agents at all. It also correctly identifies moral autonomy as an essential ingredient of any good life for human beings in association with others. Finally, it points to the need for the members of any good society to possess some capacity to reexamine their own projects and values critically. The flaw in this version of liberal theory arises when its proponents go on to claim that political and social institutions should be based on the assumption that a life of personal autonomy is intrinsically superior to relatively nonautonomous ways of life or to suggest that social arrangements should be designed to maximize personal autonomy, and to conclude that a society that fails to do these things must ipso facto be seriously defective. This flaw stems, I think, from the failure of Mill, Raz, and other advocates of the perfectionist line of reasoning to distinguish clearly between agency, moral autonomy, and personal autonomy and to analyze the different roles each of these distinct attributes plays in enabling human beings to be effective agents.

In the United States, many people probably grow to adulthood with significantly impaired capacities for autonomy$_1$, that is, for conceiving and pursuing projects and values. In an environment in which it does not seem worthwhile to formulate complex or long-term projects and in which no value more expansive than the value of self-defense seems appealing, people will fail to develop the skills required to become agents beyond a rudimentary stage. Many people probably also grow up, within different social classes, with seriously defective capacities for moral autonomy or for personal autonomy, or both. Most people—not necessarily all—in the United

States probably have *some* sense of justice and *some* ability to appraise their own values critically. For many, though, those abilities are probably very limited.

Although both agency and moral autonomy, as well as some degree of personal autonomy, are *necessary* attributes for human beings to develop in order to have a good life in association with others, the development of these attributes is not *sufficient* for a good life. A good society must do things other than enable its members to be autonomous, at least to some degree, in all these senses. So although the Autonomy Principle, as qualified in the preceding pages, tells us something significant about the shape a good society should take, it cannot do all the work needed to develop a persuasive account of the bases of social criticism. In order to make meaningful lives for themselves in accordance with their projects or plans, individuals must also have resources with which to work. I shall now turn to a liberal theory in which resources play a central role.

CHAPTER FOUR

Political Liberalism

IN ORDER TO CONSTRUCT worthwhile lives for themselves in association with others, human beings have to develop their capacities as agents as well as their capacity for a sense of justice. But human beings also need resources in order to shape their lives in ways that will be meaningful to them. Rights-based and perfectionist approaches to liberal theory do not ignore resources, of course. In John Rawls's theory of justice as fairness, however, in contrast to these other approaches, questions about the nature and distribution of the resources that are relevant to political and social criticism play a central role.

In this chapter I shall discuss critically Rawls's theory of justice as fairness. Rawls considers his theory a version of "political liberalism." Political liberalism, as Rawls sees it, adopts an approach that differs fundamentally from that of perfectionist liberalism. Whereas in his view perfectionist liberalism assumes that only one rational conception of the good exists—namely the good of self-perfection in the form of personal autonomy—political liberalism "supposes that there are many conflicting reasonable comprehensive doctrines with their conceptions of the good, each compatible with the full rationality of human persons, so far as that can be ascertained with the resources of a political conception of justice."[1] Rawls's theory of justice as fairness is not the only representative of the genre of political liberalism,[2] but it is by far the most highly developed theory in this class. In this chapter I shall discuss Rawls's theory alone.

Rawls published an initial statement of some of the key ideas of his theory in the 1950s, and his major statement of the theory as a whole appeared in 1971. Since that time the theory has been subjected to voluminous criticism. Because the critical tradition that has grown up around Rawls's theory has given rise to a variety of impressions, not all of which are accurate, and because the theory has evolved considerably over the years, it will be useful

---

[1] *Political Liberalism* (New York: Columbia University Press, 1993), p. 135. Rawls's view that perfectionism assumes that only one rational good exists is incorrect. Although some perfectionists have developed comprehensive doctrines in Rawls's sense, *liberal* perfectionism is just the view that personal autonomy is essential for a good life. That view is compatible with considerable value pluralism, since there is more to a good life, according to perfectionists, than personal autonomy.

[2] For another example, see Charles Larmore's *Patterns of Moral Complexity* (Cambridge: Cambridge University Press, 1987) and his article "Political Liberalism," *Political Theory* 18 (1990): 339–60. See also J. Donald Moon's fine recent book, *Constructing Community: Moral Pluralism and Tragic Conflicts* (Princeton: Princeton University Press, 1994).

to begin with a brief sketch of the main ideas of the theory and the way they fit together. I shall focus on the theory in its present form without calling attention to the ways in which it has changed except where by doing so I can contribute to the clarity of my argument. (Readers who are well versed in Rawls's theory may want to skip section I and go straight to section II.)

I

The principal motivation behind the theory of justice as fairness was Rawls's desire to formulate a powerful alternative to utilitarianism. It seemed to him that utilitarianism was the most comprehensive and systematic body of theory available to provide a basis for comparison between alternative social institutions and practices. Yet in Rawls's view utilitarian theory is unsatisfactory in at least two major ways.

First, in his judgment utilitarian theory fails to account for our considered conviction that individuals have rights that should not be subject to the calculus of social interests.[3] The central proposition of utilitarian theory, at least in its classical form, is the greatest happiness principle.[4] According to this principle, the best arrangement is that which maximizes the aggregate happiness of the members of society as a whole. However, in some plausible circumstances it might turn out that the way to maximize *aggregate* happiness is to impose considerable suffering on one or a few members of a society. Suppose that you and I are members of a society of one hundred people. Suppose further that ninety-five of us could be made very happy by enslaving the other five, forcing them to do all the unpleasant and demeaning chores in our society and leaving ourselves free to do only the more enjoyable and rewarding tasks. It might turn out that this arrangement would produce greater aggregate happiness than any alternative in which no one is enslaved, even when the misery of the unfortunate five slaves is taken fully into account. According to classical utilitarianism, the best arrangement is the one that maximizes aggregate happiness. If maximum aggregate hap-

---

[3] Rawls, *A Theory of Justice* (Cambridge, Mass.: Harvard University Press, 1971), p. 4.

[4] In the eighteenth century a popular formula was "the greatest happiness of the greatest number." Francis Hutcheson used this formula in *An Enquiry Concerning Moral Good and Evil*, in *British Moralists*, ed. L. A. Selby-Bigge (Indianapolis: Bobbs-Merrill, 1964), pp. 69–177, sec. 3, par. 8; and Bentham picked it up in his *A Fragment on Government*, ed. F. C. Montague (Oxford: Clarendon Press, 1891), preface and sec. 2. Bentham does not use this formula in his later works, though, perhaps because he realized that it requires double maximization of a kind that makes it an incoherent rule. For a history of this formula up to and including Bentham, see David Baumgardt, *Bentham and the Ethics of Today* (Princeton: Princeton University Press, 1952), pp. 35–59. For discussion of the incoherence of the formula, see F. Y. Edgeworth, *Mathematical Psychics* (London: Kegan Paul, 1881), pp. 117–18; and Jon von Neumann and Oscar Morgenstern, *The Theory of Games and Economic Behavior*, 3d ed. (Princeton: Princeton University Press, 1953), p. 11.

piness can be attained through an arrangement that enslaves a few in order to produce greater happiness for the rest, then classical utilitarianism would have to endorse that arrangement as the best. Rawls's claim is that results of this kind are irreconcilable with our considered judgment that individuals have rights that should not be subject to the calculus of social interests. If utilitarian theory leads to this kind of result, then that theory must be mistaken.

Second, Rawls believes that utilitarian theory, like perfectionist liberalism, presupposes an erroneous monistic conception of the good.[5] According to Rawls, it is a premise of utilitarian theory that if all individuals were fully informed and rational, all would agree that only one rational good exists. In classical utilitarianism, that good is mental pleasure or, more broadly, psychological well-being. In Rawls's view, that is, although utilitarians may accept that many different things *contribute* to the good, they assume that these things do so by contributing to psychological well-being, which alone *constitutes* the good. Rawls believes this assumption to be mistaken. In his view a plurality of different and even incommensurable conceptions of the good exists and would continue to do so even if all persons were highly rational and well informed. People conceive different values and formulate different projects. Some of these values and projects extend beyond their own and other individuals' experiences. That is, some individuals—many individuals, in fact—value things other than mental states or the state of psychological well-being. Utilitarians might try to explain away these values by claiming that they must be based on misinformation or irrational inferences. In Rawls's view, though, this effort would be misguided. People just formulate different and in many cases irreconcilable conceptions of the good. Any satisfactory theory of justice, he believes—correctly, in my view—must take this fact into account.

So the point of departure for Rawls's theory is his rejection of utilitarianism and, in particular, of these two features of utilitarian theory. These two points have been the two principal anchors for the theory of justice as fairness all along, both in its original form and in Rawls's more recent formulation of that theory as a representative of the genre of political liberalism. In other words, the theory's aim is to provide an account of principles that we can use to determine whether the institutions or arrangements of a society are just that will be consistent with the intuition or considered judgment that individuals have rights that should not be subject to the calculus of social interests and with recognition of the fact that *not* all rational and in-

---

[5] Rawls, "Social Unity and Primary Goods," in *Utilitarianism and Beyond*, ed. Amartya Sen and Bernard Williams (Cambridge: Cambridge University Press, 1982), pp. 159–85; and *Political Liberalism*, p. 135. Utilitarians dispute this claim. See, for example, James Griffin, *Well-Being: Its Meaning, Measurement, and Moral Significance* (Oxford: Clarendon Press, 1986), esp. chap. 5.

formed individuals would accept a single conception of the good, that people's conceptions of the good are irreducibly plural. These two anchors or fixed points go a long way toward defining the problem that Rawls's theory of justice as fairness is designed to solve.

The most fundamental idea of Rawls's theory of justice as fairness is the idea of *society as a fair system of social cooperation* among *free and equal persons* under conditions of moderate scarcity.[6] Although such a society is a cooperative venture for mutual advantage, its members typically adhere to different conceptions of the good—that is, they have different values and different projects they wish to pursue. For example, I take a great interest in children's education and believe that education of the highest possible quality is among the most important of all goods. At the same time, you take a great interest in the disadvantages to which handicapped people are subject and believe that attaining parity for handicapped people with the circumstances of those who are not handicapped is a value of outstanding importance, so much so that you believe that resources I think should be devoted to education should instead be used to alleviate the disadvantages of the handicapped. So our relations with one another, and those among the members of any society under conditions of moderate scarcity, are marked by conflict as well as mutual benefit. These relations are mediated by social arrangements that determine the distribution of advantages among individuals. Since the social arrangements that prevail in a given society are products of human practices and are therefore subject to change, a set of criteria is required for evaluating the various different feasible arrangements a society might adopt.

Rawls argues that these criteria can best be developed by reference to an idealized conception of society. Economists often attempt to understand the workings of market systems by first describing the notion of a perfectly competitive market and then proceeding to make the adjustments required to bring that initial notion into line with the conditions prevailing in an existing market. Rawls maintains that criteria for evaluating social arrangements can best be ascertained by the analogous method of describing a perfectly just society.[7] This *well-ordered society*, as he calls it, would be regulated by principles of cooperation that are intelligible and acceptable to all its members:

> Now let us say that a society is well-ordered when it is not only designed to advance the good of its members but when it is also effectively regulated by a public conception of justice . . . In this case while men may put forth excessive

[6] In this sketch of Rawls's theory, terms that describe the major concepts of the theory will be italicized when they are first introduced. Most of these fundamental concepts are described concisely in *Theory*, pp. 3–22. See also *Political Liberalism*, lecture 1.

[7] This is Rawls's own analogy drawn in "The Idea of an Overlapping Consensus," *Oxford Journal of Legal Studies* 7 (1987): 15, n. 24.

demands on one another, they nevertheless acknowledge a common point of view from which their claims may be adjudicated . . . One may think of a public conception of justice as constituting the fundamental charter of a well-ordered human association.[8]

The central question to which the theory of justice as fairness proposes an answer is, What should the terms of this charter be?

Rawls argues that a satisfactory answer to this question would consist of a set of principles designed to regulate the *basic structure* of society. A society's basic structure includes its political constitution and the main features of its economic and social system.

According to Rawls the basic structure of a well-ordered society should be the principal subject of a theory of justice for at least two reasons.[9] First, a society's basic structure has profound effects on individuals' aspirations, desires, abilities, and talents as well as other matters. Some versions of utilitarian theory treat individuals' desires as well as their abilities and other attributes as given, that is, as exogenous to the theory. In Rawls's view, though, that approach is unsatisfactory. Human beings are profoundly social creatures. A theory that purports to tell us how to rank alternative institutions or social arrangements while failing to take into account the impact those arrangements are likely to have on human beings by virtue of their social nature is implausible. Rawls maintains that by focusing on the basic structure of society, the theory of justice as fairness takes that impact into account.

Second, Rawls argues that certain background conditions must prevail if transactions between individuals are to be fair. These background conditions cannot be maintained simply by requiring transactions between individuals to meet certain conditions, such as those incorporated into the idea of freedom of contract. For even if a society were to begin from an initial situation of fairness, and all subsequent transactions between individuals were fair to all individuals directly involved in them, there would be a tendency for fair background conditions to erode—that is, for inequalities to develop that would eventually put individuals or their descendants into highly unequal bargaining positions in relation to one another. John Locke was aware of this tendency when he argued that consent to the institution of money implies tacit consent to the inequality that in his view inevitably

---

[8] Rawls, *Theory*, pp. 4–5.

[9] The first argument is given in ibid., pp. 7–11. The second is given in Rawls's article "The Basic Structure as Subject," in *Values and Morals*, ed. A. I. Goldman and J. Kim (Dordrecht: Reidel, 1978), pp. 47–71. See also Rawls, "A Kantian Conception of Equality," *Cambridge Review* (February 1975): 94–99. Reprinted as "A Well-Ordered Society," in *Philosophy, Politics, and Society* (5th ser.), ed. Peter Laslett and James Fishkin (Oxford: Blackwell, 1979), pp. 6–20.

results from that institution.[10] In this case, Rawls observes, "the invisible hand guides things in the wrong direction and favors an oligopolistic config-uration of accumulations that succeeds in maintaining unjustified [in]equali-ties and restrictions on fair opportunity."[11] Hence it is especially important to define standards for those basic arrangements that give rise to background conditions.

Rawls's focus on the basic structure of society has far-reaching implica-tions for his theory and is a central point in his interpretation of that theory as a *political* liberalism. In this respect Rawls's theory is quite different from both the rights-based approach to liberal theory and the perfectionist ap-proach. In fact Rawls goes to some trouble to call attention to the distinctive-ness of this aspect of his theory. The "way in which we think about fairness in everyday life," he argues, "ill prepares us for the great shift in perspective required for considering the justice of the basic structure itself."[12] In Rawls's view we cannot arrive at a plausible conception of justice for the basic struc-ture of society by applying moral principles or norms borrowed from actions and transactions on a smaller scale.

Neither rights-based political theorists like Nozick nor perfectionist theo-rists like Raz think of the basic structure of society as a distinctive subject of political theory in the way that Rawls does. Nozick, for example, argues that "moral philosophy sets the background for, and boundaries of, political phi-losophy. What persons may and may not do to one another limits what they may do through the apparatus of a state, or do to establish such an appara-tus."[13] Nozick appears to assume that we can determine what persons may and may not do to one another without considering the complex problems of coordination that arise in large societies of interdependent people. Simi-larly, Raz rejects the view that there exists "a relatively independent body of moral principles, addressed primarily to the government and constituting a (semi-)autonomous political morality."[14] Neither of these theorists regards the basic structure of society as a subject of theory sui generis. In Rawls's view, though, it is a matter of great importance that the basic structure of society should be regarded as a distinct subject of political theory in its own right. We can make sense of our actions in everyday life and of our transac-

---

[10] It "is plain, that Men have agreed to disproportionate and unequal Possession of the Earth, they having by a tacit and voluntary consent found out a way, how a man may fairly possess more land than he himself can use the product of, by receiving in exchange for the overplus, Gold and Silver . . ." Locke, *Second Treatise of Government*, in *Two Treatises of Government*, ed. Peter Laslett (Cambridge: Cambridge University Press, 1963), chap. 5, par. 50.

[11] Rawls, "Basic Structure," p. 54. I have corrected "equalities" to read "inequalities."

[12] Rawls, "Kantian Constructivism," p. 551.

[13] Nozick, *Anarchy, State, and Utopia* (New York: Basic Books, 1974), p. 6.

[14] Raz, *The Morality of Freedom* (Oxford: Oxford University Press, 1986), p. 4.

tions on a smaller scale because of the place those actions and transactions occupy within a larger scheme. The norms we apply to those actions, to the rules of social life, and to our own characters can be criticized or justified by reference to that scheme. The basic structure of society *is* that scheme. It is reasonable to suppose that the questions that can be raised about that structure are sufficiently distinctive to make it a worthy, distinct subject of theory.

Rawls's idea of society as a fair system of social cooperation, his notion of persons as free and equal, and his claim that principles of justice should be formulated specifically to apply to the basic structure of an ideal or well-ordered society are some of the most fundamental ideas of his theory of justice. But these ideas are only pieces of the conceptual foundation for that theory. They prepare the ground for his argument, the most substantive parts of which still lie ahead of us in this sketch.

Now, Rawls believes that we cannot formulate a satisfactory set of principles of justice to regulate the basic structure of society simply by asking ourselves what principles we would prefer. If a number of individuals were to ask themselves this question, they would probably produce a variety of different answers. Some might be swayed by self-interest to prefer principles they expect to be especially beneficial to themselves. Even if people were not motivated by self-interest narrowly construed, they would be motivated by their particular values, which differ from one person to the next. If it seems to me that a given set of principles of justice would help justify increased investment in the education of children, then I would probably prefer those principles to others. You, however, might be swayed to approve of principles whose acceptance you expect to help direct resources toward amelioration of the disadvantages of handicapped people. If we were to ask ourselves what principles of justice we would prefer, we would probably find that many different answers gain some support. In Rawls's view this result is unacceptable. A just society needs a fundamental charter, a public conception of justice that all its members can accept as a public point of view from which competing claims to resources can be adjudicated. Yet no fundamental charter can emerge from a procedure that merely asks each of us what conception of justice we would prefer. For in response, we would offer diverse answers, not the single answer that would be needed as the basis of a fundamental charter expressing a single public conception of justice.

In order to circumvent this difficulty, Rawls proposes that we undertake a thought experiment. Suppose that we are charged with the task of founding a well-ordered society. We do not know the positions we will occupy within that society. We do not even know what conception of the good we will possess within it, what values we will have and what projects we will want to pursue. In short, we must choose principles to regulate the basic structure of the envisaged society from behind what Rawls calls a "veil of ignorance," which prevents us from applying our particular desires, aspirations, and ideals to the choice we are asked to make. Rawls calls the hypothetical point of view we adopt when we conduct this thought experiment the *original position*. He calls those who occupy this point of view—that is, us, when we conduct the thought experiment—the "parties" in the original position.

Rawls argues that if we were to think carefully and rationally of ourselves as parties in the original position (or co-founders of a well-ordered society), we would endorse three conclusions about that society. The first is a conclusion about what we would want the members of that society to be like. The second is a conclusion about the principles we would want to regulate the basic structure of that society. The third is a conclusion about the basis on which we would measure the relative advantages of the members of that society.

The first conclusion is that we would want the members of a well-ordered society to be what Rawls calls "moral persons." Moral persons are persons who have two moral powers. First, they possess a capacity for a sense of justice. Rawls describes a sense of justice as "the capacity to understand, to apply, and to act from the public conception of justice which characterizes the fair terms of social cooperation." A sense of justice expresses a willingness to act in relation to others on terms that all can publicly endorse. Second, moral persons possess a capacity for a conception of the good, which Rawls describes as "the capacity to form, to revise, and rationally to pursue a conception of one's rational advantage or good."[15]

The attributes of a moral person as that idea is worked out in Rawls's theory of justice correspond roughly to those I have described in chapter 3 as *agency* (Rawls's "capacity for a conception of the good") and *moral autonomy* (Rawls's "capacity for a sense of justice"). There are differences of wording and emphasis between his account and mine. For instance, Rawls's description of the capacity for a conception of the good as the capacity to "pursue a conception of one's rational advantage or good" has an egoistic ring that I hope is avoided by my corresponding description of the capacity to formulate and pursue projects and values.[16] And Rawls's description of the capacity for a sense of justice as the capacity to act from "*the* public concep-

---

[15] I am using here Rawls's discussion in *Political Liberalism*, p. 19. Rawls discussed the idea of moral personality in *Theory*, but he placed relatively little emphasis on that idea there. He first emphasized the idea of moral personality as a central feature of his theory of justice in his lectures on "Kantian Constructivism," a revised version of which appears as part 1 of his book *Political Liberalism*.

[16] Textual evidence suggests that Rawls does not intend this egoistic implication. For example, in *Theory* Rawls explicitly denies that his argument for his principles of justice as fairness rests on egoistic assumptions (see p. 129). Nevertheless, the wording Rawls chooses to describe the attributes of a moral person carries a strong egoistic ring, whatever his intentions may be.

tion of justice" seems to link the sense of justice to endorsement of a particular public conception of justice, whereas I think it better to define the sense of justice in more general terms as a developed capacity to recognize other human beings as agents with projects and claims that count as a reason for a person to exercise restraint in the pursuit of her own projects and claims. Still, the two moral powers as described by Rawls seem to me approximately equivalent to the developed capacities for agency and moral autonomy.[17]

The second conclusion we would reach as parties in the original position would be an agreement on principles of justice to regulate the basic structure of the well-ordered society of which we would be the co-founders. The two principles to which Rawls believes we would agree can be summarized as follows:

1. Each person has an equal right to a fully adequate scheme of equal basic liberties which is compatible with a similar scheme of liberties for all.
2. Social and economic inequalities are to satisfy two conditions. First, they must be attached to offices and positions open to all under conditions of fair equality of opportunity; and second, they must be to the greatest benefit of the least advantaged members of society.[18]

I shall call the first of these two principles Rawls's *basic liberties principle*. I shall call the first part of his second principle the *equal opportunity principle* and the second part, following common usage and Rawls's own usage, the *difference principle*. These principles taken as a whole are the principles of justice as fairness.

These principles require some explication, at least for readers who are not intimately familiar with Rawls's theory. The basic liberties principle states that each member of society should be guaranteed certain liberties that are to be specified by a list. Rawls suggests two different ways in which a specific list of basic liberties might be derived.[19] The first way is to survey the constitutions of democratic states, note the liberties normally protected, and ex-

---

[17] For a more critical interpretation of Rawls's conception of moral personality, see William A. Galston, *Liberal Purposes: Goods, Virtues, and Diversity in the Liberal State* (Cambridge: Cambridge University Press, 1991), chap. 6. See also Thomas W. Pogge's careful discussion in *Realizing Rawls* (Ithaca: Cornell University Press, 1989), pp. 94–106.

[18] Rawls, *Political Liberalism*, p. 291. This statement of his two principles of justice as fairness differs significantly from his account of these principles in *Theory* and in Rawls's other works published before 1982. The main difference lies in his statement of the first principle, which in *Theory* refers to "an equal basic right to the *most extensive* total system of equal basic liberties compatible with a similar system of liberty for all" rather than to a *fully adequate* scheme of liberties. Rawls also reverses the original order of the two parts of his second principle; originally the clause stating that inequalities must be to the greatest benefit of the least advantaged members of society came before the clause about fair equality of opportunity. Rawls discusses some of the reasons for these changes in *Political Liberalism*, lecture 8.

[19] Rawls, *Political Liberalism*, pp. 292–93.

amine the role of these liberties in the constitutions that have worked well. The second way is to consider which liberties are essential social conditions for the adequate development and exercise of the two powers of moral persons. Rawls does not attempt to supply a complete list of the basic liberties, but he mentions prominently the political liberties, such as the right to vote and freedom of the press; freedom of thought; liberty of conscience, including freedom of worship; freedom of association; and other personal liberties such as freedom from arbitrary arrest and imprisonment, the right to a trial when charged with a criminal offense and to due process of law, and so forth.

Rawls's principal claim is that any set of political and social arrangements—here he has in mind the constitution of a democratic state—that fails to protect these basic liberties is unjust. Further, according to him the basic liberties principle is lexically prior to both parts of the second principle of justice. In other words, the protection for the basic liberties stipulated by the first principle must be guaranteed fully before the provisions stipulated by the two parts of the second principle come into play. The business of protecting the basic liberties takes priority over and is more urgent than the business of guaranteeing fair equality of opportunity or that of ensuring that social and economic inequalities work to the net advantage of those who are least advantaged by those inequalities.

The equal opportunity principle means that of all the possible political and social arrangements that would protect individuals' basic liberties, those which would best ensure that offices and positions within the society that lead to unequal rewards are open to fair competition on a basis of equal opportunity are more just than those with offices and positions that are not filled in a fair, competitive manner. This fair equality of opportunity should be underwritten, Rawls says, by education for all; no one should be excluded from a chance to obtain a favored position by lack of access to a good education.[20] Again, the equal opportunity principle is lexically prior to the difference principle. That is, the basic institutions of a society must be arranged so that conditions providing for fair equality of opportunity are met as fully as possible before the difference principle comes into play. The difference principle applies within a framework that is structured by the basic liberties principle and the fair equality of opportunity principle.

The difference principle is more complex than the other two principles and is probably the most distinctive feature of Rawls's theory. The central idea of the difference principle is that social and economic inequalities should work to the advantage of the least advantaged members of society.

An illustration may help to make this principle clearer. Suppose you are a member of a society with a total of one hundred members. Assume further that each person's "position" or "deal" within that society can be measured

---

[20] Rawls, *Theory*, p. 87.

on a scale numbered from one to ten. A person at position 1 would be in the worst possible position, whereas a person at position 10 would be in the best. Moreover, the scale is an interval scale, so that a person at position 8 has twice as good a deal as a person at position 4, and a person at position 8 is better off than one at position 7 by just the same amount as a person at position 4 is better off than one at position 3.

Now, imagine that you and the other members of your society are in a position to choose between two alternative social structures. In structure A, twenty-five people would be at position 9, fifty would be at position 6, and twenty-five would be at position 3. In structure B, twenty-five would be at position 7, while fifty would be at position 5 and twenty-five would be at position 4. We could represent these two alternative structures schematically as follows:

	Structure A	Structure B
10		
9	25	
8		
7		25
6	50	
5		50
4		25
3	25	
2		
1		

If we think of our scale as measuring how well off the members of our society will be under the two alternative social structures, and if each unit of being well off is equal to every other unit (so that a person at position 6 is precisely twice as well off as one at position 3, while a person at position 9 is three times as well off as one at position 3 and 50 percent better off than one at position 6), then we could say that the total units of being well off yielded by structure A is $(25 \times 9) + (50 \times 6) + (25 \times 3) = 225 + 300 + 75 = 600$ units. At the same time, the total units of being well off yielded by structure B is $(25 \times 7) + (50 \times 5) + (25 \times 4) = 175 + 250 + 100 = 525$ units.

If we believe that alternative social arrangements should be weighed against the yardstick of aggregate utility, as classical utilitarians argued, and if we think of our units of being well off as units of utility, then we would choose structure A over structure B, since structure A yields 600 units of total utility compared with structure B's 525 units. Aggregate utility is greater in structure A than in structure B. If, however, we accept Rawls's difference principle, and both structure A and structure B satisfy the basic liberties principle and the equal opportunity principle equally well, then we would choose structure B in preference to structure A. For the difference principle identifies the position of the least advantaged, rather than aggregate utility, as the crucial variable. From a Rawlsian point of view, those who would be well off in structure A—those at positions 9 and 6—would be taking unfair advantage of those who are worst off, who stand at position 3. Perhaps those at position 3 would lead a miserable life, and perhaps they would not. But it is known that they would be better off if we were to adopt structure B. The difference principle stipulates that social and economic inequalities should work to the advantage of the least advantaged. Therefore the inequalities that would result from adoption of structure B would be just, but those that would result from adoption of structure A would be unjust. Of course, if another alternative were available that would leave the least advantaged members of society in a better position than they would be under structure B, then that alternative would be more just than either structure A or structure B. The key point of Rawls's difference principle is that the position of the least advantaged members of society is what should count when we are comparing alternative social structures or arrangements (after we have taken into account the basic liberties and provisions to guarantee fair equality of opportunity).

For the purpose of composing this illustration I have made several simplifying assumptions. Most of these are unimportant for my purposes, but one *is* important, namely, the assumption that we can ignore the difference between the concept of utility, which utilitarians use to measure the relative positions of different people in a social structure, and the concept of *primary goods*, which Rawls uses to measure those relative positions. That primary goods constitute the appropriate measure is the third major conclusion Rawls believes we would endorse if we were to imagine ourselves in the original position. Since the concept of primary goods plays a central role in the theory of justice as fairness and in my own discussion as well, an explanation of that concept is needed.[21]

According to Rawls, a basic function of a conception of justice is to formulate a public understanding of a basis on which citizens' competing claims for scarce resources may be weighed in relation to one another. Now, Rawls assumes that individuals in a well-ordered society will have different, conflicting, and at least in some cases incommensurable values and projects (or conceptions of the good, as he calls them). This means that at least in some cases, comparing one person's conception of the good with another's will be like comparing apples with oranges. Their values and projects are just qualitatively different, and meaningful comparison is not really possible. Nor is it possible, according to this view, to compare meaningfully the extent to which different individuals attain their ends or realize their values. This lack

---

[21] For this discussion I rely mainly on Rawls's "Social Unity" and *Political Liberalism*, lecture 5, pp. 178–90.

of comparability gives rise to a serious problem, namely, the problem of how to count or to weigh conflicting claims in relation to one another. I consider it vitally important that children learn to speak Japanese before they graduate from high school at the latest. You think it is vitally important that handicapped people not be disadvantaged in comparison with those who are not handicapped, at least with regard to physical mobility. To realize either of these values would cost money, but the value of these attainments cannot be measured in money alone, and in any case you and I assign markedly different values to the same things. On what basis should we balance these competing claims?

Rawls's answer is that the concept of primary goods provides a public basis for comparisons. He argues that despite the fact that different individuals have markedly different values and projects, nearly all the values and projects that citizens could pursue in a well-ordered liberal society would require for their advancement roughly the same set of goods. Rawls calls these goods primary goods. Although he does not claim to have drawn up a complete list, Rawls identifies primary goods of five basic types: 1) basic rights and liberties, 2) freedom of movement and free choice of occupation from among diverse opportunities, 3) offices and positions of responsibility, together with their powers and prerogatives, 4) income and wealth, and 5) the social bases of self-respect.

These primary goods, Rawls argues, are necessary for the advancement of all or nearly all values and projects, however diverse these may be in other respects. Moreover, they are necessary for individuals to develop and to exercise the powers of moral persons, that is, to act as agents with a sense of justice. Primary goods can be interpreted as the goods that provide for citizens' needs.

Rawls rejects the view that individual's relative positions should be measured in units of utility because he believes that the concept of utility presupposes a misguided, monistic conception of the good. He argues that it is simply not feasible, practically or conceptually, to compare utilities when individuals adhere to markedly different values and pursue highly diverse projects. The only feasible basis of comparison is the means—or resources in a broad sense—available to individuals as specified by a list. So shares of primary goods, rather than utility or welfare attainment or desire satisfaction or any similar utilitarian concept, constitute the only appropriate basis for making comparisons among different individuals' competing claims on resources. Individuals should be thought of as being allocated a share of these primary goods. It is up them how they use those shares; that is a matter for which the individuals themselves, rather than society or its institutions, are responsible.

The principal conclusions of Rawls's theory, then, are as follows. First, the members of a perfectly just society would be moral persons—that is, they would be agents with a capacity to pursue projects and values, and they would have a sense of justice. Second, the basic structure of a perfectly just society would guarantee that each member enjoys the basic liberties and that social and economic inequalities are distributed in a way that guarantees fair equality of opportunity and ensures that inequalities work to the advantage of those who are least advantaged. Third, the measure of each person's position or relative advantage would be the "size" of that person's share of primary goods. According to Rawls, these conclusions define the basic terms of a charter to which we would agree if we were to imagine ourselves in the original position as co-founders of a new society, a charter that would actually apply in a perfectly just society.

For Rawls, the terms of this charter define the "right." In his view the right is prior to the good. In other words, norms of justice that apply to the basic structure of society take priority over individuals' projects, values, and comprehensive conceptions of the good (insofar as individuals have such conceptions). If a person makes a claim in light of her particular values or of a project in which she is interested, and fulfillment of that claim would violate justice, then her claim must be denied. Of course, for individuals the pursuit of projects and the attempt to adhere to and realize values is essential. Individuals make meaningful lives for themselves by pursuing projects and attempting to realize their values or conceptions of the good. But Rawls assumes that different people pursue different projects and hold different values, and that these diverse projects and values—or comprehensive conceptions of the good—are equally reasonable. That is, for him, the defining assumption of political liberalism. The principles of justice are intended to guide adjudication of people's *conflicting* claims, so that each person's capacity to pursue her own conception of the good will be protected, as long as that conception is consistent with justice. So although the right is prior to the good in the sense that principles of justice take priority over individuals' projects and values, the ideas of the right and the good are complementary. As Rawls puts it, "justice draws the limit, the good shows the point."[22]

One further aspect of Rawls's theory of justice remains to be explained: his conception of the function and status of the principles of justice as fairness. In A *Theory of Justice* Rawls likened his project to that of constructing a moral geometry.[23] Ideally, in the view he adopted there, the reasoning used by the hypothetical parties in the original position (that is, by us when we undertake the thought experiment of imagining ourselves as if we were those parties) would be strictly deductive, and the outcome would be the unique solution to the problem posed by the original position. That outcome would constitute an "Archimedean point"[24] from which alternative social

[22] Rawls, "The Priority of Right and Ideas of the Good," *Philosophy and Public Affairs* 17 (1988): 252. See also *Political Liberalism*, p. 174, and *Theory*, p. 253: "This priority of the right over the good in justice as fairness turns out to be a central feature of the conception."
[23] Rawls, *Theory*, p. 121 and, more generally, pp. 118–26.
[24] Ibid., pp. 260–63, 520, 584.

systems can be judged without reference to particular desires or wants or any particular conception of the good. The theory should enable us to fix our ideas about justice permanently, to define once and for all what is to count as just and unjust.[25]

Now, Rawls has conceded that his theory of justice falls far short of the deductive rigor to which he aspired. One reason for this shortcoming is that the argument he makes via the original position is relative to a given list of alternative conceptions of justice.[26] The hypothetical parties in the original position do not deduce the principles of justice. They merely select the most reasonable set of principles from a list of possibilities to which additional possibilities can always be added. So the argument for a given set of principles is always, according to Rawls, relative to the list of alternatives to which those principles are preferred.

A second and more important reason why Rawls's argument fell short of the deductive rigor to which he aspired is that his argument from the original position was not really a "proof" of his theory in any case. In Rawls's view the real test of a theory is the capacity of its principles to account for our considered judgments in reflective equilibrium.[27] Perhaps when he wrote *A Theory of Justice* Rawls supposed that the test of reflective equilibrium could lead to conclusions as rigorous as those that flow from a deductive chain of reasoning. Whether he held it at that time or not, that supposition seems misguided. The test of reflective equilibrium is subject to interpretation and is necessarily probabilistic and fallible. It does not support conclusions in the rigorous way a deductive proof does.

In the series of works culminating in the publication of his *Political Liberalism* Rawls adopts a different conception of the function and status of his theory of justice. There he sees his theory of justice as a "political conception" of justice worked out specifically for the narrow, but vital, case of the basic structure of society.[28] Rawls argues that a political conception of justice should be understood in contrast to a comprehensive conception of the good. The objective of a political conception of justice is narrower than that of a comprehensive conception of the good. Further, the function of a political conception of justice is to serve as a basis for public justification in a society, a basis on which competing claims can be weighed and a decision on those claims can be defended. A political conception of justice can serve this purpose insofar as it can be the subject of an "overlapping consensus," a consensus among people who hold differing values and comprehensive conceptions of the good but who nevertheless can agree on certain principles of justice to regulate their common affairs.

[25] Ibid., pp. 4, 12.
[26] Ibid., pp. 122–26.
[27] See the discussion in chap. 1, sec. III.
[28] Rawls, *Political Liberalism*, pp. 11ff.

Rawls does not argue that *any* agreement that might be reached by the members of a society is necessarily just. In *A Theory of Justice* he pointed out that it is possible for a society to have a publicly accepted conception of justice that is itself unjust,[29] and he says nothing in his later works to suggest that this is not a possibility.[30] But Rawls does appear in this more recent work to renounce the idea of *proof* in political philosophy. The purpose of political philosophy, as he conceives it now, is public justification, justification of the basis on which public decisions are made and justification of political institutions and practices in comparison with alternative possibilities to a society whose members are assumed to have different values and conceptions of the good.

For the sake of brevity I have had to omit many features of Rawls's theory from this exposition and to simplify others. Nevertheless, we now have in hand the principal elements necessary for an assessment of the theory. To summarize: the most fundamental ideas of the theory are the ideas of society as a fair system of social cooperation and that of persons as free and equal. The theory uses the idea of society as a fair system of social cooperation to generate the ideal of a perfectly just society (a well-ordered society) whose members would be moral persons—persons with the developed capacity to formulate and to pursue projects and values and with a sense of justice—and whose basic structure would be regulated by the two principles of justice as fairness (the basic liberties principle and the equal opportunity and difference principles). The relative positions of individuals would be measured in shares of primary goods. According to Rawls, this ideal of a perfectly just society constitutes a public basis of justification—and criticism—for real societies. The component parts of this ideal define what should count when we compare alternative institutions or reforms and weigh conflicting claims on public resources.

II

I want now to assess Rawls's theory of justice as an account of the bases of political criticism. For this specific purpose several kinds of questions that might be raised about his theory can be set aside. I shall query neither Rawls's procedure of focusing on the idea of a perfectly just society nor his

[29] Rawls, *Theory*, p. 352.

[30] Richard Rorty has argued that Rawls's view, as developed in the 1980s, is that justification rests on "whatever subjective reflective equilibrium may be obtainable, given the contingent make-up of the subjects in question" ("The Priority of Democracy to Philosophy," in *The Virginia Statute for Religious Freedom*, ed. Merrill D. Peterson and Robert C. Vaughan [Cambridge: Cambridge University Press, 1988], p. 270). This statement expresses a more historicist and relativist view than Rawls accepts. For a denial from Rawls that his view is relativist or historicist, see Rawls's "Domain of the Political and Overlapping Consensus," *New York University Law Review* 64 (1989): 251–52, n. 46.

claim that the basic structure of such a society is the appropriate subject of a theory of justice. These claims raise important questions in their own right, but I shall not pursue those questions here.[31] I want also to set aside his highly controversial claims for his argument from the original position along with Rawls's allegedly detached conception of the self.[32] As I have suggested in the preceding, the argument from the original position, though important to Rawls and useful for the development of his theory, does not constitute a *proof* or attempted proof of that theory anyway. Both the original position and the idea of the hypothetical inhabitants of that position are mere "devices of representation," as Rawls has called them,[33] intended to help us clarify our thoughts and see the force of some of the arguments for justice as fairness. These ideas do not constitute Rawls's substantive claims.

I mean to focus on those substantive claims, that is, on Rawls's claims about the bases of political criticism. The most significant of these claims are 1) that the members of a perfectly just society would be moral persons, 2) that the basic structure of a perfectly just society would be regulated by the basic liberties principle and by the equal opportunity principle and the difference principle, applied in that order, and 3) that individuals' positions should be compared with one another on the basis of their shares of primary goods.

Of these substantive claims, I shall here set aside the first, namely Rawls's claims about moral personality. This set of claims has to do with the characters that the members of a perfectly just society would have. I have dealt with this topic already in chapter 3. My conclusion there is similar to Rawls's. Like Rawls, I think the members of a good society (or a perfectly just society, in his terms) would be agents. They would have a developed capacity to formulate projects and values and to act to advance those projects and to realize those values. I also think the members of a good society would have to have a developed capacity for a sense of justice. My interpretation of these features of character differs in some respects from Rawls's, but these differences are not great enough to warrant further discussion here.

[31] For one type of question, about the range of institutions and practices that should be thought of as parts of the basic structure, see Susan Moller Okin, *Justice, Gender, and the Family* (New York: Basic Books, 1989).

[32] For that allegation, see Sandel, *Liberalism and the Limits of Justice* (Cambridge: Cambridge University Press, 1982). For a forceful reply in defense of Rawls, see Pogge, *Realizing Rawls*, chap. 2; and on liberalism more generally, see also Kymlicka's *Liberalism, Community, and Culture* (Oxford: Clarendon Press, 1989); and Rosenblum's *Another Liberalism: Romanticism and the Reconstruction of Liberal Thought* (Cambridge, Mass.: Harvard University Press, 1987).

[33] Rawls, *Political Liberalism*, pp. 24–27, 35, 75.

I shall focus, then, on Rawls's two principles of justice and on his claim that shares of primary goods should constitute the basis for comparison of individuals' relative positions in society, that is, for determining what kind of deal individuals have received. As before, the question motivating my inquiry is, How adequate is the account of the bases of political and social criticism comprised by Rawls's conclusions?

III

The first principle of justice as fairness declares that in a perfectly just society each person would have an equal right to a fully adequate scheme of equal basic liberties that is compatible with a similar scheme of liberties for all. According to Rawls, this basic liberties principle is lexically prior to the second principle of justice, which regulates social and economic inequalities. However, Rawls also maintains that the priority of the first principle holds only under "reasonably favorable conditions."[34] Reasonably favorable conditions are social circumstances in which the effective establishment and full exercise of these liberties is possible, provided the political will to enact and enforce them exists. These conditions are determined by a society's culture, its traditions, its institutional skills, and its level of economic advance, and perhaps other factors as well.

Rawls has offered two distinct and alternative arguments in favor of the basic liberties principle and its priority at different times, the first in *A Theory of Justice* and the second in his lecture on "The Basic Liberties and Their Priority."[35] These arguments cast that principle in two rather different lights.

In *A Theory of Justice* (sec. 82) Rawls conjectured that in the early stages of civilization human beings were interested primarily in gaining economic and social advantages. As conditions improved and the quantity and security of material means available to them increased, however, their interest in liberty grew stronger, and the marginal significance to them of further economic and social advantages decreased. In addition, they came to aspire to control the laws and rules regulating their association. In time individuals began to take an interest in determining plans of life for themselves, and eventually this interest assumed priority over their other interests. In this statement of his theory Rawls supposed that the priority of liberty flows from these developments.

After his book had been published, Rawls noticed that for various reasons

[34] Ibid., p. 297.

[35] Rawls, "The Basic Liberties and Their Priority," in *The Tanner Lectures on Human Values*, ed. Sterling M. McMurrin (Salt Lake City: University of Utah Press, 1982), pp. 1–87 (reprinted in *Political Liberalism* as lecture 8).

this argument provides inadequate support for the basic liberties principle.[36] Three problems with that argument are noteworthy.

The first difficulty is that Rawls's argument in *Theory* treats liberty in general as a good rather than picking out the specific liberties he intended to protect with the basic liberties principle. The basic liberties principle was intended to protect a short list of *basic* liberties, not to protect liberty as an undifferentiated good. The liberties Rawls believes require protection are, roughly, those that in the United States we generally regard as constitutionally protected. So Rawls's historical account of the priority of liberty constitutes an inadequate explanation of the content of the specific liberties protected by his basic liberties principle and of their relative standing or weight in relation to one another.

A second difficulty with the argument Rawls offers in *A Theory of Justice* for the priority of the basic liberties is that it suggests that our interest in the basic liberties is continuous and commensurable with our other interests, so that at some marginal point we would be willing to exchange a portion of our basic liberties for an equally valuable portion of some other good. This implication is strictly inconsistent with Rawls's claim that the basic liberties principle should be lexically prior to his second principle of justice and a fortiori to all other considerations that we might want to take into account in comparing alternative social arrangements. Lexical priority can be justified only if our interest in the good to which we give priority is of a different order from our interest in other, subordinate goods. If we were willing to exchange some portion of our basic liberties for some other good, by definition we would not hold those liberties to be lexically prior in importance to that other good, even though we may in general assign greater *weight* to the good of liberty than to other goods. It would be inconsistent to say both that one principle has *lexical priority* over another and that it has *greater weight* than the other. These two ways of stipulating the relative importance of different principles are different in kind.

A third, most serious difficulty with the argument for the priority of the basic liberties Rawls makes in *Theory* is that it implies that the priority of the basic liberties is contingent on the preferences individuals happen to have. The story goes that as the level of material wealth increased, people came to acquire a greater preference or taste for liberty in comparison to material goods. But this implication is strictly inconsistent with the intent of Rawls's theory of justice as a whole. According to Rawls's theory, the right is prior to

---

[36] Rawls credits H.L.A. Hart with calling attention to these weaknesses in his argument. For Hart's arguments, see his "Rawls on Liberty and Its Priority," *University of Chicago Law Review* 40 (1973): 534–55, reprinted in *Reading Rawls*, 2d ed., ed. Norman Daniels (Stanford: Stanford University Press, 1989), pp. 230–52. For Rawls's own discussion of the flaws in this argument, see "Basic Liberties," esp. p. 87, n. 83. My discussion of the difficulties with Rawls's argument borrows from his but extends it.

the good. An implication of the claim that the right is prior to the good is that the principles of justice are categorical imperatives.[37] That is, they apply necessarily rather than contingently, and their prescriptive force is not contingent on our acceptance of a given preference or our desire to achieve a given end. Rawls's historical account of the priority of right entails just the wrong conclusion, namely, that liberty has priority only because individuals prefer it to other goods. For Rawls's purposes, this conclusion puts things the wrong way around.

In light of some of these difficulties, Rawls formulated a revised argument for the basic liberties principle and its priority in his long Tanner lecture on this topic.[38] The key to this argument is the notion of moral personality, which played little role in *A Theory of Justice* but has assumed considerable importance in Rawls's more recent statements of his theory. Rawls's line of reasoning runs as follows. In order to be fully participating members of a just society, individuals must develop the capacities of moral persons, namely the capacities of an agent and the capacity to have an effective sense of justice. The basic liberties guaranteed by the first principle of justice are among the social conditions necessary for the adequate development and exercise of these capacities. Hence individuals in the original position would decide to guarantee these liberties by according them lexical priority over all other considerations that might be taken into account in evaluating political and social arrangements.[39]

This argument is a significant improvement over Rawls's initial line of reasoning for the priority of the basic liberties. For unlike that line of reasoning, this argument does not depend in any way on individuals' contingent preferences. Instead, it relies on the far more solid claim that in order to make meaningful lives for themselves in association with others, individuals must develop certain capacities, at least the capacity to conceive and to act on projects and values and the capacity to have an effective sense of justice. Although these capacities may not be particularly difficult to develop, some social conditions are required for their development, just as some social conditions are required for human beings to develop their natural capacity to learn to speak and understand a language. Moreover, Rawls's claim that some basic liberties are among the social conditions required for the development of the attributes of moral personality seems plausible. If we grant this claim for the sake of the argument, then Rawls's argument as a whole for the basic liberties principle has considerable force.

Still, that argument does not have quite the force Rawls claims for it. For

---

[37] "The principles of justice are also categorical imperatives" (Rawls, *Theory*, p. 253).

[38] Rawls, "Basic Liberties."

[39] For this argument see ibid., esp. secs. 5–8. The fullest account of Rawls's theory of moral personality is offered in "Kantian Constructivism," esp. the first lecture, "Rational and Full Autonomy," sec. 4.

the fact is that protection of the basic liberties is not the *only* social condition required for the members of a just society to develop the attributes of moral personality, regardless of the specific liberties that might happen to end up on our list of those we consider basic. Individuals must have care, at least when they are children, nourishment, perhaps some encouragement, a degree of security not only from violence but also from hunger and disease, and probably some other conditions as well. Rawls's argument suggests that *all* the conditions required to develop our capacities for agency and for a sense of justice should enjoy the same degree of protection, the same priority, as the conditions he calls the basic liberties. He offers no argument for his view that the basic liberties should be considered prior in importance to these other social conditions that individuals need to develop their capacities as agents with a sense of justice.

Rawls might respond by reminding us that the priority of the basic liberties is contingent on the presence of reasonably favorable conditions. But that response is a way of running around the problem rather than resolving it. For in effect it suggests that establishment of these favorable conditions has priority even over establishment and protection of the basic liberties themselves. What counts most fundamentally, according to this line of reasoning, is the establishment and protection both of those conditions *and* of the basic liberties. Though Rawls's claim for the priority of the basic liberties principle is not incorrect in a strict sense when his qualifications of that claim are taken into account, it *is* misleading to single out these liberties for prominent attention while merely gesturing toward other, vaguely identified social conditions that are required for the development of the attributes of moral personality.

Although this objection may seem to be merely a matter of emphasis, it is more than a quibble. For a political theory, as Rawls knows, is a practice. Theories *do* things. Rawls's claim for the priority of the basic liberties principle picks out the basic liberties for special attention and concern while relegating other conditions that are of at least equal importance for the development of agency and of a sense of justice to a barely recognized, dimly perceived background in our field of vision.

It is not difficult to grasp Rawls's motive for claiming special status for the basic liberties. That motive is clear in the opening paragraphs of *A Theory of Justice*, where Rawls asserts that "each person possesses an inviolability founded on justice that even the welfare of society as a whole cannot override."[40] In a just society, he continues, "the liberties of equal citizenship are taken as settled; the rights secured by justice are not subject to political bargaining or to the calculus of social interests."[41] Rawls believes that any

[40] Rawls, *Theory*, p. 3.
[41] Ibid., p. 4.

sound principles of justice must rule out the possibility, acceptable according to some forms of utilitarian theory, that some human beings might be
victimized or taken advantage of for the sake of securing greater happiness
for others.

Yet the priority Rawls claims for the basic liberties principle does too
much. If Rawls's argument that individuals must enjoy certain basic liberties
in order to develop their capacities for agency and for a sense of justice is
correct, then a powerful case can be made for the conclusion that protection
of basic liberties is *necessary* in any good society. But Rawls's arguments do
not support his claim that protection of these liberties is a matter of greater
priority—or urgency—than provision of the other social conditions required
for individuals to develop their capacities as moral persons.

IV

Rawls's second principle of justice states that social and economic inequalities should satisfy two conditions: first, they must be attached to offices and
positions open to all under conditions of fair equality of opportunity; and
second, they must be to the greatest expected benefit of the least advantaged
members of society. According to Rawls, this principle has lexical priority
over all other considerations we might want to take into account in comparing alternative political and social arrangements except the basic liberties
principle. Further, the first part of this principle, which I have called the
equal opportunity principle, has lexical priority over its second part, the
difference principle.

At first glance, the equal opportunity principle and the difference principle seem to be at loggerheads with each other. The first of these two parts of
Rawls's second principle insists on equality of *opportunity*. It states that
social and economic inequalities are justified if those inequalities are attached to offices and positions for which all members of society may compete on a footing of fair equality of opportunity. Clearly, though, the results
of such a competition for offices and positions will not be equal even if the
competition for them is fair. (The equal opportunity principle is after all
intended to justify inequalities.) Moreover, those results may not be beneficial to those who lose out in a fair competition. Those people just lose out.
The fact that they had a fair opportunity to compete for offices and positions
that would have enabled them to be better off does not make them actually
better off afterward.

The difference principle, however, focuses on *results* rather than opportunities. It states that inequalities are justified insofar as they work to the
greatest expected benefit of those who are least advantaged by those inequalities. While the difference principle, like the equal opportunity principle, is designed to justify inequalities, it does so on a basis that differs from

and is prima facie in conflict with the basis on which the equal opportunity principle justifies inequalities. The first of these two principles focuses on opportunities without regard to results, whereas the second focuses exclusively on those results.

Of course, the fact that Rawls stipulates that the equal opportunity principle is lexically prior to the difference principle suggests that these two principles cannot really be at odds with each other in his scheme of principles of justice as a whole. Lexical priority is supposed to specify the way in which the two principles apply in relation to each other. However, Rawls's discussions of this relation are in fact quite ambiguous. I shall accept Thomas Pogge's suggestion, which is based on a thorough discussion of the relation between the two parts of Rawls's second principle of justice, that the equal opportunity principle should be construed as a requirement of *formal* equality of opportunity, leaving the difference principle to do most of the real work of regulating inequalities.[42]

Assuming this interpretation of Rawls's second principle of justice, I see two main difficulties with that principle. The *first* has to do with the relation between individuals' needs, actions, and values on the one hand and their shares of primary goods on the other. One way to open up this difficulty is to focus on the notion of individual responsibility. A theory of the bases of social criticism that rests on the premise that individuals are free as well as equal beings, as Rawls's theory does, must take seriously the concept of individual responsibility. Rawls has argued vigorously that his theory does take individual responsibility seriously. In fact the emphasis he places on individual responsibility can be seen as a significant advantage of his theory over utilitarian theories. Some utilitarian theories treat individuals' desires or preferences as given, or as exogenous to the theory. But this approach gives rise to the well-known problem of expensive tastes. Suppose a utilitarian-inspired theory were to stipulate that all individuals should have their desires equally satisfied or achieve equally blissful mental states. Then if people's desires are unequal, they will need *unequal* amounts of resources to achieve *equal* degrees of satisfaction or happiness.[43] In Rawls's view, though, individuals are responsible for their preferences and tastes. It would be unfair for some individuals to receive greater resources than others in order to

---

[42] Pogge distinguishes four possible interpretations of the relation between the two parts of Rawls's second principle of justice in *Realizing Rawls*, chap. 4, and identifies the interpretation on which I draw as the most satisfactory. It is noteworthy that in *Theory* Rawls made the difference principle the first part of his second principle of justice, placing it ahead of the equal opportunity principle. Although he has reversed this order in more recent statements of the principles of justice as fairness, he still devotes far more discussion to the difference principle than to the principle of equal opportunity.

[43] I discuss this problem very briefly in the opening section of chap. 5. For a full-length discussion, see Ronald Dworkin's "What Is Equality? Part 1: Equality of Welfare," *Philosophy and Public Affairs* 10, no. 3 (1981): 185–246.

enable them, with their expensive tastes, to achieve a level of satisfaction equivalent to that achieved by others who have less expensive tastes. If some individuals want to cultivate expensive tastes, they may do so, in Rawls's view, but they must accept the consequences of their tastes, namely the prospect that those tastes may be much harder to satisfy than more modest preferences would be, so that they may consequently find themselves more frustrated than others.

So individual responsibility is an important theme in Rawls's theory, one that plays a key role in determining the structure of that theory as a whole. Yet if we interpret Rawls's second principle of justice in a way that leaves the difference principle to do most of the important work, it appears that in a perfectly just society of justice as fairness there would be no relation between individuals' needs or actions on the one hand and the minimum shares of primary goods to which they would be entitled on the other. That share would be determined by the difference principle, which states that the shares of primary goods enjoyed by those individuals who are least advantaged should be maximized, apparently without regard for their actions or needs.

Suppose now that we are considering alternative social arrangements for a society that happens to be quite wealthy. The set of arrangements we would choose if we were to apply Rawls's two principles of justice would guarantee a high income for every member of the society, including those who engage in little or no productive activity, some of whom are perfectly able to do so. The society is sufficiently wealthy to make this kind of provision for even its least advantaged members. In effect these individuals would receive a gift from the society as a whole and would not be held responsible for providing anything in return, even if they were able to. This seems to me to be an unwelcome implication of Rawls's difference principle.

A defender of the difference principle could produce two responses to this objection. First, she might point out that Rawls's entire theory of justice presupposes circumstances of moderate scarcity, whereas I am applying the principles of that theory inappropriately to a society that enjoys circumstances of abundance. Yet, as Rawls has emphasized in his more recent writings, moderate scarcity can be caused by subjective as well as by objective factors. Even if our society were wealthy enough for us to teach all children Japanese *and* provide the resources needed by handicapped people to be as physically mobile as those who are not handicapped, you and I would probably find other uses to which we would want to put our society's resources, and our ideas about this subject would not always converge. Because the circumstances of justice are subjective as well as objective in origin, even a wealthy society is likely to be a society of moderate scarcity by Rawls's definition.

Second, a defender of the difference principle might call attention to the fact that the implication of the difference principle I have suggested violates the spirit of Rawls's theory. At the heart of that theory is an idea of reciprocity. Rawls's view is that free and equal persons can accept the fact that inequalities are deeply influenced by contingencies if and insofar as the inequalities in question result in improvements for all, including the least advantaged members of society.

I agree that this implication violates the spirit of Rawls's theory. In fact that is my point. I endorse the spirit of Rawls's theory. The idea of generalized reciprocity of which that theory is an elaboration is a powerful basis for a theory of distributive justice. The problem is that the difference principle expresses that idea in a defective way.[44]

Of course, if we isolate the difference principle from the other principles of justice as fairness and apply it directly to a decidedly nonideal society such as the United States in the 1990s, powerful arguments that appear to work in favor of that principle can be made. The circumstances of the least advantaged members of American society are appallingly poor. Our social arrangements fail to provide many individuals with basic nutritional, medical, and housing needs. In some instances they barely gesture in the direction of providing those individuals with the educational resources that would be required to ensure fair equality of opportunity. Political decisions are notoriously subject to undue influence by those who possess disproportionate shares of financial and other resources. Many individuals are denied the means necessary to participate on an equal footing with others in political affairs. No doubt many of Rawls's readers have interpreted his difference principle in light of their awareness of these problems and have thereby been led to regard it as a sorely needed call for their rectification.

In fact Rawls's difference principle does not address *these* circumstances in *this* nonideal society at all. For these circumstances are clearly at odds with the first principle of justice, which provides, among other things, that individuals should enjoy the political liberties and that the value of those liberties to all citizens should be equal. Rawls presents the difference principle as a criterion for evaluating proposed social arrangements that already satisfy this first principle. The social arrangements that currently prevail in our nonideal society do not meet this test.[45]

[44] For a similar conclusion about the defects of the difference principle reached by a different route, see Will Kymlicka's excellent discussion in *Contemporary Political Philosophy: An Introduction* (Oxford: Clarendon Press, 1990), chap. 3.

[45] The unequal value of the political liberties is illustrated by Robert Dahl's comment, made in the mid-1950s, that "I suppose that it would be no exaggeration to say that Mr. Henry Luce [the publisher of *Time* magazine] has a thousand or ten thousand times greater control over the alternatives scheduled for debate and tentative decision at a national election than I do" (*A Preface to Democratic Theory* [Chicago: University of Chicago Press, 1956], pp. 72–73). The power of the national media in the United States has not declined perceptibly in the past forty years.

Rawls argues in favor of the difference principle by asking, By what principle can free and equal moral persons accept the fact that inequalities are deeply influenced by contingencies?[46] His answer is that this fact is acceptable as long as the inequalities in question result in improvements for all, including the least advantaged members of society. This reasoning leads him to believe that the difference principle would be included among the principles of justice that would be chosen by individuals in the original position. But Rawls's reasoning neglects the idea of reciprocity that is the very basis of his theory. The notion of generalized reciprocity provides that individuals' *needs* should be met on the assumption that those individuals are, or at some time have been or may be, contributing members of society. This notion does not suggest that individuals should have shares of means to provide for their *wants* that are stipulated without regard for their actions or their contributions to the society. Yet that is what the difference principle seems to suggest.

I am not suggesting that the contribution principle, according to which each person should receive from society resources equivalent in value to the contribution that person makes to society, should be adopted or regarded as a basic principle of distributive justice.[47] That suggestion would reflect a rigid, case-by-case view of reciprocity rather than the *generalized* reciprocity that is in the spirit of Rawls's theory. I do think, though, that a set of principles to regulate the distribution of resources to members of a society should incorporate *some* relation between contribution and reward for those who are clearly in a position to contribute. Even generalized reciprocity works both ways, from individual to others (or to "society") as well as from society to individual.

The principles of distributive justice that prevail in a good society would ensure that every member of that society has adequate means to provide for her genuine needs. On this point Rawls and I agree. But Rawls's difference principle does not say merely that we should make sure everyone's needs are met. It says that the shares of primary goods enjoyed by those who are least well off should be maximized without regard for differences in people's needs, actions, or values. That prescription is a distortion of the idea of generalized reciprocity on which Rawls's theory is based.

The *second* troubling feature of Rawls's second principle of justice has to do with the maximizing implications of the difference principle. That principle states that social and economic inequalities are justified if those inequalities benefit the least advantaged members of society. An implication of this principle is that if we are in a position to choose between two alternative sets of institutions for our society, both of which satisfy the basic liberties principle, we should choose those institutions that would leave those who are least

---

[46] I have paraphrased the question as Rawls frames it in "Basic Structure," p. 64.

[47] Rawls discusses and rejects the contribution principle in *Theory*, pp. 303–10.

advantaged (where advantage is measured by an index of primary goods) in the best position. We should, in other words, maximize the shares of primary goods enjoyed by those who are least advantaged, those who are (or will be) at the minimum position in our society.

This feature of the difference principle is troubling because maximizing rules are so demanding. That is one reason why Rawls reformulated his basic liberties principle. His original formulation of that principle (in *A Theory of Justice*) was a maximizing formulation. It stated that "each person is to have an equal right to the *most extensive* total system of equal basic liberties compatible with a similar system of liberty for all."[48] Strictly applied, this principle would have had libertarian or quasi-libertarian implications and would have left little, if any, room for the second principle of justice to come into play. Since Rawls stipulated that the basic liberties principle is to take lexical priority over the second principle of justice, that first principle would have to have been satisfied fully before the second principle could come into play. But a maximizing principle cannot really be satisfied fully. Unless two alternative proposals for the structure of institutions and practices in a society happen to have *identical* implications for the extent of liberty, the choice between them would have to be determined by the basic liberties principle alone, given its original formulation. Hence Rawls's decision to scrap the phrase "most extensive" in favor of "fully adequate."[49]

Yet a difficulty similar to that which was raised by Rawls's initial, now discarded, formulation of the basic liberties principle is created by his current formulation of the difference principle, which Rawls has not changed significantly since the publication of *A Theory of Justice* in 1971. Since the difference principle tells us that we must maximize the position of the least advantaged members of society, as measured in shares of primary goods, that principle, strictly applied, would leave little or no room for any other variables to come into play in our choice of social arrangements (other than the basic liberties principle, which takes priority over the second principle of justice). If we were to apply Rawls's principles of justice strictly, those principles would yield a strong ordering of all possible alternative social arrangements. That is, they would yield an ordinal ranking of alternatives in which two alternatives never (or rarely) occupy the same rank.

A strong ordering is too strong a result for a liberal political theory to yield.[50] In a liberal society, individuals will formulate diverse projects and values. In pursuing those projects and attempting to realize those values, those individuals will generate a unique social world. But a strong ordering

---

[48] Ibid., p. 302, emphasis added.

[49] Rawls's formulation of the basic liberties principles in recent writings, recall, has been: "Each person has an equal right to a *fully adequate* scheme of equal basic liberties which is compatible with a similar scheme of liberties for all" (*Political Liberalism*, p. 291, emphasis added).

[50] See chap. 1, sec. II herein.

would rank the different social worlds that might be generated in this way; it would identify some of these social worlds as better than others. So an ordering of this kind would in practice impose strict limits on the projects and values that individuals could pursue. Only those pursuits that would lead to a social world in which the position of the least advantaged is maximized would be permissible.

This implication is incompatible with liberal principles. If we endorse the idea that human beings have the capacity to be agents and should be free to pursue diverse projects and to create and attempt to adhere to a range of different values—an idea that is fundamental to liberal political theory—then we have to accept the conclusion that a liberal political theory should yield an ordering of alternative social arrangements of only moderate strength. In a liberal political theory, the point of a conception of political health is to help us to determine whether a political community is healthy or not. We need only a rough classification of alternative regimes, not the strong ordering of alternatives the difference principle would produce.

Notice that the problem with the difference principle is *not* that it is a "patterned" principle of distributive justice, to use Nozick's useful term. Patterned end-state principles of distributive justice do not necessarily produce strong orderings and are not inherently inimical to pluralism. *Maximizing* principles *do* produce strong orderings, however, and so are inherently antipluralistic.[51]

Rawls does not intend the difference principle to have antipluralistic implications. Rawls is a liberal theorist, and one of his foremost concerns is to formulate principles of justice that will protect individuals' freedom to pursue diverse projects and to conceive and try to realize diverse values. Recognition of the fact that people's conceptions of the good are irreducibly plural has been one of the principal anchors for the theory of justice as fairness from the beginning and is the key idea of political liberalism as Rawls conceives it. Moreover, Rawls plainly believes that his principles of justice, taken as a whole, are consistent with a range of possible, equally just arrangements.[52] But Rawls's intentions and beliefs are not the point. The fact is that the difference principle, taken literally, is incompatible with those intentions, just as the basic liberties principle was in its original form. The difference principle should be replaced with a principle that stipulates that all members of society, including the least advantaged, should receive *adequate shares* of resources instead of providing that the shares of the least well off should be maximized.

---

[51] Although I think the reasons they give for rejecting the difference principle are flawed, then, I agree with Nozick and Walzer that that principle as Rawls formulates it should be rejected. See Nozick, *Anarchy*, pp. 153–74, and Walzer, *Spheres of Justice: A Defense of Pluralism and Equality* (New York: Basic Books, 1983), pp. xv, 14–16.

[52] In *Theory*, chap. 5, Rawls argues that the principles of justice as fairness could be satisfied either by a property-owning democracy or by a liberal socialist regime.

V

I now turn to Rawls's theory of primary goods. Rawls argues that in a just society, shares of primary goods would constitute the basis on which individuals' relative positions in society would be compared. Even if we were to reject the two principles of justice as fairness altogether, this argument would constitute a significant claim. The main types of primary goods that Rawls identifies are basic rights and liberties, freedom of movement and free choice of occupation from among diverse opportunities, offices and positions of responsibility, income and wealth, and the social bases of self-respect. Rawls leaves open the possibility that we might add to this list if necessary.[53]

The point of departure of Rawls's argument for the primary goods is the observation that individuals' ends are diverse. People conceive and choose to pursue different values and projects. Typically these values and projects conflict with one another. I want children to learn Japanese in school, whereas you want disabled persons to have the same freedom of movement enjoyed by those who are not disabled. Further, according to Rawls these projects and values (or conceptions of the good) typically are incommensurable with one another. *I* know how much value *I* place on freedom of movement for the disabled and how much I place on children's learning Japanese, and *you* know how much value *you* place on these two things, but no common measure on which we might reconcile our differing valuations exists. Because our ends are diverse, and because no definitive yardstick for comparing the relative values of their attainment or partial attainment exists, it makes sense, in Rawls's view, to compare the shares of *resources* available to us to pursue those ends. Rawls's thought is that roughly the same resources can be used to pursue a wide variety of different ends. The primary goods are the resources to which individuals have access as means to pursue their ends.

Since the late 1970s, Rawls's theory of primary goods has been subject to a critique led by Amartya Sen. We may identify the strengths and weaknesses of Rawls's concept of primary goods by considering Sen's important objections.

The point of departure for Sen's critique is the observation that just as individuals' *ends* are diverse, so do individual *needs* differ from one person to the next. People whose needs differ will need *different* resources to attain the *same* ends. For example, if I am deprived of the use of my legs because of a disability, I will need greater resources than a person whose legs function normally to achieve the same degree of physical mobility. Or if I have a kidney problem and need to use a dialysis machine to function normally, I will need greater resources to function normally than a person who does

---

[53] Rawls, *Political Liberalism*, p. 181.

not need kidney dialysis. A disabled person cannot function in the same way as an able-bodied person with the same resources. So according to Sen, Rawls's claim that the relative positions of different people can best be compared by examining the shares of resources available to them is defective.

Sen broadens his point by suggesting that there are in general two sources of variation in the relation between a person's means or resources (primary goods) and the ends that person is able to achieve.[54] One is *inter-end* variation. Inter-end variation is just the diversity of people's projects and values (conceptions of the good, in Rawls's terms). The other is *inter-individual* variation. Inter-individual variation is the diversity of people's needs and abilities to achieve ends. In Sen's view, Rawls's theory of primary goods takes inter-end variation fully into account but neglects inter-individual variation.

Sen argues that inter-individual variation is a problem with more than just hard cases, such as the case of a person whose legs are disabled or that of the kidney dialysis patient.[55] Human diversity is ubiquitous and fundamental. Different people have different needs and different abilities to use resources to achieve ends depending on age, sex, mental and physical abilities, and even body size (which affects nutritional and medical requirements). This diversity means that there can be significant variations among different individuals' abilities to convert resources into achievements, even among people who do not have special disabilities or handicaps.[56] So in Sen's view, we cannot solve the problem of inter-individual variation by treating the cases of people with disabilities or handicaps as exceptions for which adjustments can be made after a theory based on the idea of primary goods has been put into place, as Rawls has suggested.[57] According to Sen, "Human diversity is no secondary complication (to be ignored, or to be introduced 'later on'); it is a fundamental aspect of our interest in equality."[58]

The obvious question raised by Sen's critique is, What is the alternative to the primary goods approach to the comparison of different individuals' relative positions? *What should we count*, if not primary goods or resources? Like Rawls, Sen rejects the utilitarian view that what counts is individual utility defined as attainment of some mental state, such as the state of happiness or the satisfaction of desires.[59] That view, as Sen puts it, focuses only on

---

[54] Sen, *Inequality Reexamined* (Cambridge, Mass.: Harvard University Press, 1992), p. 85.

[55] Sen, "Equality of What?" in *The Tanner Lectures on Human Values*, ed. S. M. McMurrin (Salt Lake City: University of Utah Press, 1980), pp. 157f., and *Inequality Reexamined*, pp. xi, 19–21.

[56] Sen, *Inequality Reexamined*, p. 19n and p. 33.

[57] Rawls suggests that these are "hard cases" that "distract our moral perception by leading us to think of people distant from us whose fate arouses pity and anxiety" ("A Kantian Conception of Equality," p. 96).

[58] Sen, *Inequality Reexamined*, p. xi.

[59] Ibid., pp. 53–55.

achievements and disregards freedom.[60] But in Sen's view the freedom to pursue objectives is itself valuable, distinctly from and in addition to the attainment of those objectives. So the utilitarian (or welfarist, as Sen calls it) approach cannot be accepted. However, Sen also rejects the resources approach represented by Rawls's theory of primary goods.[61] For that approach, according to Sen, focuses only on *means* and disregards differences that arise because of inter-individual variation in individuals' abilities to attain ends they value.

Sen calls his own proposal the *capabilities* approach. According to him, this approach focuses on the *extent* of freedom rather than just on the *means* to freedom.[62] The extent of a person's freedom is a function of her "capability set."[63] Sen describes a person's capability set as the set of "functionings" she is in a position to achieve, given the resources available to her and her needs and physical and mental abilities. A functioning can be anything from a basic attainment such as being well nourished, being in good health, or avoiding premature mortality to more complex achievements such as being happy, having self-respect, taking part in the life of one's community, and so on.[64] In general, functionings are real-world states (or states of being) that a person has reason to value. The extent of a person's freedom, then, is just the size of her capability set, that is, of the set of functionings she is in a position to achieve. Of course, "size" in this context should not be conceived in too simplistic a way. Functionings can be weighted for their values, so that having a particularly valuable functioning, such as having self-respect, in one's capability set counts for more than having two or more relatively trivial functionings in that set. So the extent of a person's freedom is the size of her capability set where that size is determined by the sum of the functionings in that set weighted by their relative values.

Sen's point, then, is that statements about and comparisons of individuals' positions—the "deals" they receive—should be based on their capability

---

[60] I agree with Rawls and Sen in rejecting the utilitarian view, but I would put the point in a different way. In my view one problem with utilitarian theory is that it fails to take seriously the idea that human beings are capable of being *agents* who conceive values and projects that are not necessarily about, or do not necessarily focus on, their own experiences. This point constitutes a critique of classical utilitarianism and all forms of utilitarianism in which the attainment of mental states is the variable of central importance, but it does not necessarily apply to desire-fulfillment versions of utilitarian theory, such as the view for which James Griffin argues in *Well-Being*. Sen is not convinced that the desire-fulfillment view is as distinct from the mental-state view of classical utilitarianism as Griffin claims; see *Inequality Reexamined*, pp. 53–54. Utilitarianism also raises the important problem of expensive tastes, which I discuss briefly in chap. 5.

[61] And by Dworkin's theory of equality of resources. See his "What is Equality? Part II: Equality of Resources," *Philosophy and Public Affairs* 10 (1981): 283–345.

[62] Sen, *Inequality Reexamined*, p. 34.

[63] Ibid., pp. 33–34, 40.

[64] Ibid., p. 39.

sets, not on their shares of resources. According to Sen, the importance of resources is derivative: we value resources because we can convert them into the fulfillment of goals or into the freedom to pursue those goals.[65] Of course we can expect there to be a positive relation between individuals' shares of resources and their capability sets, since in general people can achieve more things with greater resources than with less. But a person's capability set is a product of her needs and abilities as well as of her resources. In evaluating the kinds of deals individuals receive, we must take inter-individual variations into account.

Now, Rawls has suggested that Sen's objection to the idea of primary goods is misconceived. He concedes that the importance of primary goods (resources) is derivative but points out that "an index of primary goods is not intended as an approximation to what is ultimately important as specified by any particular comprehensive doctrine with its account of moral values."[66] In reply, Sen argues that "a disadvantaged person may get less from primary goods than others *no matter what comprehensive doctrine* he or she has."[67] As Sen sees it, his objection to Rawls's idea of primary goods does not presuppose a particular comprehensive conception of the good, contrary to Rawls's perception.

Sen offer the following example to illustrate his point.[68] Consider persons 1 and 2. Person 2 is disadvantaged in some respect, for example, is physically disabled. Persons 1 and 2 do not have the same comprehensive conception of the good. Person 1 values A more than B, whereas person 2 values B more than A. Both person 1 and person 2 value 2A more than A and 2B more than B, so that overall their orderings of these goods (which represent the relevant parts of their respective comprehensive conceptions of the good) are as follows:

Person 1	Person 2
2A	2B
2B	2A
A	B
B	A

Now suppose that with a given share of primary goods, person 1 can achieve any member of this set of goods: 2A, 2B, A, or B. Because of her disability, however, person 2, with the same primary goods, can achieve only A or B. Person 1 proceeds to achieve 2A, her most highly preferred outcome, whereas person 2 has to settle for B, which is the best feasible outcome for

[65] Ibid., p. 19 n. 20.

[66] Rawls, "Priority of Right," p. 259. See also Rawls's expanded response to Sen's objection in the revision of this essay in *Political Liberalism*, pp. 182–86.

[67] Sen, *Inequality Reexamined*, p. 83.

[68] Ibid., pp. 83–84.

her but not the outcome she would most prefer. In this scenario, as Sen points out, person 2 is at a disadvantage regardless of her comprehensive conception of the good, that is, whether she adheres to her comprehensive conception or to person 2's conception of the good. Contrary to Rawls's assumption, Sen's objection does not presuppose any *particular* comprehensive conception of the good.

Sen is correct in suggesting that his *objection* to Rawls's theory of primary goods does not presuppose a particular comprehensive conception of the good, but his *alternative* to that theory—the capabilities view—cannot be made to do the work Sen wants it to do without presupposing some particular conception of the good. The capabilities view, remember, is the proposal that what counts is the extent of freedom as determined by one's capability set, which consists of the various functionings one is in a position to attain, weighted for their values. Consider the following example. Both person X and person Y value the functionings A, B, C, D, and E. Person X ranks these functionings in alphabetical order, from A to E. Person Y values them in the order C, D, E, A, B. Both person X and person Y assign a numerical value to each functioning, so that the most valuable functioning is given a value of 5 while the least valuable has a value of 1. So the orderings and valuations of the five functionings given by person X and person Y are as follows:

Person X	Person Y
A (5)	C (5)
B (4)	D (4)
C (3)	E (3)
D (2)	A (2)
E (1)	B (1)

Person X and person Y live in a world of moderate scarcity. So they cannot achieve all five functionings. However, person X's capabilities are equivalent to person Y's. In other words, given their resources plus their mental and physical abilities, person X and person Y are able to achieve the same things. *Both* person X and person Y may choose *either* the set (A, B, C) *or* the set (D, E).

If person X chooses the set (A, B, C), the value to her of that set of functionings is $5 + 4 + 3 = 12$. If she chooses set (D, E), the value to her is $2 + 1 = 3$. If person Y chooses set (A, B, C), the value to her is $1 + 2 + 5 = 8$; if she chooses set (D, E), the value to her is $4 + 3 = 7$. Both person X and person Y are able to achieve the same functionings. But the value to person X of her best choice is 12, whereas the value to person Y of her best choice is only 8. If the extent of freedom is a product of the set of functionings that a person is able to achieve weighted for their values, then the extent of person X's freedom is considerably greater than the extent of person Y's freedom, *despite the fact that person Y's capability set is identical to person X's.*

Sen is able to equate the capability set with the extent of freedom only by tacitly assuming that individuals assign roughly the same values to the same functionings—that is, by presupposing what Rawls calls a monistic conception of the good. This assumption seems plausible in many of the cases he considers because Sen focuses almost exclusively on a specific class of "functionings," namely those that are directly related to well-being or "well-being freedom," that is, the freedom individuals have to pursue their well-being. It seems reasonable to suppose that most people value the functionings closely related to well-being, such as being adequately nourished, being in good health, avoiding premature mortality, and so on in roughly the same way. However, once we move away from functionings closely related to well-being toward the other sorts of projects and values people wish to pursue, this rough similarity among different individuals' ends breaks down.[69] So even though Sen's objection to Rawls's theory of primary goods does not presuppose a particular conception of the good, his alternative to that theory, the capabilities view, does tacitly presuppose something like a particular (and monistic) conception of the good. Without that assumption, the idea of equating the extent of a person's freedom with her capability set does not work.

There are two further difficulties with Sen's proposal, both of which are quite serious. The first is that it does not seem possible even to *fill in* the idea of a capability set, let alone equate that set with the extent of freedom. Even people with virtually identical resources plus needs and physical and mental abilities may discover quite different things to do with these resources and abilities, things that cannot be foreseen by a theorist attempting to analyze their positions or the extent of their freedom. Given a few sticks of wood, some cloth material, and various mechanical parts, the best that one person may be able to do is to build a makeshift hut. But another may discover how to construct a flying machine. The first person may be as industrious, intelligent, and imaginative as the second; it just did not occur to him to use the materials at his disposal to make a flying machine. After the fact, we can see that making a flying machine was one of the functionings in both people's capability set. Before the fact, though, we could not have foreseen that functioning.

The second problem is that the difficulties of collecting data relevant to determining the composition of individuals' capability sets are so formidable that the entire proposal is probably unworkable. Sen is aware of this problem. He concedes that "when the data simply do not exist to calculate the

---

[69] The most relevant discussion in Sen's writings to this point is in ibid., chap. 4.

extents of the respective capability sets, there is no option but to settle for the chosen functioning combination as the basis for forming a view of the opportunities that were actually enjoyed."[70] This concession understates the problem. In general, sufficient data exist to calculate the extent of people's capability sets only in artificial situations—situations imagined by a theorist, that is—or in exceptionally constrained real-life situations, such as situations of considerable deprivation or poverty in which people's capability sets are relatively small and the bulk of people's efforts go into providing for their basic needs. These situations are of great importance, of course,[71] but they are not a useful basis for the construction of theories intended to apply to situations of *moderate* scarcity. In situations of this latter type, in which individuals conceive values and pursue projects that go well beyond provision for their basic needs, estimations of people's capability sets are impossible to make in practice.

Sen's capabilities view, then, does not seem to be a promising alternative to Rawls's theory of primary goods. If Rawls neglects what Sen calls interindividual variation, then Sen neglects inter-end variation, despite his protestations to the contrary. Or to put the point a different way: Sen fails to take seriously enough the idea that human beings are capable of being agents, beings who are able to conceive a wide and unpredictable variety of projects and values and who can use their imaginations to do unforeseen and unforeseeable things. Contrary to Sen's suggestion, if we accept the fact of reasonable value pluralism, as Rawls calls it (or inter-end variation, to use Sen's term), it does *not* seem possible to get beyond means, as Sen wants to do. On this general point, Rawls's notion of primary goods holds up quite well to Sen's critique.

Nevertheless, the fact that Sen's capabilities view does not seem to be a plausible alternative to the theory of primary goods does not mean that his objection to Rawls's theory should be dismissed. That objection makes an important point, namely that variations in individuals' mental and physical capabilities should somehow be taken into account. Rawls has argued in response to Sen's critique that as long as everyone has the capacity to be a "normal cooperating member of society," variations among individuals should be ignored, and that the problem of people who do not have this capacity can be dealt with through special provisions for health care with the aim of restoring people so that once again they can be fully cooperating members of society.[72] But this suggestion does not seem to take Sen's point seriously enough, in part because many people may not have the potential

[70] Ibid., p. 135.

[71] They are also the situations with which Sen has been most concerned in his substantive work, which has focused on poverty and famines.

[72] Rawls, *Political Liberalism*, p. 184.

to become fully cooperating members of society and in part because there is so much variation in abilities *within* the class of people who *do* have the capacity to be normal cooperating members of society. Sen's critique suggests that Rawls's account of the primary goods should be modified, but it does not establish the capabilities view as a credible alternative.[73]

VI

Before going on let us review briefly the main points I have sought to make about Rawls's account of the bases of political criticism.

The principal substantive conclusions of Rawls's account of the bases of political criticism are, first, that the members of a just society would be moral persons, that is, agents with a sense of justice; second, that the basic structure of such a society would be regulated by the basic liberties principle, the equal opportunity principle, and the difference principle; and third, that individuals' positions would be compared with one another on the basis of their shares of primary goods.

As we have seen, the case for the first of these conclusions is quite strong. I cannot imagine a good (or just) society whose members are not agents, beings who are capable of formulating and trying to realize projects and values. Nor can I imagine a good society whose members do not have a sense of justice. I have quibbles with the precise way in which Rawls describes the two attributes of moral persons, but the main thrust of this claim seems to be on target.

The case for Rawls's second conclusion—that the basic structure of a perfectly just society would be regulated by the principles of justice as fairness—is more mixed. Some basic liberties are necessary for the development and exercise of human beings' capacities as agents with a sense of justice, so to that extent the first principle of justice as fairness seems sound enough. But Rawls has not been able to formulate a good argument for the priority of this principle, and I do not think a convincing argument for that conclusion can be made. The second principle of justice is even more problematic. The difference principle, which appears to be the core of Rawls's second principle of justice, is, if strictly construed, a maximizing principle. As such, it is incompatible with the pluralistic intentions of Rawls's theory—intentions with which I am in full agreement. On the other hand, *some* pat-

---

[73] Similar, though not identical, objections apply to Martha C. Nussbaum's version of the capabilities view. For one recent statement of this view, see Nussbaum, "Human Functioning and Social Justice: In Defense of Aristotelian Essentialism," *Political Theory* 20 (1992): 202–46. For a general statement that deals sympathetically with both Sen's and Nussbaum's views, see David A. Crocker, "Functioning and Capability: The Foundations of Sen's and Nussbaum's Development Ethic," ibid., pp. 584–612.

terned principle to regulate the distribution of resources in society seems appropriate in light of the liberal assumption that human beings should be able to construct meaningful lives for themselves.

The case for Rawls's third conclusion, that individuals' positions should be compared on the basis of their shares of primary goods, is again reasonably strong, though some modification of Rawls's account of the primary goods is needed. Sen's objection to the idea of primary goods identifies an important weakness in Rawls's particular account of those goods. But Sen's own proposal that we should compare individuals' positions on the basis of the *extent* of their freedom rather than by the *means* available to them does not seem workable in light of the diversity of individuals' values and ends. We should aim for an account that focuses on means, as Rawls's does, even if Rawls's own account stands in need of modification.

CHAPTER FIVE

Humanist Liberalism

RAWLS'S POLITICAL LIBERALISM focuses attention on the fact that human beings reasonably conceive diverse and conflicting values and projects, or
"comprehensive doctrines with their conceptions of the good,"[1] as he prefers
to put it. Yet recognition of this fact runs through the family of liberal political theories as a whole instead of being distinctive to Rawls. The assumption
of reasonable value pluralism, as I have called it, is a pragmatic implication
of the more fundamental liberal premise that human beings are agents, beings who conceive values and formulate plans, including plans that involve
states of the world that are not related to their own experience. According to
liberal theories, human beings should count equally as agents and not
merely as sentient beings. A central implication of this claim is that an account of the bases of political and social criticism should accommodate, insofar as it is possible to do so from a general point of view, individuals' diverse
and conflicting values.

In this chapter I develop the idea that human beings should count equally
as agents into an account of the bases of political and social criticism that
differs significantly from Rawls's theory as well as from the works in the
other genres of liberal theory that I have examined. Like Rawls, I assume
that human beings reasonably conceive diverse values. I also focus, as he
does, on means. In many other respects, though, the picture of liberal political theory that I shall describe here casts liberalism in different colors from
those used to compose the theories I have examined up to this point.

The account of the normative bases of political criticism I offer here is
rough and rudimentary. It would have to be developed and refined in many
respects in order to assume the form of a complete political theory. Like
Nozick, however, I think it would be unreasonable to demand that new
theories be presented only after all the important questions they raise have
been answered. What follows is a sketch of a plausible alternative, which I
believe helps to highlight the inadequacies of the best existing theories
while also taking advantage of those theories' strengths. I hope this sketch
will help us to begin progressing toward a better theory, one to which we
might apply the label *humanist liberalism*.

At the focus of my argument is the claim that *we human beings have a
generalizable interest in having the means necessary to pursue the projects*

---

[1] Rawls, *Political Liberalism* (New York: Columbia University Press, 1993), p. 135.

we formulate and to try to realize the values we conceive—the means, that is, to shape at least some part of our world in ways that will give our lives meaning for us. We need these means to be effective agents. This claim, I suggest, provides a point of reference around which the other features that constitute a full picture of liberal theory should be grouped. We must return to it frequently to maintain an appropriate perspective on these features and the questions they raise.

In order to protect their interest in having the means necessary to try to realize their values, individuals need rights. Yet the foundation of liberal political theory is not the idea of individual rights but rather the idea of individuals' generalizable interest in having the means to pursue their diverse and conflicting values and projects. The notion that we could construct a complete account of the bases of social criticism by multiplying rights is bound to fail.[2] Perfectionist liberalism adds an essential element to this rights-based strategy of liberal argument by identifying our generalizable human interest in developing the capacities that enable us to be agents and to have an effective sense of justice, without which human beings could not construct meaningful lives for themselves in association with other human beings. But the perfectionist strategy of argument places more weight on the idea of individual autonomy than that idea is capable of bearing and insists on an interpretation of the idea of individual autonomy that is too strong to be supported by liberal premises. Although it is true that values and projects that are formulated under circumstances of coercion or misinformation and those that are distorted by inferential errors or other cognitive defects do not have the same standing as values formulated in the absence of these distorting influences, the view that only those values and projects that result from a process of reflective self-evaluation "really count," or that a life lived in any way other than that of reflective self-direction is inferior, conflicts with the assumption of reasonable value pluralism.

Rawls's political liberalism of justice as fairness assigns a central role to basic individual rights and incorporates some of the strongest points made by perfectionist liberals in the form of the idea of a moral person, a person with the capacity for a conception of the good and the capacity for a sense of justice. Rawls also adds to the picture an extensive discussion of resources in the form of his theory of primary goods and his account of the principles regulating their distribution. But Rawls's theory, as we have seen, stands in need of reconstruction. That theory correctly identifies the need for basic liberties, but it exaggerates their importance; it offers an account of primary goods that is seriously incomplete; and it proposes distributive principles that, strictly construed, are inconsistent with the notion of generalized reci-

---

[2] As Michael Walzer suggests in *Spheres of Justice: A Defense of Pluralism and Equality* (New York: Basic Books, 1983), p. xv, and as I argue in chap. 2.

procity on which the theory is based and are incompatible with Rawls's own pluralistic intentions.

In this chapter I shall reconstruct Rawls's theory of primary goods as the core element in an account of the bases of political and social criticism. Since I am using Rawls's theory as the point of departure for developing my own account, it may be useful to point out in advance some of the ways in which my account will differ from his.

First, I amend Rawls's list of the primary goods. I shall argue that although that list may be a good beginning, it must be reshaped if we are going to use it to develop an account of the bases of political and social criticism. I shall argue in section I that we should add individuals' physical and mental powers to the list of primary goods. In section II I shall argue that we should also revise the list Rawls offers by the addition of status and recognition as primary goods or basic means people need to be effective agents. To avoid confusion, I shall call the list of goods people need that emerges from these revisions an account of the *basic means* we require to be effective agents. A person's share of these basic means determines what might be called her *agency prospects*, that is, her prospects for acting in an effective way to realize her values.

Second, these basic means occupy the central position in the account of the bases of political criticism that I shall offer here. In Rawls's theory, of course, the central purpose of the notion of primary goods is to serve as a metric by which we can compare the relative advantages of individuals for the purpose of applying the second principle of justice as fairness. In my account, though, the basic means serve as a general account of the means that individuals need to pursue the projects they formulate and to try to realize the values they conceive. Rather than single out rights and liberties for special treatment by *both* including them among the primary goods *and* formulating a separate principle of protection for them—in effect counting rights and liberties twice—I treat rights and liberties as basic means much like any others. Rights and liberties are essential means that individuals need to be effective agents, but they need not be given priority over all other means.

Third, I argue that in order to develop a plausible account of the bases of political criticism, we must distinguish between basic means that differ in kind. In general, goods are diverse. The basic means are no exception. I argue (in section III) that we cannot just lump the basic means together without first asking what parts these diverse means play in relation to one another in enabling people to be effective agents.

Fourth, I maintain (in section IV) that qualitatively different basic means should be distributed in different ways. Rather than apply a single, relatively simple principle, such as the difference principle, to all the basic means, I suggest that each good on the list of basic means should be examined to determine an appropriate distribution for that good. The appropriate distributions of different goods conform to some general principles, but these goods should not all be distributed in the same way.

Like Rawls, I rely on the notion of generalized reciprocity as a frame within which to compose my account. My project might also be seen as an attempt to interpret and to modify two well-known formulas in Marx's work. In the first, which is contained in the *Manifesto of the Communist Party*, Marx and Engels envisage "an association, in which the free development of each is the condition for the free development of all."[3] In the second, from his much later *Critique of the Gotha Program*, Marx imagines a communist society regulated by the prescription "From each according to his ability, to each according to his needs!"[4]

Suitably qualified, Marx's formulas are consistent with the interpretation I shall develop presently of the liberal premises that only individuals count, that all individuals count equally, and that all individuals count as agents. Marx and some (not all) of his followers part ways with liberalism not over these premises but over their tragic failure to recognize and accept the assumption of reasonable value pluralism, an assumption that suggests that the free development of one individual can in some circumstances *conflict* with the free development of some others as well as, in different circumstances, *contribute* to the free development of others. Like nearly all the early Reformers in the sixteenth century and many of the leading figures in the eighteenth-century Enlightenment, Marx truly believed that if people could just clear their minds of the clutter of mystifying ideologies, they would all discover the truth about what is valuable in human life, a truth that would constitute a basis of agreement that would render the most divisive kinds of human conflict obsolete. History suggests that this belief is false.

The intent of my reconstruction of the theory of primary goods is to produce an account of the means that individuals need to pursue the projects they formulate and to try to realize the values they conceive that will be useful as a basis for criticism of existing political and social institutions and practices and for evaluating proposals for reform. Before proceeding with this reconstruction, I want to clarify a few points, in part to remind the reader of some things I have already said in chapter 1.

1. My purpose is *not* just to give an account of what the state can or should do. Political theorists sometimes focus on the state as if it were the only significant actor or agent of reform. I view the state as one exceptionally important complex of institutions and practices among others in modern societies. My aim is to develop an account of the bases of political and social criticism, criticism that

[3] Karl Marx and Friedrich Engels, "Manifesto of the Communist Party," in *The Marx-Engels Reader*, 2d ed., ed. Robert C. Tucker (New York: Norton, 1978), p. 491.
[4] Marx, "Critique of the Gotha Program," in ibid., p. 531.

might be directed at the institutions and practices that comprise the state or at other institutions and practices, including the practices that help constitute a particular culture.

2. I seek to define a range of equally acceptable social arrangements, not to define a single arrangement as the sole optimal possibility or to produce a rule that would prescribe a single optimal arrangement. An account of the bases of political and social criticism should produce a ranking of actual and possible arrangements that is more like the rough, relatively weak ranking of individuals that would be yielded by classifying individuals by health than the strong ordering we would get if we were to classify individuals by height.

3. My account is universalistic in aspiration. That is, I am aiming for an account of the bases of political and social criticism that could be used to consider critically the institutions and practices of any society, regardless of the culture that prevails in that society or of any of its other distinctive characteristics. In the liberal view as I interpret it, all individuals count equally as agents *in all societies*, no matter what cultures prevail in those societies. Liberalism, in this view, is compatible with a wide range of possible cultures but not with all. It is not compatible, for instance, with cultures that enshrine hierarchy or domination of one caste over another, one race over another, or one gender over another. The *liberating* potential of the liberal tradition cannot be sustained unless we hold open the possibility that cultural understandings, even if widely shared, can themselves be unjust. I call the account of the bases of political criticism that I describe here *Humanist Liberalism* to evoke the thought that that account is for *all* human beings—female and male, old and young, of whatever culture—rather than only for some.[5]

For the better part of this chapter I shall focus on the *content* of the basic means that people need to be effective agents rather than on the *distribution* of these means. This procedure is the reverse of that adopted by many writers in recent years. Ronald Dworkin, for example, whose theory of equality of resources[6] is a major alternative to Rawls's theory and a significant source of fruitful ideas about distributive justice, develops his entire theory of distributive justice without discussing the nature of the goods to be distributed at all. Rawls does discuss the content of the list of primary goods, though in view of the important role they play in his theory of justice it is surprising that he has never devoted more than a handful of the many hundreds of pages he has written about his theory of justice to an account of these goods. Yet a theory of distributive justice is only as good as the account of the things

---

[5] Inclusiveness is a central theme in Susan Moller Okin's "Humanist Liberalism," in *Liberalism and the Moral Life*, ed. Nancy L. Rosenblum (Cambridge, Mass.: Harvard University Press, 1989), pp. 39–53.

[6] Dworkin, "What is Equality? Part 2: Equality of Resources," *Philosophy and Public Affairs* 10 (1981): 283–345.

to be distributed on which it relies. My approach is intended as a step toward rectification of this neglect. I shall accordingly set aside all discussion of the distribution of the basic means that people need to be effective agents until after I have considered the content of those means at some length.

My argument proposes a revision of existing liberal theories, not an entirely new theory drawn, as it were, from a hat. In the foregoing chapters of this book I have called attention to a number of points on which existing liberal theories of the bases of political criticism are flawed. I have also noted the strengths of some of these existing theories, strengths on which I have drawn to put together the account I offer here.

Like Rawls, I focus on the means that social arrangements make available, or fail to make available, to individuals to pursue their values and projects. My premise is that we, as human beings, have a generalizable interest in having the means necessary to pursue the projects we formulate and to try to realize the values we conceive. This premise may seem unnecessarily circuitous. Why not just say that we have a generalizable interest in having our desires satisfied or having our values realized?

Several difficulties render this latter approach untenable. The first of these difficulties is epistemological. People's desires are hard to discern. Even people who think they know one another well are often surprised to discover that their estimates of one another's desires are badly mistaken. Careful observation and discernment do of course make it possible for some people to make judgments of others' desires with a fair degree of confidence. But no one can make judgments of this type about a large number of people, certainly not about all the members of an entire society, if that society comprises more members than can be contained in a small village. The difficulty is even greater than it would otherwise be because people often conceal their true desires from others. In voting situations, for example, people often vote strategically, making it impossible to determine on the basis of their votes what their real preferences are. On a social scale, we cannot even acquire enough information to ascertain the content of individuals' desires, let alone to determine how fully those desires have been satisfied.[7]

A second difficulty with the desire satisfaction approach has to do with the commensurability of different people's desires and the satisfaction of those desires. Suppose I claim that my palate will be satisfied only if I can dine on caviar and fine wines, while you find no reason to complain about a dinner of lentil soup with bread and inexpensive beer. Are our levels of desire satisfaction equal when both of us feel that we have had a good meal, despite the vastly different content and expense of our respective dinners? What if I,

---

[7] Jon Elster emphasizes this difficulty and gives references to some of the literature on the subject in "The Market and the Forum," in *Foundations of Social Choice Theory*, ed. Jon Elster and Aanung Hylland (Cambridge: Cambridge University Press, 1986), pp. 103–32, sec. I.

with my expensive tastes, am exceptionally difficult to please and complain even after I have had the dinner for which I asked, while you are easily satisfied? Would we have to invest in a cook and waiter, together with a linen tablecloth, silver, and china for me while leaving you with plain stoneware and stainless steel to equalize our levels of desire satisfaction? How should we compare the satisfaction each of us derives from our respective dining experiences with that which we would experience from going for a bicycle ride? We do not have a means for comparing levels of desire satisfaction across individuals and across experiences that can be applied in practice, nor do I think we know how to construct one.[8]

These two difficulties constitute different dimensions of the problem, familiar in the history of utilitarian theory, of interpersonal comparisons of utility (or of levels of desire satisfaction). The desire satisfaction approach also raises a third type of difficulty, which is related to the concept of fairness. Suppose we *could* compare the level of satisfaction I attain with my expensive tastes in foods with the level you attain with your more modest tastes? Would it be fair for us to equalize the degree to which our different desires are satisfied, even though to do so I would have to be given greater resources than you? A problem that is in some ways even more serious than the one raised by my expensive tastes is that posed by the person whose desires have been scaled back to a bare minimum as a result of deprivation. If one person's desire for food can be satisfied with a daily bowl of rice while another person demands caviar and wine, would it be fair to fulfill their desires equally, assuming that we are in a position to know when their desires are equally satisfied? It does not seem as though it would.[9]

Some of these problems would be alleviated by the adoption of an approach that focuses on the satisfaction of *informed* desires, though that approach certainly does not solve all of them. But insofar as the informed desire approach becomes more credible, it also becomes less distinctive. As the most persuasive recent advocate of this approach has acknowledged, at the societal level we can really undertake no more than to try to ensure that people have sufficient *resources* to satisfy their desires.[10] As a basis for comparing alternative social arrangements and considering reforms, a plausible informed desire approach turns into an approach that focuses on means.

---

[8] But see the interesting collection of papers related to this topic collected in *Interpersonal Comparisons of Well-Being*, ed. Jon Elster and John E. Roemer (Cambridge: Cambridge University Press, 1991).

[9] For a thorough discussion of this question, see Ronald Dworkin's "What Is Equality? Part 1: Equality of Welfare," *Philosophy and Public Affairs* 10 (1981): 185–246.

[10] See James Griffin's fine discussions in "Modern Utilitarianism," *Revue Internationale de Philosophie* 141 (1982): 331–75, and in *Well-Being*. For the point about resources, see Griffin's declaration "equalize all-purpose means" in the latter work, p. 248. For his discussion of the problem of interpersonal comparisons, see chap. 7 in that work.

The account of the bases of political criticism that I describe in this chapter focuses on means. This approach enables us to avoid the problem of interpersonal comparisons of desire satisfaction and provides an answer to the questions about fairness that arise within the desire satisfaction approach. In an account that focuses on means, neither the satisfaction of individuals' desires nor the frustration of those desires counts directly for the purpose of comparing alternatives and considering proposals for reform. What counts is the means that are or would be made available to individuals, not the level of desire satisfaction that different individuals attain with those means.[11] Throughout this discussion I assume that any good society would enable its members to develop the skills required to be an agent and have a sense of justice.

I

What means do individuals need to pursue the projects they formulate and to try to realize the values they conceive? Rawls's list of primary goods is the most fully developed answer to this question in the literature, but that list, as we have seen, is flawed. Rather than toss that list out and begin anew, however, I shall proceed by investigating ways in which the list of primary goods might be amended.

Rawls groups the primary goods under five headings:

1. basic rights and liberties (specified by a list);
2. freedom of movement and free choice of occupation against a background of diverse opportunities;
3. powers and prerogatives of office and positions of responsibility in the political and economic institutions of the basic structure;
4. income and wealth;
5. the social bases of self-respect.[12]

For my purposes it will be useful to draw the goods on this list under two even broader headings: liberties and opportunities, broadly construed to include opportunities for offices and positions of responsibility (comprising items 1 through 3 on Rawls's list) and resources (item 4 on Rawls's list), leaving aside for the moment the social bases of self-respect, which plays a different role in Rawls's account from the other means on the list.

We may begin by considering how this list might be altered to answer

[11] As Griffin points out, theories of the bases of social criticism that focus exclusively on means, such as Rawls's theory, are usually insufficiently sensitive to variations between individuals (*Well-Being*, pp. 107, 119). But that shortcoming does not apply to my account, which I have deliberately designed to be sensitive to these variations.

[12] Rawls, *Political Liberalism*, p. 181. See also the discussion in *A Theory of Justice* (Cambridge, Mass.: Harvard University Press, 1971), pp. 90–95.

Sen's objection that Rawls fails to take into account inter-individual variation as well as inter-end variation. For reasons we have discussed,[13] Sen's own proposal that we should focus on individuals' capability sets is unsatisfactory. Yet his objection to Rawls's theory remains a powerful one. We must find a way to answer it if we are to develop a convincing account of the bases of social criticism that focuses, as Rawls's account of primary goods does, on means.

Notice at the outset that in his critique of Rawls's list of primary goods, Sen uses the term *capability* in two slightly but significantly different ways. On the one hand, he defines a person's capabilities as the set of things the person is capable of doing. This notion of capability, which leads naturally to the idea of a capability set, predominates in the more recent versions of Sen's critique. On the other hand, Sen has also associated the notion of a person's capabilities with certain functions that the person is or is not able to perform, such as seeing, moving about, and being nourished. This latter notion leads to the idea of a person's *basic capabilities*, which is a more restricted idea than that of a full capability set.[14]

The idea of a capability set is an unsatisfactory basis on which to compare different individuals' relative positions in society. But the idea of basic capabilities, though not entirely free of difficulties, is far less problematic. To avoid confusion and to specify the idea of basic capabilities more precisely, I shall usually use the term *mental and physical powers* rather than basic capabilities. The idea of a person's mental and physical powers covers most, though not all, of what is included in Sen's notion of basic capabilities.

I suggest that we amend Rawls's list of primary goods by including individuals' mental and physical powers among the means specified by that list.[15] Although mental and physical powers are intrinsic to the person whose powers they are, these powers are developed capabilities, and whether they become developed and remain usable is determined in part by a person's circumstances. So although political and social arrangements do not result in a distribution of powers in the same way as they lead to a distribution of commodities, these arrangements are capable of affecting the development of individuals' powers in powerful ways.

[13] In chap. 4, sec. v, herein.

[14] This ambiguity runs through all Sen's writings on this subject, but the idea of a capability set predominates in the more recent writings, especially his *Inequality Reexamined* (Cambridge, Mass.: Harvard University Press, 1992), whereas the more limited idea of basic capabilities is more prominent in the earlier versions of Sen's critique, such as his lecture "Equality of What?"in *The Tanner Lectures on Human Values*, ed. S. M. McMurrin (Salt Lake City: University of Utah Press, 1980), pp. 139–62.

[15] This suggestion is in line with the apparent intention of Sen's critique in its original form, when he argued that the "focus on basic capabilities can be seen as a natural extension of Rawls's concern with primary goods" ("Equality of What?" p. 160), before Sen developed the idea of a capability set.

The most basic powers might be thought of as constituting physical and mental *well-being*. Among these powers we can include the use of a person's limbs for walking, running, lifting, carrying, and so forth; the use of hands for grasping objects and manipulating them; the full use of the senses for seeing, hearing, feeling, tasting, and smelling; the use of other parts of the body; the use of our powers of thinking and reasoning to relate means to ends in a rational way, to select ends, and to calculate; and the use of our linguistic capabilities to be able to converse in a natural language. Various additional powers, although perhaps not necessary for physical or mental well-being in the most rudimentary sense, are only slightly less basic and can be included among those needed to participate fully in the life of one's community. These include the power to read and to write (in societies in which literacy is widespread), the ability to reason mathematically, and other, more particularized skills.

All these powers are acquired through the development of innate capacities into skills, a development that is mediated by a person's external circumstances. In a given society at a given time, some level of each of these capacities is usually considered adequate or "normal." People who fail to develop these capacities to the normal degree are considered handicapped, whereas those who develop one or several capacities to an exceptional degree are considered talented. The idea of adequacy or normality is of course socially constructed and variable from one society to another and from one time to another, but within a given society at a given time the idea of adequacy or normality usually has a reasonably firm basis in the organization of that society's practical affairs. For example, in a society in which the only way to acquire the necessities of life routinely is to buy them with currency, the ability to perform the arithmetic operations of addition and subtraction is a basic skill, without which a person would be considered at least mildly handicapped. Similarly, in a society in which information is exchanged extensively through the written word, lack of literacy is a handicap. Although these relatively mild handicaps may not affect a person's well-being in the most basic sense directly, they do affect her power to participate in the life of her community, and they may also indirectly affect a person's ability to acquire the means to maintain even her most basic well-being.

My proposal, then, is that we add mental and physical powers to the list of basic means alongside the other major types of items Rawls identifies, namely liberties and opportunities and resources. By including these powers among the basic means, we can address Sen's objection that Rawls's list fails to take into account inter-individual variation without slipping into the insuperable difficulties raised by Sen's concept of the capability set.

In order to clarify this proposal, let us compare it with some alternative ways of coping with the problem of inter-individual variation in mental and physical powers. I shall discuss three alternatives: the approach Rawls suggests in his reply to Sen's claims, Dworkin's approach in his theory of equality of resources, and Sen's own arguments about the role well-being should play in evaluating alternative social arrangements.

In response to Sen's objections, Rawls makes three points about his own theory.[16] First, he points out that throughout his theory he assumes that while all citizens do not have equal capacities, they do have at least the essential moral, intellectual, and physical capacities to be fully cooperating members of society. Second, when people's physical capacities and skills are damaged by illness or accidents, they should receive the health care necessary to restore to them the powers necessary to be fully cooperating members. Third, variations in moral and intellectual capacities and skills among those who do have at least the minimum powers to be fully cooperating members of society are dealt with, Rawls argues, by the social practices of free competition against a background of fair equality of opportunity, including fair equality of opportunity in education, and through regulation of inequalities in income and wealth in accordance with the difference principle.

Rawls's proposal for dealing with variations in people's powers that leave them unable to be fully cooperating members of their society is at least a partially satisfactory response to Sen's objections, though his apparent assumption that only physical disabilities deprive people of the power to be fully cooperating members of society is puzzling. In general, though, the notion that individuals whose powers fall short of those necessary to participate fully in the life of their society should receive health care with the intent of enabling them to regain this ability is convincing. The only significant remaining question about this type of case is why Rawls treats it as an addendum of sorts by assuming that all citizens possess sufficient powers to be fully cooperating members of society and then treating the problem of disabilities as a minor correction that can be disregarded in formulating the principles of justice. It seems more sensible to include mental and physical powers on the list of primary goods than to approach the problem of interindividual variations by the circuitous route Rawls follows, which conveys the impression that these variations are mere theoretical marginalia.[17]

Rawls's response to the problem of variations in powers among people who possess the basic capabilities necessary to be fully cooperating members of society is more problematical. His assumption seems to be that these

[16] For his discussion, see Rawls, *Political Liberalism*, pp. 182–86. I omit from my summary some points Rawls makes that are not addressed to the issue of the way in which we should take account of mental and physical powers.

[17] Rawls does suggest that the index of primary goods used in any actual society should be sufficiently flexible to "consider basic capabilities" (ibid., pp. 185–86), but he does not further explain this suggestion. In any event, he does not include basic capabilities—or powers—on his own list of primary goods.

powers are significant only as means for obtaining other primary goods, especially offices and positions and income and wealth. That assumption is false. Skills contribute to a person's ability to pursue her values and projects in many ways other than by contributing to her ability to obtain positions and wealth. For instance, articulateness is in general a highly valuable skill. A person who is especially articulate can communicate better with others than a person who is not. If two people have identical positions, incomes, and other means, but one is far more articulate than the other, the more articulate person has more means at her disposal to pursue her values and projects than does the other. She may be better able to persuade other people to see things from her point of view and to convince them to take an interest in her projects or to accept her values. She may even be able to mediate conflict within a family better than the person who is relatively inarticulate. It is misleading to represent powers or skills of this kind merely as means to other primary goods like position and income or wealth, as Rawls does. Mental and physical powers are primary goods or basic means in their own right, because they are important means that enable people to pursue their values and projects, independently of their value as means to obtain other primary goods.

In his thought-provoking argument for equality of resources, Ronald Dworkin agrees that mental and physical powers are resources, since they are used, together with material resources, to make something valuable out of one's life.[18] However, he argues that they should be treated differently from material means. The question he considers is whether, in a scheme designed to distribute resources equally to all members of a society, those individuals should be compensated to alleviate differences in physical and mental powers. Dworkin argues that for three reasons, individuals should not be compensated to *equalize* these differences. First, he suggests that the proposal that people should be compensated to equalize differences in powers raises the difficult question of defining a standard of "normal" powers to serve as a benchmark for compensation, a standard that does not now exist. Second, he points out that in some cases, such as that of a person who is born blind or mentally incompetent, no upper bound for compensation exists, because no amount of compensation could make up for the deprivation in powers suffered by a person who cannot see or cannot reason. Third, he argues that because mental and physical powers cannot be manipulated or transferred in the way material resources can be, it misdescribes the problem of handicaps to say that we must strive to make people equal in physical and mental constitution as far as this is possible. Dworkin proposes that

---

[18] Dworkin's discussion of mental and physical powers occurs in "Equality of Resources," pp. 300–304.

instead of attempting to equalize people's means by compensating them for shortfalls in mental and physical powers, we should set levels of compensation for people with shortfalls by imagining the outcome of an insurance market in which all members of a society might have participated to insure themselves against the possibility that they might suffer a deprivation of mental or physical powers.

All these are good points, and Dworkin's proposed insurance scheme is interesting and provocative. But Dworkin's analysis is limited by the fact that he equates resources, generally, with commodities and construes the problem of handicaps as a compensation problem. The conception of resources that Dworkin adopts is in fact one-dimensional, at least in comparison with Rawls's proposal, which recognizes the fact that primary goods differ in kind from one another. If a resource is assumed typically to be a commodity, then mental and physical powers are bound to appear as a peculiar kind of case. Dworkin's arguments are good ones for not treating powers as commodities. But his proposed insurance scheme only gets half the distance away from this narrow, commodity-based approach.

I suggest that instead of equating means generally with commodities, as Dworkin does, we should think of commodities as only one among several distinct types of means people can use to pursue their values and projects. Dworkin's arguments show that there is something wrong with treating powers as if they were commodities. But if that is true, then there is something missing in Dworkin's own approach, which treats a loss of powers as if it should trigger compensation through an insurance scheme, much as we would approach a loss of material possessions. Dworkin's discussion affirms that mental and physical powers are important means, but his proposal does not take sufficiently into account the distinctiveness of our mental and physical powers in comparison to the other means we use to make meaningful lives for ourselves. I shall argue presently, in section III of this chapter, for an approach that takes the distinctiveness of powers into account better than Dworkin's approach does, an approach that is capable of producing answers to the problems of defining a standard of normality and an upper limit on compensation.

Amartya Sen is a principal advocate of the view that mental and physical powers, or capabilities, should be considered centrally in assessing alternative social arrangements. But whereas in his initial formulation of this claim Sen argued that his focus on basic capabilities should be seen as a natural extension of the notion of primary goods,[19] in later writings Sen has argued that we should count at least the basic capabilities that constitute well-being *separately* from the other means that enable us to pursue our values and

---

[19] Sen, "Equality of What?" p. 160.

projects.[20] Sen distinguishes four different types of things that he claims should count from an evaluative point of view: well-being, well-being freedom (i.e., the freedom individuals have to obtain the things necessary for their well-being), agency freedom (i.e., the freedom people have to pursue whatever projects or values they may conceive), and agency achievements. According to Sen, "the important thing to recognize is that the well-being aspect and the agency aspect of persons have dissimilar roles in moral accounting. They invite attention in *disparate* ways."[21]

It is true that the capabilities that constitute well-being are not merely means that enable us to pursue our objectives like any other means and that people value well-being intrinsically rather than solely as a means to other ends or values. A person's well-being is not the *same thing* as her agency freedom (or agency prospects, to use my term), and it is possible that a single event can both increase a person's agency freedom and decrease her well-being.[22] But it does not follow that for the purpose of assessing alternative social arrangements, well-being should be counted separately.

Sen considers the argument that "in judging the relative advantages of different people, the proper basis of comparison should be just their respective agency freedoms. The information on agency aspect would *inter alia* include the value of each person's own well-being, in the light of whatever importance she herself gives to it in her agency objectives. Treating the person herself as the best judge of how she may be viewed by others, it might look as if the agency aspect would tell all that is relevant for others to know."[23] According to Sen, this argument is defective. For one thing, he points out, people must often make hard choices. If a person chooses to pursue objectives that are detrimental to her well-being, it does not follow that her well-being is unimportant, either to her or to others. For another, well-being and agency freedom are relevant considerations for different purposes. Sen suggests, for example, that although a society may assume responsibility for making sure that its members have the means to sustain their well-being, it may not want to assume responsibility for making sure that they are able to attain their other objectives.

Both of Sen's arguments are correct, but they do not establish the point he wishes to make, which is that well-being considerations and agency considerations should play disparate roles in "moral accounting." Some of the capabilities that constitute well-being, particularly some of the mental powers, are conditions of our being able to formulate projects and conceive values in

---

[20] See generally Sen's "Well-Being, Agency, and Freedom: The Dewey Lectures, 1984," *Journal of Philosophy* 82 (1985): 169–221, esp. pp. 205–8; and *Inequality Reexamined*, esp. pp. 69–72.

[21] Sen, "Well-Being, Agency, and Freedom," p. 206.

[22] See Sen's discussion of this point in ibid., pp. 206–7.

[23] Sen, *Inequality Reexamined*, p. 69.

the first place. Human beings who fail to develop at least these powers are not even agents. Many of the mental and physical powers that constitute well-being are essential or important means that contribute to our ability to pursue and to realize our values and projects. A person who wants to run a mile in less than five minutes, or one who just wants to enjoy a regular weekend tennis game, has to have many of the powers that constitute well-being to be able to attain these objectives. Similarly, a person who wants to write a good book, or one who just wants to do a crossword puzzle, has to have some of the powers that constitute well-being to do these things. A person has to attain some degree of well-being as a condition of conceiving any values or projects at all, and has to have many of the powers that constitute well-being to be able to pursue many values and projects in an effective manner. In short, the mental and physical powers that constitute well-being are a *condition* for our *conceiving* and a *means* for our *pursuing* values and projects generally. Sen offers no good reason why we should "count" these powers other than as such a condition and means. To do so would be to engage in double counting.

Of course, Sen has been deeply concerned throughout his career with poverty, famine, and other social issues closely related to well-being, and it is natural that he should emphasize well-being prominently. I agree with Sen that well-being is vitally important. But it is important because it enables agents to conceive and pursue the objectives they wish to pursue, not as a separate consideration.

The claim I have advanced here—that a person's physical and mental powers should be included among the list of basic means available to her to advance her projects and to attempt to realize her values—leads to a certain view of the distinction between persons and the means available to them and assigns aspirations, desires, projects, and values to the person and mental and physical powers to her means. The idea behind this distinction is that an account of the bases of social criticism should focus on the means available to people to pursue their projects and values, assigning responsibility for formulating these projects and values to the individuals whose projects and values they are and not ranking these projects and values for their worthiness. In reality, of course, a person's powers cannot be disentangled from her values as neatly as this distinction may suggest. People develop some of their powers and not others in part because they want to realize some values rather than others. Nevertheless, people find themselves in a position to develop their powers, or find themselves unable to develop them, in large part because of the social arrangements that shape their lives. If the distinction between powers on the one hand and values on the other is far from clear in practice, it is at least reasonably clear conceptually, and I shall argue in section IV that it would be possible to arrange social institutions in a way that would respect the distinction in practice, even if it is not possible to disentangle precisely the share of our powers for which we can consider our circumstances accountable from that for which we, as persons with particular aspirations and values, are responsible.

II

In order to pursue their values, human beings need resources as well as mental and physical powers (and liberties and opportunities). The principal resources that Rawls includes on his list of primary goods are income and wealth. I want to argue that Rawls's list should be amended to include status and recognition as a resource.

Before turning to this argument, however, I want briefly to defend Rawls's treatment of income and wealth within his account of primary goods. Rawls has often been criticized, especially from the left, for focusing too much attention on income and wealth in a way that tends, mistakenly, to justify capitalist market society.[24] Although I agree in part with this criticism in that I think Rawls's account of the primary goods neglects some goods or means that are of great importance, I do not think the criticism is entirely on target and would like to clarify some points that are relevant to my discussion of the means people need to pursue their values.

First, when Rawls discusses wealth as a primary good, I take him to mean wealth in Adam Smith's sense. By "wealth" Smith meant a fund or stock of the "necessaries and conveniencies of life,"[25] that is, a stock of useful goods. Although Smith is often considered—justifiably, in my view—a founder and the most outstanding representative of the classical school of political economy, his conception of wealth was still essentially Aristotelian. Unlike some of his successors, Smith linked the concept of wealth to use. In this respect Smith's view was closer to Marx's (as well as to Aristotle's) than to that of many of his successors in the classical school of political economy. His concept of wealth is identical to Marx's concept of use-value and different from Marx's concept of value, the attribute of commodities that, in Marx's view, ultimately determines the ratios in which they are exchanged in capitalist societies. According to Marx, commodities have a twofold nature that results from the fact that they embody both use-value and value, and this twofold nature of commodities accounts for many peculiarities and malfunctions of production and exchange within capitalist economic systems.[26] So far as I can tell, Rawls's notion of wealth is identical to Adam Smith's and Marx's concept of wealth as use-value. Considered strictly as a use-value, wealth is

[24] See, for example, Adina Schwartz, "Moral Neutrality and Primary Goods," *Ethics* 83 (1973): 294–307.

[25] Smith, *An Inquiry into the Nature and Causes of the Wealth of Nations* (New York: Random House, 1937).

[26] Marx, *Capital* (New York: International Publishers, 1967), vol. 1.

certainly an important general means that contributes to individuals' abilities to pursue their values.

Second, it is true that Rawls says of the primary goods generally that within his theory of justice, it is assumed that people would prefer more rather than less of them, whatever their ends may be.[27] This statement has sometimes been taken to imply that Rawls assumes that human beings necessarily desire to receive as much income and to accumulate as much wealth as possible. But Rawls also says that "beyond some point [wealth] is more likely to be a positive hindrance, a meaningless distraction at best if not a temptation to indulgence and emptiness."[28] This observation suggests that Rawls does not intend his comment about individuals preferring more rather than less of the primary goods to be interpreted as an endorsement of unlimited accumulation. Moreover, it is important to bear in mind that Rawls's theory presupposes a society in which conditions of moderate scarcity prevail, and to recall that in *A Theory of Justice* Rawls placed great emphasis on what he later called the "objective" circumstances of justice, that is, the shortage of available resources in relation to wants. In a situation in which resources are in relatively short supply, the comment that people generally can be expected to want more rather than less of those resources does not seem to imply acceptance of a favorable attitude toward unbridled accumulation.

It is true that more wealth does not always enhance a person's agency prospects or improve her ability to pursue her values, particularly if she already possesses considerable wealth. More wealth rather than less does not always add to our ability to pursue our values, any more than more muscle rather than less always adds to our physical abilities; beyond a certain point, more can mean too much. I think it is reasonably clear that Rawls recognizes this fact, even though he does have an unfortunate and misleading tendency in many of his writings to use income and wealth as surrogates for the primary goods as a whole. Whatever Rawls's view of this matter may be, however, the significant point is that in recognizing the fact that wealth in the sense of access to material goods is a means people need to pursue their values, we are not committed to the (mistaken) view that it is always better to have more of these goods than less of them. Access to an adequate share of material goods is important to everyone, but maximization of those shares may not be a good thing.

I want now to argue that we should include status and recognition on the list of primary goods or means people need to pursue their values and projects. Status and recognition differ in kind from other resources, such as income and wealth. They are "distributed" by the members of society to one

---

[27] Rawls, *Theory*, p. 92.
[28] Ibid., p. 290.

another, not by a state to its citizens. Status and recognition are generally neglected by political theorists, probably because they are less susceptible to institutional control and less easily measurable than other resources.[29] If we want to take account of the principal means that individuals need to pursue their values, however, we must consider status and recognition.

On his own list of primary goods, Rawls includes the social bases of self-respect as one of the most important goods. Rawls's notion of the social bases of self-respect overlaps with, but is not identical to, the concepts of status and recognition. An exploration of the differences between these ideas will help to clarify my proposal.

Rawls argues that the social bases of self-respect should be included among the primary goods for two reasons.[30] First, a person must have self-respect in order to sustain the conviction that her values are worth realizing, her projects worth carrying out. Without self-respect, nothing may seem worth doing. Second, self-respect implies confidence in a person's own ability to carry out her intentions. Lacking that confidence, a person might also lack the will to try to realize her values. Self-respect, then, is not valuable just in the way any other good might be. It is valuable because a person must have self-respect in order to value other things, to conceive values with real conviction and commitment, and because self-respect enables us to act in such a way as to realize our values.

Rawls argues that in a just society, the need for the social bases of self-respect is met by the recognition that each individual receives by virtue of her acceptance by her fellow citizens as an equal citizen entitled to equal fundamental rights and liberties within a scheme of just institutions, together with the support individuals receive through their participation in voluntary associations.[31] A key feature in the provisions for self-respect he envisages is that the members of a just society should, in their capacities as citizens, avoid assessing the relative value of one another's ways of life[32] (though in his more recent writings Rawls has emphasized that citizens may see things differently in their personal affairs from how they see them in their public roles as citizens).[33] This public recognition belongs to the political conception of justice that Rawls believes all the members of a perfectly just society should endorse.

---

[29] Michael Walzer, however, devotes a chapter to discussion of status and recognition in *Spheres* (chap. 11).

[30] Rawls, *Theory*, pp. 440–46.

[31] Ibid., p. 544.

[32] Ibid., pp. 327ff., 442.

[33] A sharp distinction between the qualities of individuals *qua* citizens and their qualities *qua* private persons flows from Rawls's emphasis in his recent writings on the claim that his conception of justice is a *political* conception as distinct from a comprehensive moral theory or part of a comprehensive moral theory. See especially "Political Not Metaphysical," *Philosophy and Public Affairs* 14 (1985): 223–51, sec. v.

Rawls is right to suggest that a sense that our values are worth realizing and that we are capable of acting effectively on those values is essential to a good life. Self-respect is one of the necessary conditions individuals must attain in order to create meaningful lives for themselves. It is probably as basic in importance, or nearly so, as the capacities for agency and for a sense of justice.

I want to suggest, though, that status and recognition are essential or primary goods for reasons that go beyond their role in enabling people to attain self-respect. *In addition* to their role as sustainers of our self-respect, status and recognition are means, resources of great importance that individuals can use to advance their values. Further, I want to argue that the provisions Rawls envisages for supporting self-respect—public recognition by citizens *qua* citizens of the equal rights and liberties to which all are entitled plus the support provided by membership in free associations—are inadequate. Individuals need real recognition from the other members of their society as whole persons, and not merely in their role as citizens, in order to pursue their values effectively. In a pluralistic society—one whose members differ from one another in physical and cultural characteristics as well as holding different values—this kind of recognition can prevail only if the members of that society have a vigorous sense of justice, the kind that pervades a person's life and conduct rather than affecting her only within the confines of a given role such as that of a citizen.

To see my point, consider black America.[34] Black Americans have shorter and more painful lives than whites. The unemployment rate among blacks over the past thirty years has typically been twice the rate for white Americans. Black Americans who do have jobs earn only about three-quarters the amount earned by white Americans with jobs. Blacks are almost completely unrepresented in many professions, where the most highly paid and most satisfying jobs are found. Most black children attend schools that are segregated de facto. Most black families live in neighborhoods that are segregated de facto, despite the fact that most blacks, when asked, express a preference for integrated neighborhoods. The rates for teenage pregnancy and single parenthood are far higher among blacks than whites. The strains that come with being black impose heavy burdens on black married couples. Blacks disproportionately commit violent crimes and disproportionately are imprisoned. Black Americans who "make it" in a white world do so usually by reining in their opinions and emotions in ways white Americans are seldom, if ever, called on to do.

Some of the disadvantages that white America imposes on black Americans would be eliminated if black Americans enjoyed genuine fair equality

---

[34] In the next several paragraphs I draw on the useful collection of data and discussion in Andrew Hacker's *Two Nations: Black and White, Separate, Hostile, Unequal* (New York: Ballantine Books, 1992).

of opportunity in employment and education with whites. In reality, of course, black Americans do not enjoy fair equality of opportunity in either education or employment, even when the relatively small but well-publicized effects of affirmative action policies are taken into account. But suppose counterfactually that black Americans did enjoy fair equality of opportunity with whites. Suppose also that white Americans genuinely accepted the proposition that black Americans are entitled to the same basic rights and liberties of equal citizenship that all other Americans enjoy (most white Americans do accept this proposition, at least in the abstract). Would black and white Americans then be on an equal footing with one another in American society?

Clearly they would not. Black Americans are not at a disadvantage in relation to whites only because they are deprived of the rights and liberties of equal citizenship, or because white Americans fail to accept that they are entitled to these rights and liberties, or because they do not enjoy fair equality of opportunity in education and employment with whites. Black Americans are at a disadvantage because of the identity whites impose on them on a daily basis, that is, because of the expectations and perceptions whites have of blacks. White Americans think of black Americans as "different" from themselves. For white Americans, black Americans are defined by their being black. White Americans form impressions ("stereotypes") of black Americans based on their skin color and physical characteristics, features that tell nothing about who they really are or what they have made of themselves. Whites routinely regard black Americans with suspicion in situations in which they would not regard a white person with suspicion, and they often regard black Americans with hostility. Whites are systematically unsure of black Americans' intentions unless they receive reassuring signals that they do not demand from other whites. Whites, including those who think of themselves as liberals, harbor deep-seated suspicions that black Americans' abilities are inferior to those of whites. In a letter Thomas Jefferson wrote fifteen years after composing the Declaration of Independence—a document that affirms as "self-evident" that all human beings everywhere are "created equal"—he says that "nobody wishes more than I do to see proofs that nature has given to our black brethren talents equal to those of the other colors of men, and that the appearance of a lack of them is owing merely to the degraded condition of their existence in Africa and America."[35] As Andrew Hacker points out, Jefferson was torn, as are some liberal whites today, between the hope that blacks are equal and the suspicion that they are not.

---

[35] Letter from Thomas Jefferson to Benjamin Banneker of 30 August 1791, in *Thomas Jefferson: Writings*, ed. Merrill D. Peterson (New York: Library of America, 1984), quoted in Hacker, *Two Nations*, p. 25.

For the most part white Americans do not believe that black Americans should be denied the rights and liberties of equal citizenship or fair equality of opportunity in education and employment. But white Americans do believe that they—whites—should be entitled to send their children to schools of their choice, even if that means avoiding schools that have black enrollments they perceive as too high (too high, for most whites, means enrollments that result in a percentage of blacks among the total population of students in a school comparable to or slightly higher than the overall percentage of blacks in the national population, i.e., about 12 or 13 percent). White Americans believe they are entitled to live in neighborhoods of their choice, even if this means avoiding neighborhoods that are more than 10 or 15 percent black. White Americans believe they have a right to be suspicious of whomever they please, even if this means that they will systematically suspect blacks in situations in which they would not be suspicious of whites. White Americans believe they have a right to expect black Americans to behave like whites and to avoid blacks when they fail to prove that they are indistinguishable in conduct and attitudes from whites.

These beliefs reveal a deep inability on the part of white Americans to extend acceptance and recognition to black Americans equivalent to the recognition they extend to whites as a matter of course. The problem is not that whites believe blacks should be deprived of the rights and liberties of equal citizenship. The problem is that whites do not really view blacks as *persons* in the same way as they do other whites. Whites tend not to think of black Americans as agents with values they want to realize and projects they would like to pursue. They tend to think of black Americans as blacks, to define the identities of the black people they meet by reference to their physical characteristics and to their imputed African origins. This tendency is called racism.

Racism imposes limitations on the things black Americans can *do*. Black Americans cannot, for the most part, live in integrated neighborhoods. If blacks manage to gain a footing in a neighborhood, whites quickly get the message and move out. Black Americans cannot, for the most part, send their children to integrated schools. Blacks cannot walk down a street frequented by whites without wondering whether they are being perceived with suspicion or hostility. Blacks cannot travel across the country by car without being aware that they may be met with overtly racist reactions at some stop or other along the way.

Racism and its consequences certainly tend to diminish black Americans' self-respect. Rawls's inclusion of the social bases of self-respect among the primary goods entails the conclusion that those consequences should be eliminated. However, diminution of black Americans' self-respect is not the only consequence of white Americans' inability to recognize black

Americans as agents with projects and values much like their own. By withholding this recognition, whites deprive blacks of a resource blacks need to participate fully as equals in the public life of their own society. Black subcultures are born in part out of a necessity whites impose on blacks that pushes many blacks out of the main streams of American public life and forces them to rely entirely on their own resources, to create their own lives separately from, and often in repudiation of, the lives of whites.

Black Americans are not the only group in American society that suffers from a shortfall in status and recognition, though they probably suffer a greater shortfall than any other sizable group. Although middle-class women in America have gained ground rapidly in relation to men during the past quarter-century, women as a group still are not really recognized as equal *persons* by many men in American society, even by men who accept, at least as an abstract proposition, that women deserve the same rights and liberties of equal citizenship as they do. In fact many American *women* do not accept that they and other women are entitled to be regarded as persons with their own integrity and their own values and projects, just as men are. Moreover, the sexism that pervades American culture is mild compared with that which prevails in most other cultures and countries in the world. Even where women's rights and liberties of equal citizenship are apparently secure, their status in society is inferior to that of men.

Unlike the distribution of income and wealth, the distribution of status and recognition cannot be manipulated easily by the state. Recognition is a good that the members of a society give to one another. It cannot be given by the institution called the state,[36] even in the form of a constitution that provides rights and liberties of citizenship that are equal for all citizens. The state or its representatives can affect the distribution of honors and positions, but it cannot impose a tax on recognition or make transfer payments of recognition to those of its members who suffer shortfalls of this good. Yet the fact that status and recognition are relatively resistant to state control does not make these goods any less important than other means people may use to advance their values or pursue their aims. Status and recognition are means in this sense as important as any others, including income and wealth. A person who possesses these goods can accomplish things that cannot be achieved by a person who does not possess them. She can get people to do things they will not do for those who have little status or low status.

Status is as universal a good as any we can identify. The desire for status

---

[36] It is possible, of course, to bring certain kinds of *official* recognition under state control, but that is not the kind of recognition I intend.

is as widespread as any motive that can be traced in the historical record of human societies. This desire is at least as fundamental as the desire for wealth.[37] In fact in the economically more developed societies, income and wealth seem to be desired largely because a person's share of these goods goes a long way toward determining his status. My point, however, is not just that status is widely coveted. It is that status is a means, a resource of great importance in determining what people can do with their lives and how effectively they are able to pursue their values and the projects they conceive. Without status and recognition—recognition that goes beyond acceptance of the proposition that all members of society are entitled equally to the rights and liberties of equal citizenship—it is difficult or impossible for people to live good lives in association with others, to pursue projects and seek to realize values in a social setting in ways that tend to make their lives meaningful to them.

No general list of the means that individuals need to pursue their values is likely to be complete, nor need it be. A list of primary goods or basic means may be more or less adequate, but a definitive list of these means is probably beyond our grasp. If our aim were to draw up a blueprint for a perfectly just society that we could then attempt to implement, our inability to construct a definitive list would be troubling, because an omission might result in a major flaw in our design. But my aim is to compose an account of the normative bases of social criticism to which we can refer in comparing existing practices with proposed reforms, not to design a perfectly just society from the ground up. For this purpose incompleteness in our list need not be considered a flaw. A list of the basic means should remain open-ended, ready to accommodate additions or revisions in the event that persuasive arguments for them are made. I do think, though, that by amending Rawls's list of the primary goods, which emphasizes liberties and opportunities on the one hand and income and wealth on the other, to include mental and physical powers and status and recognition, we arrive at a workable and reasonably robust list of those general means that individuals need to pursue their diverse values which can be affected in different ways by different social arrangements.

By including mental and physical powers and status and recognition on our revised list of primary goods, we address two different types of variation among individuals to which Rawls's own list is blind. The first is the type of inter-individual variation on which Sen focuses, that is, inter-individual var-

---

[37] "The outstanding discovery of recent historical and anthropological research is that man's economy, as a rule, is submerged in his social relationships. He does not act so as to safeguard his individual interest in the possession of material goods; he acts so as to safeguard his social standing, his social claims, his social assets" (Karl Polanyi, *The Great Transformation: The Political and Economic Origins of Our Time* [Boston: Beacon Press, 1957], p. 46).

iations in people's basic capabilities and needs. Adding mental and physical powers to our list of primary goods enables us to take account of those variations and to provide for individuals' diverse abilities to convert resources into desired goals. The second type of variation among individuals that our modification is intended to address is variation in individuals' physical or otherwise relatively fixed characteristics that leads others to treat those individuals in discriminatory ways. Adding status and recognition to our list of basic means gives us a way of characterizing unwarranted discriminatory treatment and of taking it into account in estimating individuals' shares of basic means.

Any general list of the means individuals need to pursue their values will in practice be culture- or society-specific to a degree. Certainly mental and physical powers are in part culture-specific. For example, skills of logical and mathematical reasoning play a greater role in determining people's relative advantages in a society like that of the United States, where science and technology play enormously influential roles and where considerable scientism, or admiration (whether well-founded or not) for science and the appearance of science, is prevalent in the general culture, than these skills play elsewhere. Similarly, the ability to read and write is highly important in societies in which literacy is widespread and the written word is a crucial means of disseminating information, but it plays no role in those societies (now virtually extinct) that do not have a written language. The other items on our list are also partially culture-dependent. Wealth, for instance, exists in all societies, but can take markedly different forms. In societies that have adopted the institution of money, wealth is usually equated (somewhat misleadingly) with the possession of money in some form, but in the many historical societies that have lacked this institution wealth has taken a variety of other forms. Even basic liberties would take somewhat different forms in different societies.

It is true, then, that to some degree goods are always local and particular in character.[38] Yet a general account of the basic means that people need to pursue their values is still useful. These means are only *partly* culture-dependent. Mental and physical powers are essential for people to pursue their values in every culture, and many of the most significant of these powers hardly vary at all from one culture to the next. Liberties and opportunities in some form help constitute the means that people use to pursue their goals in every society. Similarly, wealth exists in every society, as do status and recognition. These goods may take different forms in different societies, but they play important roles in determining individuals' abilities to pursue their values in every society.

---

[38] As Walzer points out in *Spheres*, p. xv.

III

Let us take stock for a moment of the account of the means that individuals need to pursue their values produced by the amendments to Rawls's list of primary goods that I have suggested. A useful way to bring this revised account into focus might be to compare it side by side with Rawls's own list.

Primary Goods (justice as fairness)	Basic Means (humanist liberalism)
	1. Mental and physical powers
1. Liberties and opportunities:	2. Liberties and opportunities
a. Basic rights and liberties	(including items a through c on
b. Freedom of movement and free choice of occupation	Rawls's list)
c. Powers and prerogatives of offices and positions of responsibility	
2. Resources:	3. Resources:
d. Income and wealth	a. Income and wealth
3. The social bases of self-respect	b. Status and recognition

The list of means I adopt for my account of humanist liberalism differs from Rawls's list of primary goods by the addition of mental and physical powers considered as a means and by the substitution of status and recognition for Rawls's more narrowly construed notion of the social bases of self-respect. These revisions are intended, as I have said, to take account of two types of variations among individuals to which Rawls's list is blind: inter-individual variations in people's basic capabilities and needs and inter-individual variation in people's physical or otherwise relatively fixed characteristics that lead others to treat those people in discriminatory ways. Notice that the list remains blind, or at least as blind, probably, as it is possible for any general list of this type to be, to what Sen calls inter-end variation, that is, to variations in people's values and goals. This blindness is appropriate—in fact it is required—in an account of the means people need to pursue their values and objectives that accepts the assumption of reasonable value pluralism and seeks to accommodate as wide a range of diverse values and conceptions of the good as possible. The result of these revisions is a list that classifies means roughly into three basic types: mental and physical powers, liberties and opportunities, and resources, including status and recognition as well as income and wealth.

Each of the three major categories on the revised list of basic means is internally complex. Mental powers are not the same as physical ones: a person can be mentally incompetent yet enjoy perfect physical health, or can be mentally quite healthy and active, yet physically disabled. A person can enjoy some kinds of liberties while lacking others. A person may possess considerable material wealth while having very poor status, or can have high status, but little wealth. Moreover, the internal complexity of these means is deeper than I have already indicated. It is possible for a person to have considerable wealth in the form of access to material resources while lacking access to some particular kinds of material resources that are vitally important, such as foods. If it were possible to draw up an exhaustive account of each of these goods—and I doubt that it is—the result would be a very elaborate affair.

A list of the means people need to pursue their values and objectives gets us some way toward an account of the bases of political and social criticism that rests on the premise that human beings have a generalizable interest in having the means necessary to pursue the projects they formulate and to try to realize the values they conceive. But a list alone leaves some important questions still to be answered. One of these questions has to do with the way in which the different items on the list of means are related to each other. I want now to consider this question.

In order to simplify matters, I shall focus on the heterogeneity of the three major types of means I have suggested people need to pursue their values—mental and physical powers, liberties and opportunities, and resources—setting aside for now the fact that each of these types of means is itself internally complex and heterogeneous. I shall assume, in a deliberately artificial and counterfactual way, that each of these types of means is simple and homogeneous. This simplifying assumption will enable us to make some progress toward a view of the way we should take into account the functional relations between the different means that contribute to individuals' abilities to pursue their values. Real-world complexity could of course be reintroduced after some of the more basic theoretical issues have been dealt with.

In his discussion of equality of resources, as we have seen in section 1 above, Dworkin observes cogently that in some cases, such as that of a person who is born blind or mentally incompetent, no amount of compensation in the form of money or other material goods could make up for the deprivation in powers imposed on that person by his circumstances. This observation calls attention to the important fact that different kinds of means play different functional roles in enabling people to pursue their values and aims.

Dworkin's observation leads him to reject the suggestion that we should seek to equalize differences between different people's means caused by impairment of their mental or physical powers by compensating them with resources of other kinds. He proposes that instead of attempting to equalize people's means, a task that would be impossible at least in the case of a person who is mentally incompetent, we should imagine the level of compensation for which people would want to insure themselves against the possibility that they might become disabled in some way. According to his proposal, the level of compensation people should receive for shortfalls in

mental and physical powers would be determined by imagining a hypothetical market in insurance people take out to indemnify themselves against the
possibility of an accident or some other disabling event.

I want to suggest an alternative to Dworkin's approach to the problem of
shortfalls. I intend the approach I suggest to apply to shortfalls in any of the
major types of means that contribute to people's abilities to pursue their
values: mental and physical powers, liberties and opportunities, and resources. The guiding thought throughout is that the purpose of these means
is to enable human beings to pursue the projects they formulate and to try
to realize the values they conceive, that is, to be effective agents. I assume
that in a good society, all members would have the means to be effective
agents, insofar as that society's institutions and practices can be arranged to
enable them to do so.

I shall assume for the moment that some plausible way of defining the
notion of an adequate (or "normal") share of overall means can be devised.
Dworkin, remember, cites the difficulty of defining a standard of normality
in mental and physical powers as a benchmark for compensation as one of
his reasons for rejecting the proposal that we should try to equalize differences in mental and physical powers through compensation. I shall consider
the problem of defining the notion of an adequate share of means in section
IV. For now, though, I wish to set that problem aside.

As Dworkin observes, no amount of compensation in the form of material
goods can make up for severe deprivations of mental or physical powers. A
similar observation could be made about deprivations of both the other
major types of means. No amount of compensation in the form of material or
other resources can enable a person who is utterly deprived of liberties and
opportunities to be an effective agent. Similarly, neither mental and physical
powers nor liberties and opportunities can be sufficient to enable a person
to be an effective agent if that person is deprived of the basic material necessities of life. Each of these types of means contributes to enabling people to
be effective agents in a distinctive way. To a limited extent substitution of
one type of good for another may help sustain a person's effectiveness as an
agent. For example, it may be possible to compensate a person who has
unusually limited material resources or wealth by making greater opportunities available to that person than to others. The general point, though, is that
substitutions of this sort are possible only within relatively narrow limits.

We can describe this situation generally by saying that the different types
of means are *functionally complementary*. In considering how to make provisions for people to have the means to be effective agents, we must take into
account the fact that different means contribute in diverse ways.

Suppose, now, that we were to try to construct an overall index of basic
means like the index of primary goods Rawls suggests. I shall call the imagined index a *means index*. Such an index would represent the overall extent

of a person's means as a value on a scale in order to determine whether that person has adequate means to be an effective agent. Suppose further that we were to stipulate, as a matter of convention, that the value of an adequate share of basic means should be represented by the number 1. (Recall that I have postponed the substantive problem of defining the concept of an adequate share to section IV of this chapter.) Then in principle we could express the value of the means available to any given individual to pursue her values as a number less than, equal to, or greater than 1. According to our convention, a person whose means have an overall value less than 1 has an inadequate share of means, whereas a person whose means have a value of 1 has an adequate share, and someone whose means have a value greater than 1 has a more than adequate share.

Before continuing, I should say that I do not mean these simple mathematical conventions to be taken too literally. In his *Nicomachean Ethics* Aristotle observes that we should search "for that degree of precision in each kind of study which the nature of the subject at hand admits."[39] I do not think the study of the means that enable people to be effective agents is amenable to precise measurement in real life of the sort that would be necessary to make the kinds of mathematical calculations I shall imagine here useful. My purpose is illustrative, not literal. I want only to use mathematical symbols to convey an intuitive idea, not to propose that we make use in real life of mathematical calculations of the kind I shall imagine.

If the different types of means that empower people to pursue their values are functionally complementary, then the value of a person's overall share of means cannot be determined by addition as though, say, an adequate share of mental and physical powers had a value of .33, a similar share of liberties and opportunities had the same value of .33, and an adequate share of resources had a value of .34, with a sum of $.33 + .33 + .34 = 1.0$. If it were possible to calculate the value of a person's means index by addition, then compensation problems of the kind Dworkin identifies would not arise. Clearly, though, these problems do arise. For example, we could not adequately compensate a person with no mental and physical powers (with a value of 0) by increasing the value of her share of resources to .67, bringing the sum of the values of the means available to her to $0 + .33 + .67 = 1.0$. The idea that a person with this set of means should be regarded as having the means to be an effective agent is plainly absurd.

A more plausible approach to calculating the value of a person's means would be to treat the major types of means as factors whose values can be multiplied to produce a figure representing the overall value of her means.

[39] Aristotle, *Nicomachean Ethics*, ed. Martin Ostwald (Indianapolis: Bobbs-Merrill, 1962), book 1, chap. 3, 1094b 25.

For example, we might say that an alert, energetic, intelligent, and vigorous person's mental and physical powers have a value of 1, whereas a comatose person's mental and physical powers have a value of or close to 0. Similarly, we could say that the value of a fully adequate share of liberties and opportunities equals 1, as does the value of a fully adequate share of resources. Then the means index value for a person who enjoys a fully adequate share of mental and physical powers, liberties and opportunities, and resources would be $1 \times 1 \times 1 = 1$. Similarly, the means index value for a person who has a fully adequate share of liberties and opportunities and of resources, but who has less than adequate intelligence or a moderate physical disability (with a value of 0.8) would be $0.8 \times 1 \times 1 = 0.8$.

Although this rather fanciful mathematical illustration is not to be taken literally, it can help us to express some of the consequences of the fact that the different types of means that enable people to be effective agents are functionally complementary. For example, it can help us to express the intuition that although people who are mildly deprived of some types of means can be compensated by being provided with means of another type, compensation becomes more difficult the more severe the deprivation happens to be. If we use the letter P to represent a person's mental and physical powers, the letter L to represent her liberties and opportunities, and the letter R to represent her resources, then if her mental and physical powers fall only moderately short of the level considered adequate, it may be possible to make up that shortfall by providing her with a more than adequate share of some other means. If, say, $P = 0.8$ while $L = 1$, but $R = 1.25$, then the value of her overall means index is $0.8 \times 1 \times 1.25 = 1$. However, if her shortfall in one of the major types of means is more serious (so that, say, $P = 0.5$), then a disproportionately greater share of other goods will be needed to bring her overall means index to an acceptable level (if $P = 0.5$ and $L = 1$, then the value of R will have to be 2 to yield a product of 1). Similarly, the illustration can be used to express the fact that shortfalls of more than one type of means tend to have compounding effects. For instance, if a person with adequate mental and physical powers ($P = 1$) has moderately inadequate liberties and opportunities ($L = 0.8$) and similarly inadequate resources ($R = 0.8$), that person's overall means index value will be a meager $1 \times 0.8 \times 0.8 = 0.64$. This is roughly the position that many black Americans find themselves in today.

Again, I do not intend this illustration to be taken literally. I use it only to convey in a symbolic way some intuitions connected with the fact that the different types of means that empower people to be effective agents are functionally complementary in relation to one another. I do not want to encourage a fetishistic taste for mathematical precision in matters in which that kind of precision cannot really be attained. In the real world, calculating the value of a person's means index would be a rougher and more intuitive exercise than it appears in these simple illustrations. It would not, however, be a meaningless exercise.

The idea of a means index composed of functionally complementary components, as a particular way of expressing the notion that human beings have a generalizable interest in having the means necessary to pursue the projects they formulate and to try to realize the values they conceive, suggests three points that, taken together, define an approach to the problem of shortfalls that differs from the compensatory approach that underpins Dworkin's insurance scheme.

First, if different types of means are functionally specific, then a compensatory approach to the problem of shortfalls should be adopted only if it is not feasible to correct the shortcoming in kind. In other words, if a person has an inadequate share of one type of means, the most appropriate response would be to ensure that her share of *that* means is adequate rather than to compensate her by providing her with a larger share of some other good. If, for example, her mental powers are inadequately developed because of social conditions that fail to provide the opportunities, encouragement, and support that people need to develop their mental skills, the most appropriate response would be to improve those conditions so that she and others will be able to cultivate their mental powers. If her liberties or opportunities are inadequate for her to be an effective agent, then her liberties or opportunities should be improved. Political and social arrangements are acceptable when they empower people to be effective agents to an adequate degree. If people lack the means necessary to be effective agents, the appropriate response is to eliminate the deprivation, not to compensate those people for it.

Second, if it is not feasible to eliminate deprivation of one type of means, compensation in the form of a larger than usual share of some other means is appropriate if and only if that step can be expected to raise the *overall* value of a person's "means index." Again, the central idea behind the approach to the comparison of alternative social arrangements that I am describing here is that human institutions and practices should enable people to acquire the means necessary to pursue the projects they formulate and to try to realize the values they conceive. If compensation can help people do that, then it should be considered.

Third, if no amount of compensation can bring the overall value of a person's means index up to an adequate or near-adequate level, then compensation is inappropriate. If we want political and social arrangements to serve our generalizable interest in having the means necessary to be effective agents, then it makes no sense to compensate people for shortfalls in those means in ways that still leave them unable to pursue projects or try to realize the values they conceive. We must accept the fact that, as human beings, we cannot solve every human problem that may arise or guarantee the full, rich life of an effective agent to every human being. We must work to eradicate deprivation wherever we can, but we cannot create a society in which no deprivation or suffering whatsoever occurs.

These implications of the idea of a means index suggest why the worries Dworkin raises about the lack of an upper bound on compensation for people who are severely deprived of one type of means do not arise in the agency prospects approach. Those worries arise only when we lose sight of the *purpose* of means. That purpose is to empower individuals. Political and social arrangement should make available to people the means they need to pursue the projects they formulate and to try to realize the values they conceive. Within the perspective of humanist liberalism, compensation that does not serve this purpose—such as that which, on Dworkin's insurance scheme, might be given to a person who is mentally incompetent—would be inappropriate.

The idea of a means index composed of distinct, functionally complementary types of means points to a reason why we would want at least some basic types of rights and liberties to be protected in a virtually absolute way by any set of political and social institutions and practices. That reason is that rights and liberties are among the distinctive types of means people need to conceive and pursue values in an effective manner. If our rights or liberties were to be violated, or if we were to trade some of them away, the consequence would in nearly every case be to diminish the means available to us to be effective agents. This approach, then, offers a basis for the conclusion that protection of basic rights and liberties is a *necessary* feature of any good society. It does *not* suggest the conclusion that protection of those rights and liberties should have *priority* over all the other desiderata we might apply to political and social arrangements, since it also suggests that the other principal means that enable people to be effective agents—adequate mental and physical powers and adequate resources—are also necessary.

I do not suppose that the overall list of basic means for which I have argued—mental and physical powers, liberties and opportunities, and resources, including status and recognition as well as income and wealth—is complete. The list can be further amended if amendments turn out to be warranted. There is no way to know in advance whether additional revisions will be needed or what the content of these revisions might turn out to be. The list is by nature open-ended and subject to revision on the basis of convincing arguments. I do think, though, that the list I have proposed is an improvement over the narrowly focused account based on material resources that underpins Dworkin's theory of equality of resources and the more extensive and variegated, but still flawed, account of primary goods that Rawls offers in his theory of justice as fairness.

I have discussed the content of the basic means individuals need in order to pursue their goals and values at some length in part because recent discussions within liberal theory that focus on means, such as Dworkin's and Rawls's, have relatively less to say about this topic than about the distribution of these goods. Yet a theory that claims to explain the way in which goods should be distributed can only be as good as the substantive account of those goods on which it relies. My main aims in this discussion have been to demonstrate the need for a more richly textured account of these basic means than either Dworkin or Rawls offers and to suggest some amendments to Rawls's theory of the primary goods that seem to me necessary to construct a credible account of the bases of political and social criticism for a pluralistic society.

It might be argued that the account of basic means for which I have argued is *too* broad. The claim behind this objection is that in extending the idea of basic means in the way I have suggested, we make that idea too unwieldy to be useful for the purpose of social criticism. Items like "mental and physical powers" or "status and recognition" may be more difficult to measure than apparently better-defined items such as "basic rights and liberties" or "income and wealth." Further, by multiplying the number of items on our list of basic means, it could be argued, we make the task of social criticism too complicated. In light of this objection, Rawls's more compact list of primary goods may seem preferable to my account of basic means.

If the purpose of a list of basic means were to specify goods whose provision to individuals should be ensured by the state and its officials or to produce a blueprint for an ideal society, then my list might well be too broad, as well as inappropriate in other ways. At least one of the major categories on that list—status and recognition—cannot be provided to individuals by the state and its officials in any case; it is a good that can only be given to citizens by one another. But the purpose of the list of basic means is not simply to provide guidelines for public officials or to specify objectives for public policy. The state and its officials are neither the sole important agents of political and social change nor the only possible objects of political and social criticism. The culture and practices that prevail in a society can be objects of social criticism, too. The culture of racism, for example, is resistant to state control.[40] Even if it were possible to establish state control over that culture, we should not want to establish that control. To do that would be to endow the state with too much power, power that would be oppressive and inconsistent with a liberal society. Yet a culture of racism makes a great deal of difference to the way in which a society works, to the things the members of that society are able to do. It blocks recognition of the fact that all members

---

[40] At least that culture is resistant to state control in the short term. In the longer term, cultural practices are susceptible to state manipulation at least to a degree. Nationalism, for example, can be seen as a product of deliberate state policies. For an interpretation of nationalism along these lines, see Benedict Anderson, *Imagined Communities: Reflections on the Origin and Spread of Nationalism*, 2d ed. (New York and London: Verso, 1991).

of society are agents whose claims to the means necessary for a person to pursue her values and projects should have standing equal to the claims of all others.

The purpose of an account of the bases of political and social criticism is to identify the key attributes that distinguish a good society from a bad one, regardless of the source of those attributes or of the strategies that are most likely to be effective in bringing about their reform. If those attributes fall easily within the competence of the state and its officials, as basic rights that can be guaranteed by a constitution and a legal and judiciary system do, then the state and those officials are likely to be the most appropriate avenue for their reform. If they fall elsewhere, then other avenues will have to be pursued. Political theory cannot restrict its focus to one domain of action that is defined in advance by a given structure of institutions and practices. To assume that criticism and proposals for reform must focus on the state, the government, or public officials is to condemn political theory to a subsidiary role, one that cannot even consider challenges to the status quo in the largest sense. Indeed, cultural criticism may be the kind of criticism to which political theories that are willing to confront that status quo lead most naturally. If we review the great figures in the history of political philosophy—Plato, Machiavelli, Hobbes, Rousseau—we find that none of these writers confined his attention to political institutions and practices in the narrow sense. All in fact mounted trenchant attacks on cultural norms that were prevalent in their times, attacks that were integral to their analyses of the shortcomings of their societies.[41] If we want to come to grips with the flaws in our own society, we cannot restrict our scope to the state, as some of our political theorists in recent times have been inclined to do.

IV

I shall now take up a question I have deliberately set aside up to this point: how should the basic means required for people to be effective agents be distributed? A theory of distributive justice is only as good as the account of the things to be distributed on which it relies. But a theory of the basic means people need to be effective agents would be empty if it were not accompanied by some account of the way in which these means should be allocated to persons.

In this section I shall describe briefly the shape I think such an account should take. My aim is not to offer a complete theory of distributive justice.

[41] For some representative discussions in the secondary literature, see Eric Havelock, *A Preface to Plato* (Cambridge, Mass.: Harvard University Press, 1963); David Johnston, *The Rhetoric of Leviathan: Thomas Hobbes and the Politics of Cultural Transformation* (Princeton: Princeton University Press, 1986); and Jean Starobinski, *Jean-Jacques Rousseau: Transparency and Obstruction* (Chicago: University of Chicago Press, 1988).

It is to identify in a general way the distributions that need to occur if a society is to be a good society, not to develop a prescription that would determine how every good should be distributed. So the goods on which I shall focus will be those that belong on a list of the basic means people need generally to pursue their values. Moreover, I shall not discuss the distribution of these goods in detail. Instead, I shall identify some principles to which I think we should appeal when we have to consider particular distributions of the goods that constitute the basic means people need to be effective agents. My main concern will be to describe the notion of an *adequate share* of these means.

One note before proceeding further: to identify principles that describe the way in which a good should be distributed is not to identify a particular agent as the one that should be responsible for ensuring that actual distributions conform to these principles. I do not assume that the state should be the sole or even the principal agent enforcing the principles I describe. To ask what the principles of distributive justice should be is not to ask how those principles should be realized; these are two distinct questions, and although they are related to each other, no good is done by conflating them.

I begin with a complication. Because the basic means that people need to be effective agents are diverse, we do not just have to define the notion of an adequate share of basic means taken as a whole. An adequate share of basic means *means* an adequate share of each of several different things. A single distributive pattern may not be appropriate for all these things. So the idea of looking for a single principle to describe the way in which the basic means should be distributed quickly breaks down into the task of describing appropriate distributions for several diverse types of goods.

The observation that diverse goods call for diverse distributive principles is central to Michael Walzer's arguments about distributive justice in *Spheres of Justice*. Walzer's purposes are not the same as mine: he wants to describe principles of distributive justice that apply across the entire range of distributions, whereas I seek only to formulate principles to describe an appropriate distribution of the basic means that people require to be effective agents. But Walzer is the only major theorist of justice who has considered seriously the distributive implications of the fact that goods are diverse. Since that fact is also important to my own account of the bases of political criticism, it is reasonable to think of Walzer's arguments as possible answers to the question I have formulated here.

Walzer's point of departure is a critique of the idea that there should be "a single criterion, or a single set of interconnected criteria, for all distributions."[42] To search for unity, he suggests, is to misunderstand the subject matter of distributive justice. That subject matter is diverse, and its diversity calls for a plurality of distributive principles.

[42] Walzer, *Spheres*, p. 4.

Of course, Walzer suggests, that plurality itself requires a coherent defense. There must be principles that justify our choice of distributive criteria, even if those criteria are plural. The principles that Walzer suggests focus on the notion of the social meanings of goods. These social meanings, he observes, are historically and culturally particular. They change over time and differ from place to place. Furthermore, different goods often have distinct social meanings. The general rule Walzer proposes is that distributions of goods should be faithful to their social meanings, to the understandings about the significance of those goods that the members of a community of meaning share with one another. "A given society is just," he claims, "if its substantive life is lived in a certain way—that is, in a way faithful to the shared understandings of the members."[43]

Walzer points out that the rule that goods should be distributed in accordance with their social meanings entails that when goods have distinct social meanings, their distributions must be autonomous. That is, goods should be distributed in accordance with *their* particular social meanings; the distribution of one good should be independent of the distribution of others when the meanings of those goods are distinct. In pluralistic societies, this conception of distributive principles leads to a vision of complex equality in which a variety of distinct distributions, each determined by its own independent distributive principles, coexist. This plurality of distributions makes for a plurality of ways in which individuals can do well. In a pluralistic society in which the distinct social meanings of diverse social goods prevail, someone who has a greater share than others of one good may wind up having a lesser share of the next good, so that opportunities to do well in at least *some* respect are widely dispersed among the members of the society as a whole. According to Walzer, this autonomy in the distribution of diverse goods is likely to make for greater overall equality than any other conceivable arrangement.[44]

Walzer's vision of complex equality is highly attractive. But the principle on which he relies to justify that vision—that distributions of goods should be faithful to their social meanings—is problematical and, in the end, inadequate as a basis for a theory of distributive justice. The vision of complex equality can and should be defended on a basis different from the one Walzer offers.

One difficulty with the principle underlying Walzer's vision is that it assumes that goods have commonly accepted meanings to which we can look for guidance in determining how a given good should be distributed. This assumption is true in part, but it is not true enough of the time to make Walzer's principle a useful guide to practice. When a genuine shared understanding about the social meaning of a good exists, controversy about the

[43] Ibid., p. 313.
[44] Ibid., pp. 320–21.

distribution of that good is rare. Controversies about distribution are most likely to arise when those common meanings do *not* exist. When that happens, the precept that distributions of goods should be faithful to their social meanings is not much help, because there is no accepted social meaning for the distribution of a good to be faithful to.

Walzer suggests parenthetically that when people disagree about the meaning of social goods, justice requires that the society be faithful to those disagreements by providing institutional channels for their expression and adjudication.[45] This is a reasonable suggestion, but it offers us far less than we have a right to ask from a theory of distributive justice. What such a theory might be useful for is to help us decide *how* to adjudicate disagreements. Disagreement about the meaning of social goods is the normal case, especially in the complex, pluralistic societies on which Walzer focuses. Yet his principle that distributions should be faithful to the shared understandings of people about the social meanings of goods does not seem to promise much guidance in cases of real disagreement.

Another difficulty with the principle behind Walzer's vision of complex equality has to do with its implications for societies that are not pluralistic. Walzer forthrightly concedes in his opening chapter that in "a society where dominance and monopoly are not violations but enactments of meaning, where social goods are conceived in hierarchical terms . . . there is no room, and there are no criteria, for autonomous distributions." Toward the end of *Spheres of Justice* he returns to this problem, pointing out that "in a society where social meanings are integrated and hierarchical, justice will come to the aid of inequality." Walzer illustrates the point by referring to the (inegalitarian) practices of an Indian village. He argues that justice "cannot require a radical redesign of the village against the shared understandings of its members. If it did, justice itself would be tyrannical." We could, he argues, try to convince the villagers that their doctrines are false, but we cannot justifiably compel them to change their practices in violation of their understandings.[46]

Walzer's argument about the way in which we should conduct ourselves toward villagers who hold shared understandings that are at variance with our ideas conflates two issues that should be kept distinct. The first issue is about *what justice is*. According to the principle that Walzer proposes, a just distribution of goods is defined as a distribution that is faithful to shared understandings about the social meanings of those goods. That principle tells us that if the villagers understand the social meanings of goods in ways that support an unequal distribution of those goods, an unequal distribution is ipso facto a just distribution. The second issue is about the *strategies* we

[45] Ibid., p. 313.
[46] Ibid., pp. 26–27, 313–14.

might adopt to make unjust practices more just. These strategies can themselves be more or less just.

Walzer is right to suggest that we should not ride roughshod over the shared understandings of the members of a village in order to impose our own ideas about justice. But the reason why we should not do so is that we would be forcing the villagers to live in accordance with a conception of justice they do not understand. Our coercion would be unjust (unless we were preventing a greater injustice some of the villagers would otherwise impose on one another). It would be unjust because it is unnecessarily coercive, not because the villagers' ideas about distribution are just.

Walzer, as I have mentioned, suggests that we can always try to convince the villagers that their doctrines are false. But if justice in distributions is defined as faithfulness to shared understandings about the social meaning of goods, then we would have nothing to appeal to in our effort to convince the villagers that they are wrong. Their practice would be right precisely because it is in accordance with their shared understandings. We would have no ground for complaining that that practice is unjust.

Walzer's principle—that distributions of goods are just when they are in accordance with shared understandings of the social meaning of those goods—is flawed. That principle fails to yield needed guidance in cases where shared understandings do not exist—as is normal in a pluralistic society—and yields misleading guidance in nonpluralistic, hierarchical societies where shared understandings do exist. Shared understandings of the social meaning of goods do play an important role in their distribution, but they do not play the fundamental, justice-defining role Walzer describes for them. Walzer's vision of complex equality is attractive, but the general principle he offers to support that vision is not.

The central point to which we should refer in thinking about distributive justice is that human beings have a generalizable interest in having the means necessary to be effective agents. Moreover, we *equally* have an interest in having these means. It does not follow from these claims that we all should possess equal shares of all goods. In fact, the liberal view that human beings reasonably conceive diverse values and conceptions of the good entails—pragmatically if not logically—that under most conditions, the distributions of some goods at a given time should be *un*equal. But the liberal view, or at least my humanist interpretation of that view, also entails that all human beings should have *adequate shares* of at least some basic goods.

To see why some goods should be distributed unequally, consider the following example. Suppose that all the members of a society start the year with equal shares of all the basic means—equal mental and physical powers, equal liberties and opportunities, and equal bundles of resources—but with different values. Their resources include both means of production and consumer goods. Because the members have different values, they wish to live their lives in different ways. Some, who are ambitious, use their means of production to produce as many commodities as possible. By the end of the year they have accumulated large stocks of commodities. Others devote just enough time to production to get by and spend the rest of their time enjoying their consumer goods. At the end of the year, when the members of the first group are flush with spare commodities, the members of the second have no more than the shares with which they began. Different members of the society as a whole now possess unequal bundles of commodities.

The inequality in the members' bundles of commodities that exists at the end of the year may seem unfair to an observer who enters the scene with no knowledge of the previous year's experience. But that perception is corrected once we fill the observer in on what the members have been doing over the previous year. From the viewpoint of humanist liberalism, it would be unfair to seize commodities now from the more ambitious members and redistribute them to the rest. The inequalities that exist at the end of the year have arisen entirely because of differences between the different members' values, not because some started off with advantages over others or because some have had better luck than others. Those who are worse off at the end of the year have no ground for complaining of their lot, which is a consequence of the values they pursued during the course of the year.

Of course, a great deal of the inequality that exists in real life can be accounted for by the unequal distribution of advantages and disadvantages. The point of my illustration is just to show that even in a world in which everyone enjoyed equal powers, liberties, opportunities, and resources, inequalities would still arise.

In humanist liberalism, inequalities that arise because of differences in people's values or in the projects they pursue are legitimate. These inequalities may be of many different kinds. A person who wants to become an outstanding athlete will try to cultivate her physical well-being in general as well as the more particular capabilities and skills required for the sport in which she wants to excel. A person who wants to be a professional writer will try to develop his linguistic competence to a high degree and may be relatively neglectful of his body and physical powers and skills. Someone whose ambition is to become an actor or singer with a good deal of status and fame will use the means available to her to pursue that goal. Finally, someone who just wants to have a reasonably comfortable, easy, quiet life may not cultivate any of his mental or physical powers, or accumulate any resources, in greater quantities than are necessary to attain that objective. Legitimate inequalities can arise in different types of goods.

Now to return to our question: how, in view of the fact that human beings have a generalizable interest in having the means necessary to be effective agents *and* in view of the assumption of reasonable value pluralism, should the basic means required for people to be effective agents be distributed?

I suggest that the answer to this question has two parts. The first part focuses on our equal interest in having *equal* shares of the basic means that every person requires in order to participate fully in the life of her society. The second part focuses on our equal interest in having the *different* goods that are useful for realizing our *particular* values and for pursuing the particular projects in which we take an interest.

I shall define a *fully adequate share* of basic means as the share that is sufficient to enable individuals to participate fully as equals in the life of their societies, including the activities of political deliberation through which the members of a society try to chart their future as a community. To the extent that goods are necessary to achieve this kind of participation, I shall call them *value-independent*. Value-independent goods, or value-independent shares of goods, are those shares of goods that all individuals ought to have, regardless of the particular values they want to realize and the particular projects they wish to pursue.

Goods that are not necessary and shares of goods that exceed the amount necessary for individuals to participate fully as equals in the life of their societies are *value-dependent*.

The *first* distributive principle of humanist liberalism is that every human being should have a share of basic means that is fully adequate to enable that person to participate fully as an equal in the life of her society and in the processes of political deliberation and decision making. The content of the goods necessary to achieve the status of a full participant will vary from one society to the next and over time. It will vary in part because of technological change. In a society with no written language, literacy is not among the powers that constitute an adequate share. In a society with no electronic media, access to a radio or other electronic sources of information is not one of the material goods that constitute an adequate share. In a society in which information is transmitted mainly through the written word and electronic media, both these things should be included in the bundle of means that constitute an adequate share. It will also vary in part for reasons that may be culturally specific. The ability to understand, read, speak, and write in the language or languages in which public affairs are discussed in one's society is a part of the bundle of means that constitute an adequate share, but the particular language or languages obviously vary from one society to the next.

The content of the goods necessary to achieve the status of a full participant varies from one society to the next in part because of cultural variation, but the cultural variation that is relevant to humanist liberalism differs from the kind of cultural particularism to which Walzer's theory of distributive justice points. According to Walzer's principle, a society's shared understandings of the meanings of goods *define* justice for that society. In humanist liberalism, a society's shared linguistic and other norms help to determine the content of the list of basic means that constitute a fully adequate share. Walzer's theory is radically particularist;[47] humanist liberalism is particularist in details.

The *second* distributive principle of humanist liberalism is that the distribution of goods that are not necessary for individuals to participate fully in the lives of their societies or shares of goods beyond those which are necessary—value-dependent goods—should be *value-sensitive*. In other words, these goods should be distributed in patterns that are contingent on, and are the products of, the particular values and projects that the members of that society want to pursue.

Both the content of value-dependent goods in a society and the appropriate distributive configuration or pattern of those goods will vary from one society to the next and over time as a result of the particular values and projects individuals want to pursue. Neither of these things can be determined from the outside, as it were, in the absence of knowledge of the particular values and projects that individuals have pursued over time.

The second distributive principle of humanist liberalism expresses the grain of truth that is present in Robert Nozick's critique of patterned end-state principles of distributive justice. From the viewpoint of humanist liberalism, Nozick's theory erroneously treats all goods as if they were equally value-dependent. That theory neglects the generalizable interest of all human beings in having the means necessary to be effective agents while focusing wholly on some human beings' interest in having means that are useful for the pursuit of their *particular* projects and values. But *some* goods—many goods—*are* value-dependent, or are value-dependent beyond the point at which the quantity of those goods available to a person exceeds a certain share. In humanist liberalism, unlike Nozick's theory, our *equal* interest in having the *different* goods that are useful for realizing our particular values is placed in the context of and subordinate to our *equal* generalizable interest in having the *equal* basic means necessary to be effective agents—agents who can, among other things, participate fully as equals in political deliberations to chart their society's future.

These two principles describe the overall shape that an account of the way in which goods should be distributed would take in a theory of distributive justice formulated within the framework of humanist liberalism. They do not describe particular distributions of particular goods. Since these particular distributions are dependent on variations in technology and culture as well as, to a degree, on individuals' actual values, the amount that we can say about them in a general account is limited. Nevertheless, there are some more concrete things we can say about the distribution of particular goods. In these comments, my aim is to suggest how we might develop an account of an acceptable range of distributions for some of the diverse kinds of basic

[47] This is his own description in ibid., p. xiv.

means, an account that would be consistent with the central claim that as human beings, we have a generalizable interest in having the means required to be effective agents.

.   .   .

Basic rights and liberties, like those Rawls singles out in his first principle of justice as fairness, present perhaps the simplest case. These rights and liberties are relatively value-independent. People need these rights and liberties, or some of them, to pursue almost any values they might want to pursue. In fact, without basic rights and liberties, human beings would probably find it difficult, and perhaps impossible, to develop the skills that are necessary to become agents and to acquire a sense of justice. In a good society, basic rights and liberties would be guaranteed equally for everyone.

Robert Nozick has argued that people should be able to transfer their basic rights to others, if they wish, just as they might transfer a commodity in exchange for some other good.[48] According to his account, individuals should be allowed to transfer their basic rights because those rights derive from an absolute right of self-ownership that all individuals enjoy. For Nozick, this right of self-ownership is the foundation of all our other rights. This view undercuts the distinction between basic rights and other, less fundamental rights.

From the perspective of humanist liberalism, basic rights are basic because, and insofar as, they are necessary means for people to pursue the projects and values they conceive. People whose basic rights are not guaranteed lack a means that is essential for them to be effective agents. We can reasonably assume that under ordinary circumstances, no one would be willing to give up a good that is essential for that person to be an effective agent. Hence in humanist liberalism, as in Rawls's theory of justice as fairness and most other versions of liberal political theory, basic rights and liberties are regarded as inalienable.

There are some circumstances—extraordinary or extreme ones—in which many people *would* be willing to transfer away basic liberties. For example, many parents would be willing to sacrifice their liberty to save a child from death. But in these circumstances, most people who would be willing to sacrifice their liberty would be willing to sacrifice their lives, too, if, say, that is what would be necessary to save their children. A human being's sacrifice of her liberty or basic rights is virtually equivalent to her sacrifice of her life. A sacrifice of this nature *is* a kind of death, the death of the person as an effective agent, as a being who has the means to pursue her own values and goals.

---

[48] See chap. 2 herein.

Basic rights and liberties do not, as Rawls alleges, take lexical priority over all other goods. These rights are essential, but they are not *more* essential than basic mental and physical powers or the material necessities of life. What distinguishes basic rights and liberties from other equally essential goods is the fact that basic rights and liberties are entirely, or almost entirely, value-independent. *All* these most basic means are equally essential for human beings to develop and to exercise their capacities as agents. So in humanist liberalism, they are all regarded as equally fundamental.

.   .   .

Like basic rights and liberties, some mental and physical powers are essential for people to be effective agents. But mental and physical powers are also attached to persons, and subject to their control, at least over the long term, in ways that basic rights and liberties are not. Whereas basic rights and liberties can be secured for individuals by the political institutions of their society, people must develop their own mental and physical powers. They need favorable social conditions and resources to develop these powers, of course, but even with favorable conditions, they must do the developing themselves.

According to the humanist view I have set out to describe in this chapter, human beings have a generalizable interest in having the means necessary for them to be effective agents. These means include mental and physical powers. But human beings also have a particular interest in pursuing the particular values and projects they conceive. People choose to develop different mental and physical powers in light of the different values they wish to pursue.

I have suggested in section 1 of this chapter that the claim that a person's mental and physical powers should be included on the list of basic means available to her to advance her goals and values leads to a distinction between persons and the means available to them and assigns her aspirations, desires, projects, and values to the person while assigning her mental and physical powers to her means. In reality, though, mental and physical powers cannot be disentangled neatly from aspirations and values. People develop some of their powers instead of others because they want to pursue some values rather than others; thus a person's mental and physical powers are at least partly value-dependent. Because of this fact, we cannot simply declare that in a good society all individuals would have the same mental and physical powers or even that all people would have powers of equivalent values. People choose to develop particular powers because those powers are valuable *to them*, in light of their values; the same powers might be far less valuable, or not valuable at all, to another person.

Yet a person's mental and physical powers are not entirely value-dependent. Some of these powers are valuable to human beings as such, regardless of the particular values they want to pursue. We may assume that any person—any agent—has, at a minimum, an interest in developing those powers that are necessary to maintain mental and physical well-being. These powers include the full use of one's limbs, hands, and other parts of the body; they include the use of the senses for perception; they also include the mental and physical skills required for a person to be a competent speaker; and they include the use of one's powers of thinking and reasoning to relate means to ends, to deliberate about and select ends, and to calculate at least in rudimentary ways. These capabilities and skills are needed by human beings generally to pursue all or nearly all the projects people normally conceive. People can get along without some of these capabilities, of course. A person can be deprived of one of the senses or of the use of a limb and still live a meaningful life. But we would not hesitate to agree that a person who lacks one or more of these powers is deprived, that her ability to pursue projects is in some way impaired, even if it is not destroyed by her handicap.

We may also assume, I think, that any person has an interest in having those powers that are necessary to enable her to participate fully as an equal with others in her society. Someone who participates fully as an equal with others is at least capable of becoming aware of the affairs that affect herself and her fellow citizens and of participating in deliberations with others about matters that affect the society or political community as a whole. The things that affect a society as a whole also usually affect a particular person's prospects for advancing her values or for acting on them in an effective way. So our interest in having the powers necessary to become aware of and participate in deliberations about matters of common concern is a fundamental human interest.

The powers necessary to be a fully participating member of society are, as I have said, in part culture- or society-dependent. In any society, those powers include competence in the language (or languages) in which information about matters of common concern is disseminated and in which deliberations about these matters are normally conducted. For example, the members of American society have an interest in being competent users of the English language. This interest is *contingent* in the sense that it just happens to be a matter of contingent fact that English is the language in which, overwhelmingly, public information is disseminated and public deliberations are conducted in the United States. But it is also *fundamental* in the sense that all members of American society and the projects in which they are interested are profoundly affected by the affairs that affect American society as a whole.

In the case of mental and physical powers that are either essential for well-being or necessary for individuals to participate fully as equals in their society, that society should assume substantial responsibility for ensuring that its members develop those powers. This responsibility is likely to raise controversial issues, especially where the powers or skills necessary to be a fully participating member of society are concerned. In the United States, for example, some people object to educational standards that require children who do not speak English in their homes or neighborhoods to learn that language in their schools. I do not think those objections should prevail, but there is no escaping the fact that the line separating essential from non-essential capabilities, powers, and skills is fuzzy and subject to reasonable disputes.

The farther away we move from those capabilities and skills that are essential for basic well-being and for people to become fully participating members of their society, the more value-dependent mental and physical powers become. For powers that are value-dependent, people should have roughly *equal access* to the means required to develop those powers and skills.

By equal access I do not mean mere equal opportunity. If each person in a group of one hundred people has an equal chance to win a single prize (say in a drawing or raffle), then we could say that each of those people has an equal opportunity to obtain the prize. Yet only one of those people will win the prize. In this situation, the one hundred people have equal opportunity, but highly unequal access to the prize. In view of the crucial role that mental and physical powers play in enabling people to be effective agents, equal opportunity to the means to develop those powers is not adequate. People should have equal access to the means to develop their mental and physical powers, or access that is as nearly equal as a society can maintain. This does not mean that universities should open their doors to everyone regardless of their prior training or abilities to do university-level work. It does mean that anyone with the requisite capabilities should be able to find a place in a university.

At the end of section I, earlier in this chapter, I suggested that inclusion of mental and physical powers on a list of the basic means people need to pursue their values and projects leads to a distinction between the person and her circumstances in which we assign aspirations, projects, and values to the person and mental and physical powers to her circumstances. In reality, people's powers cannot be neatly disentangled from their values, because people begin to develop certain powers rather than others at a very early age and because the relation between values and powers in real life is dynamic, closely intertwined, and mutually reinforcing. But if—and only if—all the members of society had equal access to the means necessary to develop their powers, then we would not have to disentangle those two things. For we could then assume that the powers people actually develop are those they would want to develop, and that variations in people's powers can be accounted for solely by variation in their values rather than by variation in the means available to them to develop their powers.

If people have equal *access* to the means to develop their mental and physical powers, they will *not* have equal mental and physical *powers* at the end of the day. People make decisions to develop their powers or skills based on their values. Because people's values are diverse, they will want to develop diverse skills. Moreover, some will be more ambitious than others and will be more interested in developing their powers generally than others. *This* kind of inequality is consistent with—and in fact entailed by— liberal principles, principles that should be capable of accommodating diverse goals, values, and conceptions of the good.

.   .   .

Material goods, like mental and physical powers, are in part value-dependent. But they are not *wholly* value-dependent. In considering how these goods should be distributed, we must bear in mind *both* the equal interest we have as human beings in having equal shares of the basic means people need to participate fully in the life of their society *and* our equal interest in having the *different* goods that are useful for realizing our particular values.

Every human being should have a share of material goods sufficient to maintain her mental and physical well-being and to maintain the powers required to participate fully as an equal in her society. A package of material goods of this "size" constitutes a bare, minimally adequate share, for which all human beings have a basic need. Our interest as human beings in having a share of material goods of this extent is value-independent and truly fundamental.

As in the case of mental and physical powers, the line between truly essential, value-independent material goods and truly value-dependent goods is fuzzy and liable always to be controversial. No one can say precisely where this line should be drawn, in part because the notion of participating fully as an equal in one's society is itself subject to dispute and in part because, as I have observed, this line is partially culture-dependent. The task of defining the idea of an adequate share of material goods in practice will always be difficult, and the result will always be controversial. It is no more likely that we will ever be able to produce a definitive formula to describe the bundle of material goods that constitutes an adequate share than it is that we will be able to define, once and for all, an optimal speed limit for automobile traffic on highways. Yet at the same time, the problem of defining an adequate share of material goods is no more arbitrary than is that of setting speed limits for highways. In both cases perspicuous reasoning can lead to a narrowing of the problem to within a reasonable range.

To the extent that material goods are value-dependent, they should be distributed in value-sensitive ways. Markets are in principle capable of distributing material goods in value-sensitive ways. Suitably regulated, markets can be reasonably efficient distributors of material goods, more so than any other known institution. But markets do have to be regulated to maintain conditions that approximate those of an ideal market in order to be efficient distributors. The general idea of the market as an efficient distributor of material goods can be grasped by considering carefully Ronald Dworkin's theory of equality of resources.[49] Although Dworkin's theory is really only a fragment of a theory of distributive justice, since it focuses on commodities or material goods, it offers an attractive account of the way in which we should think about the distribution of those goods insofar as they are value-dependent.

Dworkin asks us to imagine a group of shipwreck survivors who have been washed up on a desert island with abundant resources and no native population. They want to divide the island's resources equally among themselves. As a criterion for this division, they devise an envy test. The idea is that no division of resources will be considered an equal division if, once the division is complete, any of the survivors would prefer someone else's bundle of resources to his own bundle.

Dworkin argues that the best way to achieve an equal division would be through an auction in which each survivor receives an equal number of clam shells, which no one values in themselves, to bid for the island's resources. The survivors would bid for the resources they most desire in light of their particular values. Although they might not all be equally happy with the result, since some might have ambitious desires while others have relatively modest ones, at the end of the auction no one would value another person's bundle of resources more than his own, and in that sense their shares would be equal—as equal as they could practicably be made to be, that is, in light of the diversity of the survivors' desires. The survivors' ability to produce an equal division of resources—one that would pass the envy test—is of course dependent on their entering the market on equal terms (i.e., with equal numbers of clam shells).

Dworkin's concept of the auction is, of course, a deliberate simplification. Many adjustments and additions to that idea would have to be made to adapt it to the circumstances of a dynamic economy. Nevertheless, one key feature of ideal markets that is relevant for our normative purposes is already contained in Dworkin's description of the auction. That is the idea that in order for a market to produce a distribution of goods that is genuinely value-sensitive, the participants in that market have to enter it on equal terms. Markets whose participants are not equal in the resources (or clam shells) they bring

[49] Dworkin, "Equality of Resources."

to the market produce distorted results, which are highly sensitive to variations in resources and, therefore, less sensitive to variations in individuals'
values than an ideal market would be. This fact points to an important tension in the way in which markets are viewed from the normative perspective
of humanist liberalism. On the one hand, ideal markets—those in which the
participants enter on an equal footing—are the sole known efficient means
of distributing value-dependent goods. On the other hand, real markets tend
to lead to unequal shares of goods, and people who have accumulated unequal shares of goods enter markets on unequal terms. In the case of markets, our equal interest in having the different goods that are useful for realizing our particular values pulls in two different directions. In the real world
this tension may never be resolvable completely. It can, however, be amelio-
rated by regulation that is sensitive to both poles of the tension.

.   .   .

As human beings, we have a generalizable interest in being recognized by
our fellow human beings as agents with values that are distinctively our own
that we should be able to pursue. This kind of recognition is a value-independent basic means. Without it, our ability to pursue our projects or conceptions of the good would be seriously impaired, whatever the particular
content of those projects or conceptions should happen to be. Recognition
of one another as agents who should be able to pursue their particular values
and projects is a good that the members of a society give to one another.
Recognition of this sort is synonymous with a vigorous sense of justice. This
good should be given in equal shares by the members of a society to one
another as equal citizens.

People sometimes desire recognition beyond that which is due to them by
virtue of their status as equal citizens. Status or recognition in excess of that
to which all are entitled as equal citizens is a value-dependent good. Recognition of the sort that would satisfy this desire is not a basic means, in the
sense in which I have used that concept in describing humanist liberalism.

As long as all the members of a society enjoy the recognition that is their
due as equal citizens, people should be free to seek greater status in much
the same way as they should be free to seek to accumulate material goods or
any other value-dependent means. We can imagine that in a good society
there might be an ideal market in status parallel to the ideal market in material goods Dworkin envisages. People would enter this market with equal
resources, but each person's share of status and the particular type of status
each person enjoys at the end of the day would vary depending on the way
in which those people have in the meantime chosen to deploy their equal
resources.

Like material goods, of course, status is itself a differentiated good. A person can enjoy considerable status within a profession or "field" of action yet be unknown to people who are not participants in or interested observers of that field. Even most entertainers and politicians, who are among the best-known figures in the United States and many other countries, are well known only within small niches of their society.

Status is in part a positional good.[50] That is, it is a good that depends on a person's position in a hierarchy in relation to other people. To a degree, one's possession of status presupposes other people's relative lack of status. We think of some people as having high status because they have *more* status than others.

If status were a *purely* positional good, then no one could ever gain in status without causing someone else to lose status. In real life, competition for status is partly like this; when some people gain in status, the status of others tends to diminish. But it is not entirely like this. Because status is a differentiated good as well as a positional good, it is possible for people to acquire status in complementary ways. For example, one person might acquire considerable status or recognition as a visual artist, whereas another gains status as a writer. Although the two people might think of themselves as competing with each other for greater recognition, their competition is indirect and muted in comparison with that which would occur if only a single hierarchy or scale of status existed.

Although status beyond what is due to the members of a society by virtue of their equal citizenship is not a basic means of the most fundamental kind, the desire for status is historically one of the most pervasive desires we can observe. This fact suggests that the social arrangements that prevail in a good society should be capable of distributing status to the members of that society in amounts greater than would be made possible by the existence of a single hierarchy or scale. In order to do this, a society must be *socially pluralistic*: it must include a variety of different "fields" in which people can try to excel and enable people to choose fields that seem to them congenial to their talents.[51]

V

Although the sketch of a political theory I have offered here is rudimentary, its main points should be clear enough to permit comparisons with the theories I have discussed in the preceding chapters—comparisons that will, I hope, highlight the advantages of humanist liberalism over these other theories. It may be useful here to summarize some of the main features of the humanist view I have described.

[50] For the concept of positional goods, see Fred Hirsch, *Social Limits to Growth* (Cambridge, Mass.: Harvard University Press, 1976).

[51] This conclusion is consistent with Walzer's vision in *Spheres* of a society characterized by complex equality.

First, according to humanist liberalism, *any* good society would enable its members to develop the skills required to be agents and to have a sense of justice. Without these skills, human beings would be incapable of living good lives in association with others. Perhaps the most trenchant criticism of all that could be made of any society's political and social arrangements is that those arrangements fail to enable individuals to acquire and develop these skills.

Second, the major institutions and practices of any good society would be shaped by recognition of the claim that all human beings share an equal interest in having the means (or resources) necessary to pursue the projects they formulate and to try to realize the values they conceive. These resources are of qualitatively different, complementary kinds. They include mental and physical powers; rights, liberties, and opportunities; income and wealth in the sense of access to useful material goods; and status and recognition, goods that can be given only by the members of a society to one another. Because these resources vary from place to place and from time to time, no definitive list of them is possible. But any list of resources that accurately reflects our generalizable interest in having the means we need to be effective agents would be more comprehensive than Rawls's list of primary goods.

Third, in a good society resources would be fairly distributed. A fair distribution of value-independent resources—those resources that the members of a society at a given time and stage of development need to participate fully as equals in their society's affairs, including its political affairs—is an *equal* distribution. All the members of a good society would have shares of these resources that are fully adequate for them to participate as equals in their society's affairs. A fair distribution of value-dependent resources—resources that the members of a society can use to pursue their different projects and values—is a *value-sensitive* distribution. A value-sensitive distribution is the distribution that would result from an auction under ideal conditions in which each participant takes part on an equal footing with every other participant. In a society whose members have different values, such an auction would lead to uneven distributions of different goods. But the resulting distribution would nevertheless be equal—as equal as it could be, that is, in light of the differences among different individuals' values.

I BEGAN THIS BOOK by asking what counts in political and social criticism. For most of its history, theories in the liberal tradition of political thought have answered this question by focusing on two kinds of features of the social world. The first is individual rights and liberties. What seemed to count most of all, to many thinkers in the early liberal tradition, was whether political and social arrangements protected these rights and liberties. Liberals held different views about the means for protection on which reliance was to be placed—some emphasized natural and positive laws, whereas others stressed social conditions—but liberals generally agreed in treating protection of individual rights or liberties as the central concern of political theory.

In more recent years, thinkers in the liberal tradition have come to view economic justice as an essential complement to individual rights of the more traditional kind. What we should look for in comparing alternative social arrangements, from the viewpoint of many liberals in the twentieth century, is whether individuals' rights are adequately protected *and* whether they have the material resources to make worthwhile use of those rights. Liberals have of course disagreed over distributive principles as well as over the best means to achieve desirable distributions. But for many liberals in our age, concerns about the equitable distribution of economic resources have achieved parity or near-parity with concerns about rights and liberties.

These concerns no longer portray adequately the things a liberal theory must take into account if that theory is to be true to the most fundamental commitment of the liberal tradition. That commitment is to the idea that political and social arrangements should enable individuals to be effective agents. We all have an *equal* interest in having the means necessary to pursue the projects we formulate and to try to realize the values we conceive. Those means include basic rights and liberties as well as economic resources. But they also include capabilities, or mental and physical powers, which individuals need to make use of their liberties and resources. No liberal, to my knowledge, denies this fact. Yet the most widely read works of liberal theory treat it as a marginal concern, one that can safely be placed in the background of a picture of the things that really count in political and social criticism. Recognition, too, has come within the purview of liberal theories. Usually, though, recognition has played a peripheral role in liberal theories, perhaps because those theories have so often been designed on the assumption that the state is the principal agent of political and social change.

If liberal theories are to sustain their liberating potential, these concerns—
with the mental and physical powers people have and with the recognition
they receive—must be brought to the center of the picture of the things that
really count when we assess political and social arrangements in a critical
way.

Both these factors are likely to become increasingly important with the
passage of time. For both deal with diversities of kinds that are likely to
become even more prevalent in the coming years than they have already
done, both in the United States and in many other parts of the world. Theories like Rawls's theory of justice as fairness have responded intelligently
and plausibly to the fact that people conceive diverse *values*. It is one of the
great strengths of Rawls's theory that it takes the assumption of reasonable
value pluralism seriously from beginning to end. But the diversity of people's capabilities as well as their cultural and ethnic diversity are hardly less
important than the diversity of values. Liberal theories as a class have so far
failed to consider these types of diversity with a degree of seriousness conso-
nant with their significance in the real world.

Human beings have a generalizable interest in having adequate shares of
the means they need to be effective agents. An adequate share is not merely
a share sufficient to enable a person to sustain her basic well-being or to "get
by." An adequate share is a share large enough to enable a person to participate fully in the life of her society, including the deliberative processes
through which the members of that society try to shape its future. Those
processes involve individuals in acts of agency of a distinctive kind, acts they
conceive and carry out in common with other human agents. A person who
is unable to participate fully as an equal with others in shaping her social
world is at least partially disenfranchised.

An adequate share does not mean a large share of material goods or commodities. Mental powers and recognition can and should play prominent
roles. These "means" play a crucial role in determining how effective we are
as agents.

. . .

I have suggested in this book how we might rethink the idea of a liberal
theory. But how might we remake liberal practice? Although humanist liberalism is as yet only a rudimentary theory, its overall shape is already sufficiently clear to enable us to see some of its implications.

First, a society that embodies the principles of humanist liberalism would
protect the basic rights and liberties that are associated with the ideas of
constitutional government, the rule of law, and toleration. This implication
of established liberal theories should not change. Basic rights such as freedom of thought and speech, freedom of religion, freedom from arbitrary

arrest and imprisonment, and the like are among the basic means people need to be effective agents. These liberties have been fundamental to the liberal tradition since its inception, because writers in that tradition have seen the necessary connection between them and the empowerment of individuals as effective agents. Any good society would protect these basic rights, at the very least.

Although the approach to liberal theory for which I have argued in this book maintains the traditional liberal emphasis on rights, it suggests a way of thinking about rights that differs from that maintained by some liberal thinkers. Many liberal writers in recent years have seen rights as ways of defending against considerations of utility. For Rawls, the defense of individual rights against utilitarian threats was perhaps the principal motivation behind the formulation of his theory of justice as fairness. In "a just society," he declares in the second paragraph of his book, "the liberties of equal citizenship are taken as settled; the rights secured by justice are not subject to political bargaining or to the calculus of social interests."[1] Nozick sees rights as moral side-constraints that limit strictly what individuals and institutions can do in the name of utility. Dworkin, similarly, has on many occasions depicted rights as trumps, means of protecting individuals from the consequences of goal-oriented reasoning, especially reasoning based on the goal of collective welfare, in public affairs.[2]

Dworkin's reasoning about rights is particularly instructive, because it is probably more representative of widely shared views about rights than the views of either Rawls or Nozick, both of whom have developed more elaborate philosophical theories about rights than Dworkin's. Dworkin does not deny that utilitarian reasoning has a legitimate role in deliberations about public affairs. The role of rights is to trump that reasoning, not to invalidate it altogether. Consider, for example, Dworkin's reasoning about the relation between law, rights, and pornography. Dworkin defends the right of individuals to sell and to purchase literature of any content, including pornographic literature, by claiming that we have a "right to moral independence" that trumps other justifications of political decisions. "If someone has a right to moral independence," he says, "this means that it is for some reason wrong for officials to act in violation of that right, *even if they (correctly) believe that the community as a whole would be better off if they did*."[3] Dworkin assumes that utilitarianism provides the relevant account of what it would mean for a community as a whole to be better off.

---

[1] Rawls, *A Theory of Justice* (Cambridge, Mass.: Harvard University Press, 1971), p. 4.

[2] See especially Dworkin's article "Hard Cases," in *Taking Rights Seriously* (Cambridge, Mass.: Harvard University Press, 1978), pp. 81–130.

[3] Dworkin, "Do We Have a Right to Pornography?" in *A Matter of Principle* (Cambridge, Mass.: Harvard University Press, 1985), p. 359, emphasis added. See also Dworkin's "Liberty and Pornography," in the *New York Review of Books* (15 August 1991): 12–15.

Given his own hypotheses, Dworkin's suggestion that the community as a whole might be better off by denying its members their right to moral independence could be true only in a peculiar sense. For Dworkin's argument really is that it would be wrong, and therefore *worse* (in the sense of less just), for a society to violate this right than for it not to do so. The community as a whole could be *both* better off *and* worse off (in the sense of being less just) only if it would be better off by a standard that is incomplete and therefore flawed.

Dworkin's approach to the problem of pornography (as well as to many of the other public issues on which he has written eloquently over the years) is to assume that utilitarian reasoning in public affairs is valid up to a point—the point, that is, where it meets a right, by which utilitarian reasoning (in Dworkin's writings) is invariably trumped. Humanist liberalism suggests a different approach. According to humanist liberalism, utilitarian reasoning—reasoning that hinges on the maximization of pleasure or desire satisfaction and the minimization of pain—should not really play a role in reasoning about public affairs at all. What we should think about in assessing policies as well as institutions and practices is the impact they have or are likely to have on the means available to people to pursue their values and goals. Rights help to constitute those means. They do not occupy a position "outside" our ordinary reasoning about public affairs, ready to trump that reasoning when it poses a threat to them. Instead, they figure in our reasoning from the start.

The perspective framed by Dworkin's approach leads to a powerful tension between the ideas of the right and the good. According to that approach, a *just* society is one in which individuals' rights are respected. By contrast, a *good* society is one in which utility is maximized (or in which a utilitarian standard of some other kind is met). In humanist liberalism no such tension arises. Utility as such—happiness or desire satisfaction—does not count. What counts is the means available to individuals to pursue their values and goals. So from the perspective of humanist liberalism, there is no distinction between a good society and a just one.[4]

Second, the approach to liberal theory that I have sketched in this book endorses, as do other liberal theories, the use of markets as distributors of commodities as well as their regulation. But that approach suggests a distinctive ideal to which regulated markets and redistributive measures

---

[4] A distinction between the right and the good is fundamental to Rawls's theory of justice as fairness, too, but in that theory the distinction does not lead to a deep *tension* as it does in Dworkin's approach. For Rawls the ideas of the right and the good play complementary roles. Although Rawls's view of this matter differs from the view for which I am arguing, his view is closer to mine than is Dworkin's. For a clear statement of Rawls's view of the relation between the right and the good, see *Political Liberalism* (New York: Columbia University Press, 1993), lecture 5.

should approximate. Distributions of goods should meet two desiderata. First, to the extent that goods are necessary for individuals to be able to participate fully as equals in the life of their society, including its political life, regulation and redistributive measures should aim to guarantee that all individuals receive those goods. Second, to the extent that goods are value-dependent, their distributions should be value-sensitive. Within the framework of this approach, distributive justice is not a matter of simple equality. Nor can the ideal of distributive justice be defined by a single principle, such as the difference principle. Rather, distributive justice consists in each person having an adequate share of the resources needed to participate fully in the life of her society and in value-dependent goods being distributed in ways that are sensitive to individuals' values (not merely to their purchasing power). In real life, of course, institutions and practices are not likely to embody these principles perfectly even if they were designed to embody them as fully as possible. But real institutions and practices never fully embody a social ideal. Even basic constitutional rights are not protected perfectly in real constitutional regimes.

The humanist approach to liberal theory for which I have argued suggests that we should devote considerably greater attention as a society to the means available to individuals to develop their powers—that is, to education, broadly conceived.

Two main aims should guide our educational practices. The first is to provide the members of our society with the means to develop the capabilities and skills appropriate to democratic citizenship.[5]

In humanist liberalism, institutions are assessed on the basis of their success in empowering individuals to be effective agents. But empowerment is not a commodity. Institutions do not "deliver" it to people in the way they might deliver some goods. People are empowered as agents in part by participating in deliberations and in making decisions that help to determine the future shape of their own society. Democratic institutions enable people to be effective agents by involving them in democratic processes as well as by generating the right product. When we compare alternatives, the process-related contribution democratic practices make toward the attainment of liberal goals should not be left out of our accounting.[6]

To sustain a good life in association with others over time, people also need to have democratic capabilities, capabilities that can be cultivated through a democratic education. The most important of these is a vigorous sense of justice, an ability to recognize and accept one's fellow citizens as

---

[5] For a full-length discussion, see Amy Gutmann, *Democratic Education* (Princeton: Princeton University Press, 1987).

[6] For a vigorous defense of the value of democratic practices, which emphasizes them more than I do, see Benjamin Barber, *Strong Democracy: Participatory Politics for a New Age* (Berkeley and Los Angeles: University of California Press, 1984).

agents with values and projects of their own they should be entitled to pursue, even if those values conflict with one's own. A vigorous sense of justice is incompatible with nationalism (though not with patriotism), with racism, and with sexism. It is incompatible with all group identities that are sustained by defining the identity of the other—the other sex, the other race, the other nationality—in less than fully human terms.

A second, only slightly less important capability is communicative skill, which enables people to give their deliberations the public character needed for others to be able to consider their arguments and claims. Democracy is essentially a communicative practice. It requires skills, much as any other practice does, a point John Dewey made with vigor and conviction in his great work *Democracy and Education.*[7]

The second major aim that should guide our educational practices is to provide equal access to educational resources to all the members of our society. Equal access would not lead to equal educational attainments. With equal access, people would choose to learn different things, and some would choose to devote more of their time and energy to learning than others. The outcome of equal availability of educational resources would vary from one individual to the next in accordance with individuals' differing values. But if educational resources were equally accessible to all individuals, we could be confident that different outcomes—the different powers that individuals develop—reflect differences in individuals' values rather than differences in their wealth or privileges.

. . .

The first premise of liberal political theory is that only individuals count. Individuals formulate projects. Individuals conceive values. When values and projects come to fruition, individuals experience the joy of their attainment; when they fail, individuals feel the frustration that results.

Liberal individualism—the claim that only individuals count—is the substance and strength of the liberal tradition. But liberal individualism misinterpreted is the Achilles' heel of the liberal tradition. Liberal individualism is misinterpreted when it becomes transmuted into the view that since only individuals count, individuals need think only about themselves, about their shares, and about whether their rights have been respected or violated, whether they have received or failed to receive their fair share. Liberalism misinterpreted fosters the perception that people can best secure the means to be effective agents by carving out for themselves the most extensive set of rights, and the largest bundle of commodities, they can obtain.

[7] John Dewey, *Democracy and Education*, in *John Dewey: The Middle Works, 1899–1924*, vol. 9, ed. Jo Ann Boydston (Carbondale: Southern Illinois University Press, 1980).

That perception is false. It has the truth-value of the perception—a perception that is, tragically, widely shared in the United States—that since some criminals have guns, the best way to protect oneself against violence is to obtain a gun. Unfortunately, the result of this action is too often that someone gets shot, and the victim is rarely a criminal caught in a criminal act.

Democracy—and liberalism—needs *public* spaces on multiple levels. In liberal societies, we tend systematically to underestimate the need for democratic public spaces and to overestimate the importance of individual or private space to effective agency. Human beings become effective agents by going out into the public world and trying to make themselves understood in democratic settings. The importance of this kind of agency is especially likely to be overlooked in Eastern Europe, with its history of many decades in which public space was distorted or annihilated. Whether the comprehension that would be needed to restore that space can be regained is one of the largest questions that hangs over the future of that part of the world today.

Liberal principles are radical principles. They are bound to be controversial, to lead to disagreements and struggles. The struggles are and will be struggles over power, over how a world of perception and speech is going to be defined. It would be naive to suppose that we could evade these struggles by reducing liberal principles to the most consensual, least controversial common denominator we can discover in the hope that all people will at some point be brought to agree with us. As we face the future, we need to know where we stand and what we stand for. The sketch of humanist liberalism I have offered here is an effort to give voice to those convictions.

References

Ackerman, Bruce. *The Future of Liberal Revolution*. New Haven: Yale University Press, 1992.

Anderson, Benedict. *Imagined Communities: Reflections on the Origin and Spread of Nationalism*. 2d. ed. New York and London: Verso, 1991.

Aristotle. *Nicomachean Ethics*. Ed. Martin Ostwald. Indianapolis: Bobbs-Merrill, 1962.

Arthur, John, and William H. Shaw, eds. *Justice and Economic Distribution*. Englewood Cliffs, N.J.: Prentice-Hall, 1978.

Barber, Benjamin. *Strong Democracy: Participatory Politics for a New Age*. Berkeley and Los Angeles: University of California Press, 1984.

Barnett, Randy E. "Compensation and Rights in the Liberal Conception of Justice." In *Compensatory Justice: Nomos XXXIII*, ed. John W. Chapman, pp. 311–29. New York: New York University Press, 1991.

Baumgardt, David. *Bentham and the Ethics of Today*. Princeton: Princeton University Press, 1952.

Benhabib, Seyla. *Situating the Self: Gender, Community, and Postmodernism in Contemporary Ethics*. New York: Routledge, 1992.

Benn, Stanley I. *A Theory of Freedom*. Cambridge: Cambridge University Press, 1988.

Bentham, Jeremy. *A Fragment on Government*. Ed. F. C. Montague. Oxford: Clarendon Press, 1891.

Berlin, Isaiah. *The Crooked Timber of Humanity*. New York: Knopf, 1991.

———. "Two Concepts of Liberty." In *Four Essays on Liberty*, pp. 118–72. Oxford: Oxford University Press, 1969.

Braybrooke, David. "Gauthier's Foundations for Ethics under the Test of Application." In *Contractarianism and Rational Choice: Essays on David Gauthier's "Morals by Agreement,"* ed. Peter Vallentyne, pp. 56–70. Cambridge: Cambridge University Press, 1991.

———. "Social Contract Theory's Fanciest Flight." *Ethics* 97 (1987): 750–64.

Buchanan, James. *The Limits of Liberty: Between Anarchy and Leviathan*. Chicago: University of Chicago Press, 1975.

Chapman, John W., ed. *Compensatory Justice: Nomos XXXIII*. New York: New York University Press, 1991.

Christman, John. "Constructing the Inner Citadel: Recent Work on Autonomy." *Ethics* 99 (1988): 109–24.

———, ed. *The Inner Citadel: Essays on Individual Autonomy*. New York: Oxford University Press, 1989.

Cohen, G. A. "Robert Nozick and Wilt Chamberlain: How Patterns Preserve Liberty." In *Justice and Economic Distribution*, ed. John Arthur and William H. Shaw, pp. 246–62. Englewood Cliffs, N.J.: Prentice-Hall, 1978.

Crocker, David A. "Functioning and Capability: The Foundations of Sen's and Nussbaum's Development Ethics." *Political Theory* 20 (1992): 584–612.

Dahl, Robert A. *A Preface to Democratic Theory*. Chicago: University of Chicago Press, 1956.

Daniels, Norman. "Moral Theory and the Plasticity of Persons." *The Monist* 62 (1979): 265–87.

———. "Reflective Equilibrium and Archimedean Points." *Canadian Journal of Philosophy* 19 (1980): 83–103.

———. "Some Methods of Ethics and Linguistics." *Philosophical Studies* 37 (1980): 21–36.

———. "Wide Reflective Equilibrium and Theory Acceptance in Ethics." *Journal of Philosophy* 76 (1979): 256–82.

———, ed. *Reading Rawls*. 2d ed. Stanford: Stanford University Press, 1989.

Davis, Lawrence. "Nozick's Entitlement Theory." In *Reading Nozick: Essays on "Anarchy, State, and Utopia,"* ed. Jeffrey Paul, pp. 344–54. Totowa, N.J.: Rowman and Allanheld, 1981.

Dewey, John. *Democracy and Education*. In *John Dewey: The Middle Works, 1899–1924*, vol. 9, ed. Jo Ann Boydston. Carbondale: Southern Illinois University Press, 1980.

———. "The Need for a Recovery of Philosophy." In *John Dewey: The Middle Works, 1899–1924*, vol. 10, ed. Jo Ann Boydston, pp. 3–48. Carbondale: Southern Illinois University Press, 1980.

Donner, Wendy. *The Liberal Self: John Stuart Mill's Moral and Political Philosophy*. Ithaca: Cornell University Press, 1991.

Dumont, Louis. *From Mandeville to Marx: The Genesis and Triumph of Economic Ideology*. Chicago: University of Chicago Press, 1977.

Dworkin, Gerald. *The Theory and Practice of Autonomy*. Cambridge: Cambridge University Press, 1988.

Dworkin, Ronald. "Liberty and Pornography." *New York Review of Books* (15 August 1991): 12–15.

———. *Life's Dominion: An Argument about Abortion, Euthanasia, and Individual Freedom*. New York: Knopf, 1993.

———. *A Matter of Principle*. Cambridge, Mass.: Harvard University Press, 1985.

———. *Taking Rights Seriously*. Cambridge, Mass.: Harvard University Press, 1978.

———. "What Is Equality? Part 1: Equality of Welfare." *Philosophy and Public Affairs* 10 (1981): 185–246.

———. "What Is Equality? Part 2: Equality of Resources." *Philosophy and Public Affairs* 10 (1981): 283–345.

Edgeworth, F. Y. *Mathematical Psychics*. London: Kegan Paul, 1881.

Elster, Jon. "The Market and the Forum." In *Foundations of Social Choice Theory*, ed. Jon Elster and Aanund Hylland, pp. 103–32. Cambridge: Cambridge University Press, 1986.

———. *Sour Grapes: Studies in the Subversion of Rationality*. Cambridge: Cambridge University Press, 1983.

———, and John E. Roemer, eds. *Interpersonal Comparisons of Well-Being*. Cambridge: Cambridge University Press, 1991.

Feinberg, Joel. *Harm to Self*. Vol. 3 of *The Moral Limits of the Criminal Law*. Oxford: Oxford University Press, 1986.

Fiss, Owen M. "Coda." *University of Toronto Law Journal* 38 (1988): 229–44.

Flavell, John H. *The Developmental Psychology of Jean Piaget*. New York: Van Nostrand, 1962.

Foucault, Michel. *Discipline and Punish: The Birth of the Prison*. New York: Vintage Books, 1979.

Frankfurt, Harry. "Freedom of the Will and the Concept of a Person." *Journal of Philosophy* 68 (1971): 5–20.

Fukuyama, Francis. *The End of History and the Last Man*. New York: Free Press, 1992.

Galston, William A. *Liberal Purposes: Goods, Virtues, and Diversity in the Liberal State*. Cambridge: Cambridge University Press, 1991.

Gauthier, David P. *Morals by Agreement*. Oxford: Oxford University Press, 1986.

Gilligan, Carol. *In a Different Voice: Psychological Theory and Women's Development*. Cambridge, Mass.: Harvard University Press, 1982.

Gramsci, Antonio. *Selections from the Prison Notebooks of Antonio Gramsci*. New York: International Publishers, 1985.

Gray, John. *Mill on Liberty: A Defence*. London: Routledge and Kegan Paul, 1983.

Grice, G. R. "Moral Theories and Received Opinion." *Aristotelian Society*, supplementary vol. 52 (1978): 2–12.

Griffin, James. "Modern Utilitarianism." *Revue Internationale de Philosophie* 141 (1982): 331–75.

———. "Towards a Substantive Theory of Rights." In *Utility and Rights*, ed. Raymond G. Frey. Oxford: Blackwell, 1985.

———. *Well-Being: Its Meaning, Measurement, and Moral Significance*. Oxford: Clarendon Press, 1986.

Gutmann, Amy. *Democratic Education*. Princeton: Princeton University Press, 1987.

Habermas, Jürgen. *Legitimation Crisis*. Trans. Thomas McCarthy. Boston: Beacon Press, 1975.

———. *Reason and the Rationalization of Society*. Trans. Thomas McCarthy. Vol. 1 of *The Theory of Communicative Action*. Boston: Beacon Press, 1981.

———. *Theorie der Gesellschaft oder Sozialtechnologie: Was Leistet die Systemforschung?* With Niklas Luhmann. Frankfurt: Suhrkamp, 1971.

Hacker, Andrew. *Two Nations: Black and White, Separate, Hostile, Unequal*. New York: Ballantine Books, 1992.

Halévy, Elie. *The Growth of Philosophical Radicalism*. London: Faber and Faber, 1972.

Hare, R. M. "Rawls's Theory of Justice." In *Reading Rawls*, 2d ed., ed. Norman Daniels, pp. 81–107. Stanford: Stanford University Press, 1989.

Harman, Gilbert. *The Nature of Morality*. New York: Oxford University Press, 1977.

Hart, H.L.A. "Rawls on Liberty and Its Priority." *University of Chicago Law Review* 40 (1973): 534–55. Reprinted in Norman Daniels, ed., *Reading Rawls*, 2d ed., pp. 230–52. Stanford: Stanford University Press, 1989.

Havelock, Eric A. *A Preface to Plato*. Cambridge, Mass.: Harvard University Press, 1963.

Hayek, Friedrich von. *The Constitution of Liberty*. Chicago: University of Chicago Press, 1960.

Hegel, G.W.F. *Phänomenologie des Geistes*. Hamburg: Felix Meiner, 1952.

Heller, Thomas C., Morton Sosna, and David E. Wellbery, eds. *Reconstructing*

Individualism: Autonomy, Individuality, and the Self in Western Thought. Stanford: Stanford University Press, 1986.

Herzog, Don. *Without Foundations: Justification in Political Theory*. Ithaca: Cornell University Press, 1985.

Hirsch, Fred. *Social Limits to Growth*. Cambridge, Mass.: Harvard University Press, 1976.

Hobbes, Thomas. *The Elements of Law, Natural and Politic*. 2d ed. Ed. Ferdinand Tönnies. London: Frank Cass, 1969.

———. *Leviathan, or the Matter, Forme, and Power of a Commonwealth, Ecclesiastical and Civill*. Ed. Richard Tuck. Cambridge: Cambridge University Press, 1991.

Hume, David. *An Enquiry Concerning the Principles of Morals*. Ed. J. B. Schneewind. Indianapolis: Hackett, 1983.

———. *A Treatise of Human Nature*. Ed. L. A. Selby-Bigge. Oxford: Clarendon Press, 1967.

Hutcheson, Francis. *An Enquiry Concerning Moral Good and Evil*. In *British Moralists*, ed. L. A. Selby-Bigge, pp. 69–177. Indianapolis: Bobbs-Merrill, 1964.

Jefferson, Thomas. *Thomas Jefferson: Writings*. Ed. Merrill D. Peterson. New York: Library of America, 1984.

Johnston, David. "Beyond Compensatory Justice?" In *Compensatory Justice: Nomos XXXIII*, ed. John W. Chapman, pp. 330–54. New York: New York University Press, 1991.

———. *The Rhetoric of Leviathan: Thomas Hobbes and the Politics of Cultural Transformation*. Princeton: Princeton University Press, 1986.

Kant, Immanuel. "What Is Enlightenment?" In *The Philosophy of Kant*, ed. Carl J. Friedrich, pp. 132–39. New York: Random House, 1949.

Kleinig, John. *Paternalism*. Totowa, N.J.: Rowman and Allanheld, 1984.

Kohlberg, Lawrence. "Moral Stages and Moralization: The Cognitive-Developmental Approach." In *Moral Development and Behavior: Theory, Research, and Social Issues*, ed. T. Lickona. New York: Holt, Rinehart, and Winston, 1976.

———. *The Philosophy of Moral Development*. San Francisco: Harper and Row, 1981.

———. "Stage and Sequence: The Cognitive-Development Approach to Socialization." In *Handbook of Socialization Theory and Research*, ed. David A. Goslin, pp. 347–480. Chicago: Rand McNally, 1969.

Kymlicka, Will. *Contemporary Political Philosophy: An Introduction*. Oxford: Clarendon Press, 1990.

———. *Liberalism, Community, and Culture*. Oxford: Clarendon Press, 1989.

Larmore, Charles E. *Patterns of Moral Complexity*. Cambridge: Cambridge University Press, 1987.

———. "Political Liberalism." *Political Theory* 18 (1990): 339–60.

Lenneberg, Eric H. *Biological Foundations of Language*. Malaber, Fla.: Krieger, 1984.

Lindblom, Charles E. *Inquiry and Change*. New Haven: Yale University Press, 1990.

Litan, Robert E. "On Rectification in Nozick's Minimal State." *Political Theory* 5 (1977): 233–46.

Locke, John. *An Essay Concerning Human Understanding*, ed. Peter H. Nidditch. Oxford: Oxford University Press, 1975.

————. *Second Treatise of Government*. In *Two Treatises of Government*, ed. Peter Laslett. Cambridge: Cambridge University Press, 1963.

Lomasky, Loren E. *Persons, Rights, and the Moral Community*. Oxford: Oxford University Press, 1987.

Lukes, Steven. "An Archimedean Point." *Observer*, 4 June 1972.

————. "Relativism: Cognitive and Moral." *Aristotelian Society*, supplementary vol. 48 (1974): 165–88.

MacIntyre, Alasdair. *After Virtue*. 2d ed. Notre Dame: University of Notre Dame Press, 1984.

Mackie, John L. *Ethics: Inventing Right and Wrong*. Harmondsworth, Middlesex: Penguin, 1977.

Marx, Karl. *Capital*. Vol. 1. New York: International Publishers, 1967.

————. "Critique of the Gotha Program." In *The Marx-Engels Reader*, 2d ed., ed. Robert C. Tucker, pp. 525–41. New York: Norton, 1978.

————. *The German Ideology*. Part 1. In *The Marx-Engels Reader*, 2d ed., ed. Robert C. Tucker, pp. 146–200. New York: Norton, 1978.

————, and Friedrich Engels. "Manifesto of the Communist Party." In *The Marx-Engels Reader*, 2d ed., ed. Robert C. Tucker, pp. 469–500. New York: Norton, 1978.

Mill, John Stuart. *The Collected Works of John Stuart Mill*. 33 vols. Ed. John M. Robson. Toronto: University of Toronto Press, 1963–90.

————. *On Liberty*. Ed. David Spitz. New York: Norton, 1975.

————. *"Utilitarianism" and Other Writings*. New York: New American Library, 1974.

Moon, J. Donald. *Constructing Community: Moral Pluralism and Tragic Conflicts*. Princeton: Princeton University Press, 1994.

Nagel, Thomas. "Libertarianism without Foundations." In *Reading Nozick: Essays on "Anarchy, State, and Utopia,"* ed. Jeffrey Paul, pp. 191–205. Totowa, N.J.: Rowman and Allanheld, 1981.

Narveson, Jan. *The Libertarian Idea*. Philadelphia: Temple University Press, 1988.

Nielsen, Kai. *Equality and Liberty*. Totowa, N.J.: Rowman and Allanheld, 1985.

————. "Our Considered Judgments." *Ratio* 19 (1977): 39–46.

Nietzsche, Friedrich. *Beyond Good and Evil*. Trans. Walter Kaufman. New York: Random House, 1966.

Nozick, Robert. *Anarchy, State, and Utopia*. New York: Basic Books, 1974.

Nussbaum, Martha C. "Human Functioning and Social Justice: In Defense of Aristotelian Essentialism." *Political Theory* 20 (1992): 202–46.

Okin, Susan Moller. "Humanist Liberalism." In *Liberalism and the Moral Life*, ed. Nancy L. Rosenblum. Cambridge, Mass.: Harvard University Press, 1989.

————. *Justice, Gender, and the Family*. New York: Basic Books, 1989.

Paul, Jeffrey, ed. *Reading Nozick: Essays on "Anarchy, State, and Utopia."* Totowa, N.J.: Rowman and Allanheld, 1981.

Piaget, Jean. *The Moral Judgment of the Child*. New York: Free Press, 1965.

Plato. *Republic*. Trans. Richard W. Sterling and William C. Scott. New York: Norton, 1985.

Pogge, Thomas W. *Realizing Rawls*. Ithaca: Cornell University Press, 1989.

Polanyi, Karl. *The Great Transformation: The Political and Economic Origins of Our Time*. Boston: Beacon Press, 1957.

Rasmussen, David M. *Reading Habermas*. Oxford: Blackwell, 1990.

Rasmussen, Douglas B., and Douglas J. Den Uyl. *Liberty and Nature: An Aristotelian Defense of Liberal Order*. La Salle: Open Court, 1991.

Rawls, John. "The Basic Liberties and Their Priority." In *The Tanner Lectures on Human Values*, vol. 3, ed. Sterling M. McMurrin, pp. 1–87. Salt Lake City: University of Utah Press, 1982.

———. "The Basic Structure as Subject." In *Values and Morals*, ed. A. I. Goldman and J. Kim, pp. 47–71. Dordrecht: Reidel, 1978.

———. "The Domain of the Political and Overlapping Consensus." *New York University Law Review* 64 (1989): 233–55.

———. "The Idea of an Overlapping Consensus." *Oxford Journal of Legal Studies* 7 (1987): 1–25.

———. "The Independence of Moral Theory." *Proceedings and Addresses of the American Philosophical Association* 48 (1975): 5–22.

———. "Justice as Fairness: Political Not Metaphysical." *Philosophy and Public Affairs* 14 (1985): 223–51.

———. "A Kantian Conception of Equality." *Cambridge Review* (February 1975): 94–99. Reprinted as "A Well-Ordered Society," in *Philosophy, Politics, and Society* (5th ser.), ed. Peter Laslett and James Fishkin, pp. 6–20. Oxford: Blackwell, 1979.

———. "Kantian Constructivism in Moral Theory." *Journal of Philosophy* 77 (1980): 515–72.

———. "Outline of a Decision Procedure for Ethics." *Philosophical Review* 60 (1951): 177–97.

———. *Political Liberalism*. New York: Columbia University Press, 1993.

———. "The Priority of Right and Ideas of the Good." *Philosophy and Public Affairs* 17 (1988): 251–76.

———. "Social Unity and Primary Goods." In *Utilitarianism and Beyond*, ed. Amartya Sen and Bernard Williams, pp. 159–85. Cambridge: Cambridge University Press, 1982.

———. *A Theory of Justice*. Cambridge, Mass.: Harvard University Press, 1971.

Raz, Joseph, *The Morality of Freedom*. Oxford: Oxford University Press, 1986.

Rorty, Richard. "The Priority of Democracy to Philosophy." In *The Virginia Statute for Religious Freedom*, ed. Merrill D. Peterson and Robert C. Vaughan, pp. 257–82. Cambridge: Cambridge University Press, 1988.

Rosenblum, Nancy L. *Another Liberalism: Romanticism and the Reconstruction of Liberal Thought*. Cambridge, Mass.: Harvard University Press, 1987.

Ryan, Alan. *The Philosophy of John Stuart Mill*. 2d ed. Basingstoke, Hampshire: MacMillan, 1987.

———. *Property and Political Theory*. Oxford: Blackwell, 1984.

Sandel, Michael J. *Liberalism and the Limits of Justice*. Cambridge: Cambridge University Press, 1982.

Scanlon, T. M. "Contractualism and Utilitarianism." In *Utilitarianism and Beyond*, ed. Amartya Sen and Bernard Williams, pp. 103–28. Cambridge: Cambridge University Press, 1982.

Scheffler, Samuel. "Natural Rights, Equality, and the Minimal State." In *Reading Nozick: Essays on "Anarchy, State, and Utopia,"* ed. Jeffrey Paul, pp. 148–68. Totowa, N.J.: Rowan and Allanheld, 1981.

Schwartz, Adina. "Moral Neutrality and Primary Goods." *Ethics* 83 (1973): 294–307.

Sen, Amartya K. "Equality of What?" In *The Tanner Lectures on Human Values*, ed. S. M. McMurrin, pp. 139–62. Salt Lake City: University of Utah Press, 1980.

———. *Inequality Reexamined*. Cambridge, Mass.: Harvard University Press, 1992.

———. "Well-Being, Agency, and Freedom: The Dewey Lectures, 1984." *Journal of Philosophy* 82 (1985): 169–221.

———, and Bernard Williams, eds. *Utilitarianism and Beyond*. Cambridge: Cambridge University Press, 1982.

Shue, Henry. *Basic Rights: Subsistence, Affluence, and U.S. Foreign Policy*. Princeton: Princeton University Press, 1980.

Singer, Peter. "Sidgwick and Reflective Equilibrium." *The Monist* 58 (1974): 490–517.

Smith, Adam. *An Inquiry into the Nature and Causes of the Wealth of Nations*. New York: Random House, 1937.

Smith, Rogers. *Liberalism and American Constitutional Law*. Cambridge, Mass.: Harvard University Press, 1985.

Starobinski, Jean. *Jean-Jacques Rousseau: Transparency and Obstruction*. Chicago: University of Chicago Press, 1988.

Stassen, Glen. "Michael Walzer's Situated Justice." *Journal of Religious Ethics* 20, no. 4 (Fall 1994).

Strong, Tracy B. "Texts and Pretexts: Reflections on Perspectivism in Nietzsche." *Political Theory* 13 (1985): 164–82.

Sunstein, Cass. "The Limits of Compensatory Justice." In *Compensatory Justice: Nomos XXXIII*, ed. John W. Chapman, pp. 281–310. New York: New York University Press, 1991.

Taylor, Charles. *Sources of the Self: The Making of the Modern Identity*. Cambridge, Mass.: Harvard University Press, 1989.

Tuck, Richard. *Hobbes*. Cambridge: Cambridge University Press, 1991.

Von Neumann, Jon, and Oscar Morgenstern. *The Theory of Games and Economic Behavior*. 3d ed. Princeton: Princeton University Press, 1953.

Waldron, Jeremy. *Liberal Rights: Collected Papers, 1981–1991*. Cambridge: Cambridge University Press, 1993.

———. *The Right to Private Property*. Oxford: Oxford University Press, 1988.

———. "Theoretical Foundations of Liberalism." *Philosophical Quarterly* 37 (1987): 127–50.

Walzer, Michael. *Just and Unjust Wars: A Moral Argument with Historical Illustrations*. New York: Basic Books, 1977.

———. "Philosophy and Democracy." *Political Theory* 9 (1981): 379–99.

———. *Spheres of Justice: A Defense of Pluralism and Equality*. New York: Basic Books, 1983.

Weber, Max. *From Max Weber: Essays in Sociology*. Ed. H. H. Gerth and C. Wright Mills. New York: Oxford University Press, 1946.

———. *The Methodology of the Social Sciences*. Trans. Edward A. Shils and Henry A. Finch. New York: Free Press, 1949.

Weinrib, Ernest J. "Adjudication and Public Values: Fiss's Critique of Corrective Justice." *University of Toronto Law Journal* 39 (1989): 1–18.

Wolff, Robert Paul. "Nozick's Derivation of the Minimal State." In *Reading Nozick: Essays on "Anarchy, State, and Utopia,"* ed. Jeffrey Paul, pp. 77–104. Totowa, N.J.: Rowman and Allanheld, 1981.

Wolin, Sheldon S. *Politics and Vision*. Boston: Little, Brown, 1960.

Young, Robert. *Personal Autonomy: Beyond Negative and Positive Liberty*. London: Croom Helm, 1986.

Index

absolutism, 3
Ackerman, Bruce, 5n
affirmative action, 156
agency, human, 25, 26, 30, 40, 45, 67, 68, 69, 71, 72, 87, 98, 99; described, 22–24; discussed critically, 79–83; and self-authorship, 75. *See also* autonomy, moral autonomy, personal autonomy
Anderson, Benedict, 168n
anomie, 95, 96
apartheid, 4
Aristotle, 21, 25, 90, 152, 164
autonomy, 44, 70, 138; analyzed, 71–77; in distribution of goods, 171–72. *See also* agency, Autonomy Principle, moral autonomy, personal autonomy
Autonomy Principle, 77, 99; defined, 70

Barber, Benjamin, 190n
Barnett, Randy E., 20n
basic liberties, 108–12, 115, 116, 124, 127, 128, 135, 144, 146, 152, 156–61, 164, 165, 167–69, 173, 174, 177, 178, 185, 186, 188; discussed critically, 117–21. *See also* freedom, rights
basic structure, 104–8, 113–16, 135, 144
Baumgardt, David, 101n
Benhabib, Seyla, 17n
Benn, Stanley I., 71n, 88n
Bentham, Jeremy, 6, 21, 24, 25, 82, 101n
Berlin, Isaiah, 27n, 94–95, 97
Braybrooke, David, 62n, 63n
Buchanan, James, 42, 43, 58–67

capabilities, 130, 132, 145, 149, 150, 160, 161, 186; and capability set, 131, 133, 134; democratic, 190
capitalism, 3, 4
Christman, John, 71n, 88n
circumstances of justice, 26, 27, 84, 123, 132, 134, 153. *See also* justice: distributive
civil rights movement, 16
Cohen, G. A., 50n
coherence: as desideratum for theory, 27–28, 31
Coleridge, Samuel Taylor, 96

compensation, 50–52, 149, 162–67
complex equality, 171–73. *See also* equality, inequality
consent, 44, 46, 56–58
considered judgments, 33–39, 48–49, 65, 70, 101, 102, 114. *See also* reflective equilibrium
constitutionalism, 5, 17–18, 24, 187
contractarianism, 42, 58–65
contribution principle, 125

Dahl, Robert, 124n
Daniels, Norman, 33, 34n
Darwinism: social, 4
Davis, Lawrence, 62n
democracy, 14–15, 18, 25, 54, 55, 58. *See also* capabilities: democratic
demoktesis, 54–56
Den Uyl, Douglas J., 43n, 70
deontological theory, 41
despotism, 64, 65, 92
Dewey, John, 10, 191
difference principle, 14n, 108–11, 115, 116, 135, 139, 147, 190; discussed critically, 121–27
Donner, Wendy, 78n
Dworkin, Gerald, 71n
Dworkin, Ronald, 66, 122n, 130n, 141–49, 162–68, 182, 188–89

Edgeworth, F. Y., 101n
egoism, 19, 26, 84, 106, 107
Elster, Jon, 97n, 142n
Emerson, Ralph Waldo, 96
Entitlement Theory of Justice, 44–58, 62. *See also* liberalism: rights-based, Rights-Based Principle
equality, 3, 17, 21, 22, 46, 53, 173. *See also* complex equality, inequality
ethnocentrism, 36
externalities, 49

Feinberg, Joel, 70n, 71n, 92
Fiss, Owen M., 20n
Flavell, John H., 86n
Foucault, Michel, 8n

foundationalism, 9n
founding, 11, 12
Frankfurt, Harry, 80, 81, 93
freedom, 4, 21, 22, 26, 53, 63, 64n, 150; of
    contract, 104; extent of, 130–36; positive
    and negative, 94, 95; of speech, 14, 18, 187;
    of the will, 80, 81. See also basic liberties,
    rights
Fukuyama, Francis, 7n

Galston, William A., 108n
Gauthier, David P., 42, 43, 62, 63n
gender, 4
generalizable interests, 15, 17, 137, 142, 173,
    174, 176, 177, 178, 183, 185, 187
generalized reciprocity, 124, 125, 140
German Idealism, 31
Gilligan, Carol, 86n
Gramsci, Antonio, 7n
Gray, John, 88n
Grice, G. R., 36n
Griffin, James, 41n, 94, 102, 130n, 143, 144n
Gutmann, Amy, 190n

Habermas, Jürgen, 15
Hacker, Andrew, 155n, 156
Halévy, Elie, 21n
Hare, R. M., 36n
Harman, Gilbert, 32n
Hart, Herbert L. A., 118n
Havelock, Eric, 169n
Hayek, F. A., 43
Hegel, G.W.F., 74, 96
Herzog, Don, 9n
heteronomy, 93
Hirsch, Fred, 184n
Hobbes, Thomas, 3, 21, 32, 83n, 85, 169
human agency. See agency, human
Hume, David, 27n, 32, 84
Hutcheson, Francis, 101n

identity, 19, 20, 76, 87, 157
imagination, 14, 23, 36, 72, 81, 82, 84, 86, 93–
    96
individuality, 69
inequality, 104, 105, 109, 113, 121, 122, 124,
    125, 147, 172–74. See also complex equal-
    ity, equality
informational bases of theories, 28, 29, 31, 61,
    62
integration, 5
interests. See generalizable interests

Jefferson, Thomas, 156
Johnston, David, 20n, 169n
judgments. See considered judgments
justice: distributive, 3, 5, 14n, 17, 53, 169–84;
    as categorical imperative, 119; as fair-
    ness, 100–136; public conception of, 106,
    115; and public justification, 114, 115;
    theories of, 35. See also circumstances
    of justice

Kant, Immanuel, 32, 69, 72
Kantianism, 20
Kleinig, John, 70n
Kohlberg, Lawrence, 82n, 86n
Kymlicka, Will, 20n, 116n, 124n

language, 160; acquisition of, 72, 74, 82, 86,
    119, 179
Larmore, Charles E., 26n, 69n, 100n
Lenneberg, Eric H., 82n
liberal tradition, 3, 7, 8, 10, 40, 186, 188, 191
liberalism: philosophical, 17–25
libertarianism, 43, 70, 126
Lindblom, Charles E., 38n
Litan, Robert E., 62n
Locke, John, 3, 24, 40, 66, 68, 69, 83n, 104,
    105n
Lomasky, Loren, 24
Luhmann, Niklas, 15n
Lukes, Steven, 36n

Machiavelli, Niccolo, 169
MacIntyre, Alasdair, 19n
Mackie, John L., 32n
markets, 4, 18, 25, 52, 103, 182, 183, 189; and
    envy test, 182; and exchanges, 51; in insur-
    ance, 149, 163, 166, 167
Marx, Karl, 24, 31, 140, 152
Mead, George Herbert, 82n
mercantilism, 3, 13
Mill, James, 6n
Mill, John Stuart, 6, 21n, 24, 69, 77, 78, 82,
    88–92, 98
Moon, J. Donald, 100n
moral autonomy, 72–79, 95, 97–99, 107, 108,
    112, 113, 115, 116, 119, 120, 121, 135, 138,
    144, 155, 183, 185, 190, 191; discussed crit-
    ically, 83–87. See also agency, autonomy,
    personal autonomy
moral personality, 75, 107, 109, 112, 115, 116,
    119, 120, 135, 138
moral sentiments, 33

moral truth, 32, 33
Morgenstern, Oscar, 101n

Nagel, Thomas, 45n
Narveson, Jan, 42n, 60n
Nazism, 91
neutrality, 25
Nielsen, Kai, 36n
Nietzsche, Friedrich, 9, 22, 25, 32, 90, 93, 96
Nozick, Robert, 14, 25, 40n, 41–67, 79, 105, 127, 137, 176, 177

Okin, Susan Moller, 116n, 141n
ordering, 29–31, 32, 126; types of, 127
original position, 107, 108, 113, 114, 125; as device of representation, 116
overlapping consensus, 35–36, 103n, 114

paternalism, 70, 95
patterned principles of justice, 45, 53, 57, 127
perfectionism, 68–99, 77, 100, 102, 105, 138
Pericles, 90
person: concept of, 79, 80, 84, 89, 93; as free and equal, 103, 106, 115; recognition of, 157–58
personal autonomy, 75–79, 100; discussed critically, 87–99; and experimentation, 89, 92. See also agency, autonomy, moral autonomy
perspectivism, 9
Piaget, Jean, 82n, 86n
Plato, 8, 21, 22n, 25, 68, 169
Pogge, Thomas W., 108n, 122
Polanyi, Karl, 159n
pornography, 188–89
power, 6, 8, 9; of the state, 43, 47, 64
powers: mental and physical, 139, 145–52, 161–68, 173, 174, 178–81, 185–87, 190. See also capabilities
practical reasoning, 16, 28, 29
primary goods, 111–17, 122, 123, 126, 128–41, 144–49, 152–55, 157, 159, 160, 161, 167, 168, 185
progress, 89, 92
public goods, 59, 60

Québécois, 20

race, 4
racism, 157, 168, 191
ranking. See ordering
Rasmussen, David M., 15n

Rasmussen, Douglas B., 43n, 70
Rawls, John, 14n, 21n, 27n, 32–35, 37, 42–44, 75, 100–149, 152–59, 161, 167, 168, 177, 178, 185, 187, 188, 189n
Raz, Joseph, 71n, 77, 78, 79, 88n, 98, 105
recognition. See status
reflective equilibrium, 33–39, 66, 114. See also considered judgments
reflective self-direction, 69, 75, 77, 81, 89, 90, 91, 93, 95, 138. See also self-development
responsibility, 44, 122, 123
rights, 3, 5, 16, 17, 18, 25, 68, 138, 190; natural, 42, 44–58, 64, 65; of self-ownership, 42, 54–55, 177; as side-constraints, 40, 56n, 188, 191; as trumps, 66, 189. See also basic liberties, Entitlement Theory of Justice, freedom, Rights-Based Principle
Rights-Based Principle, 40–67
Rockefeller, John D., 72, 74
Rorty, Richard, 9n, 115n
Rosenblum, Nancy L., 20n, 116n
Rousseau, Jean-Jacques, 169
rule of law, 5, 18, 24, 187
Ryan, Alan, 66n, 78n

Sandel, Michael, 19n, 116n
Scanlon, T. M., 39n
scarcity. See circumstances of justice
Scheffler, Samuel, 47n
Schwartz, Adina, 152n
segregation, 4
self-development, 78, 88, 90, 100, 140, 146. See also reflective self-direction
self-interest. See egoism
Sen, Amartya K., 128–36, 145–47, 149–51, 159, 161
sexism, 158, 191
shared understandings, 11, 16, 171–73
Shue, Henry, 67n
Singer, Peter, 36n
slavery, 48–61, 65, 101, 102
Smith, Adam, 3, 13, 152
Smith, Rogers M., 69n
Starobinski, Jean, 169n
Stassen, Glen, 16n
state, 3, 4, 13, 14, 41, 44, 54, 63, 85, 108, 140, 158, 168, 169, 170, 186; democratic, 54–57, 109; minimal, 43, 45, 46, 52–55, 60. See also power
state of nature, 45, 53, 54
status, 139, 152–60, 161, 162, 167, 168, 183–87

Strong, Tracy B., 9n
Sunstein, Cass R., 20n
sympathy, 71, 72, 82

Taylor, Charles, 19n
Tuck, Richard, 32n

United States, 9, 11, 16, 63, 64n, 83, 98, 99, 118, 124, 160, 179, 180, 184, 187, 192
utilitarianism, 6, 14n, 21n, 24, 25, 41, 78, 82, 88, 101, 102, 104, 110, 112, 121, 122, 129, 130, 188, 189; and greatest happiness principle, 101, 121; and interpersonal comparisons, 143–44
utopianism, 9, 10, 37

value pluralism, 26, 27, 30, 31, 37, 91, 100, 113, 126, 128, 134, 137, 138, 140, 174, 187; contrasted with monism, 102, 133
von Neumann, Jon, 101n

Waldron, Jeremy, 26, 39n, 41n, 47, 66n, 67n
Walzer, Michael, 9, 14n, 16, 127n, 138n, 154n, 170–73, 175, 176, 184n
Weber, Max, 68, 85
Weinrib, Ernest J., 20n
well-being, 102, 146, 147, 149, 150, 151, 179, 181
well-ordered society, 103, 104, 106, 108, 111, 112, 115, 116, 117, 123, 135, 154, 159
Wolff, Robert Paul, 41n
Wolin, Sheldon S., 10n

Young, Robert, 70n